PENGUIN BOOKS

REDEMPTORAMA

Carol Flake is a poet, scholar, and journalist who grew up in Texas and who now lives in Cambridge, Massachusetts. She has been an editor at *New Orleans* magazine, the Boston *Phoenix,* and *Vanity Fair.* She has written on the subjects of popular culture and religion for such publications as *The New York Times, The Washington Post, The New Republic, The Nation, The Village Voice,* and *New England Monthly.*

REDEMPTORAMA

Culture, Politics,
and the New Evangelicalism

CAROL FLAKE

PENGUIN BOOKS

PENGUIN BOOKS
Published by the Penguin Group
Viking Penguin Inc., 40 West 23rd Street,
New York, New York 10010, U.S.A.
Penguin Books Ltd, 27 Wrights Lane,
London W8 5TZ, England
Penguin Books Australia Ltd, Ringwood,
Victoria, Australia
Penguin Books Canada Ltd, 2801 John Street,
Markham, Ontario, Canada L3R 1B4
Penguin Books (N.Z.) Ltd, 182–190 Wairau Road,
Auckland 10, New Zealand

Penguin Books Ltd, Registered Offices:
Harmondsworth, Middlesex, England

First published in the United States of America by
Anchor Press/Doubleday & Company, Inc., 1984
Published in Penguin Books by arrangement with
Anchor Press/Doubleday & Company, Inc., 1985
Reprinted 1988

LIBRARY OF CONGRESS CATALOGING IN PUBLICATION DATA
Flake, Carol.
Redemptorama: culture, politics, and the
new evangelicalism.
1. Evangelicalism—United States.
2. Christianity and culture.   3. Christianity
and politics.   I. Title
BR1642.U5F58   1985   280'.4   85-9543
ISBN 0 14 00.8265 4

Page 301 constitutes an extension of this copyright page.

Printed in the United States of America by
R. R. Donnelley & Sons Company, Harrisonburg, Virginia
Set in Garamond

TO MY MOTHER AND FATHER AND TO JOHN

AUTHOR'S NOTE

Writing about religion, particularly about a form of worship that has been part of one's life, is difficult. One tends to take the role either of apologist or apostate. And there are some clear injunctions in the New Testament about criticizing the faith and practices of others. I fear that in many cases I've cast the first stone and failed to remove the beam from my own eye. Accordingly, I've tried to use a mixture of "criticism and kindness," as one preacher advised me.

My purpose has been to explore the rift between evangelicalism and secular culture, using my own experience in both worlds as a means of seeking points of similarity and reconciliation as well as of disagreement. There has been considerable intolerance and misunderstanding on both sides. Evangelicals who mistrust secular culture often fail to see how they have appropriated its forms and themes, while skeptics who distrust fundamentalism often fail to perceive that conservative Christian culture reflects many of the implied values of secular culture. One cannot understand America without understanding fundamentalism, nor can one understand America without understanding cultural diversity.

I would like to express my appreciation to the many evangelicals I met on my pilgrimage back to my own Southern Baptist roots. I found kindness and consideration in unexpected places. Often those individuals with whom I disagreed on many points were generous with their time and courteous with their arguments. I am particularly grateful to Jim Wallis and the Sojourners for their hospitality and for the example they offer of "costly discipleship," of the kind of Christian calling that does not come easy.

I would like to express my admiration for those writers, particularly Marshall Frady and Garry Wills, who have demonstrated that one can write for both pilgrim and scoffer. And I would like to thank my agent, Tim Seldes, and those editors who encouraged me to explore my ambivalence about Christ and culture: Robert Christgau and Karen Durbin at *The Village Voice,* Elizabeth Pochoda at *The Nation,* and, most of all, Phil Pochoda at Doubleday, who had faith that my pilgrimage could become a book.

Lastly, I would like to thank John Tirman, who makes it all worthwhile, and I would like to extend my love and gratitude to my parents, whose caring, unselfish lives are a testament to the tender, loving capacity of religious faith.

Contents

REDEMPTORAMA

Culture, Politics,
and the New Evangelicalism

Introduction

It no longer fits to picture us as redneck preachers pounding the pulpit. Evangelical Christianity has become the greatest show on earth. Twenty to forty years ago it was on the edge of things. Now it has moved to the center.

Evangelist Dave Breese

According to the Chinese zodiac, 1976 was the year of the dragon, but according to *Newsweek,* it was the Year of the Evangelical. Swept along on a nationwide tide of bicentennial faith in old-fashioned, down-home decency, a Bible-quoting Southern Baptist farmer from a remote village in Georgia landed in the White House. Such was the strength of that righteous tide that a survey on the nation's religious proclivities led pollster George Gallup, Jr., himself a devout Episcopalian, to predict a national religious revival. The causes of this imminent upsurge of spirituality, ventured Gallup, were a "general turning inward to seek refuge from everyday pressures" and a "search for nonmaterial values in light of the fading American Dream."

Judging by the high percentage of Americans who had defined themselves on his questionnaires as born again, Gallup concluded that there were as many as 50 million evangelical Christians in America, an estimate that far exceeded the more modest self-tally by evangelicals, which was usually put at between 20 to 30 million. (Evangelicals accounted for the discrepancy by pointing out that Gallup's criteria probably allowed enthusiastic Catholics, Mormons, and assorted high churchers to be included among their number.) Southern Baptists alone accounted for over 13 million souls.

Conservative politicians took note of the voting bloc of some 5 to 8 million evangelicals who had cast decisive ballots in Carter's favor. Here was a fervent, ready-made constituency, not yet closely allied to any party but possessing enormous potential for single-issue crusades. Liberals, however, tended to regard evangelicals from a cautious distance, like explorers peering through the foliage at a stone-wielding prehistoric tribe. As a stringer from a national newsweekly once asked me, glancing nervously around at the cheerful multitude applauding Pat Boone during a Jesus festival, "Who *are* these people?"

Evangelicals seemed to be set off from other Americans by differences of culture as well as creed. They held notions about God, country, and family that only a generation before had been virtually a national anthem, yet they had become strangers in their own land. They wore white socks and unnatural fibers. In a study by one sociologist, they were even shown to have different (lower) IQs.

Evangelicals were not content to practice their faith in the privacy of their own churches. Nor did they leave the preaching to the ordained. By definition, evangelicals were bearers of Good News (the term evangelical is derived from the Greek work *evangelion*, meaning messenger). The central experience in their lives was the acceptance of Jesus as their personal savior, and they wanted to share it with the world. Their "I Found It!" bumper stickers haunted honking drivers during traffic jams; their toll-free numbers leaped out from the airwaves at jiggle-seekers flipping the dials on TV sets; their doorbell-ringing deacons interrupted wine-topers at dinner.

Evangelicals were working as recruiters long before the Moonies invaded the nation's airports or the Hare Krishnas took to the sidewalks. So zealous, in fact, were the most evangelical of all evangelicals—the TV preachers—that critics accused them of creating "video cults." For skeptics, all that separated, say, Oral Roberts from Sun Myung Moon was the video healer's affiliation—albeit tenuous—with the venerable tradition of American Protestantism.

Evangelicals divided the world into the saved and the lost and counted it their responsibility to transform the latter into the former. Jimmy Carter himself had rung dozens of doorbells for his faith following his own mid-life conversion experience. One day in 1966, still in the depths of a depression brought on by a decisive loss to Lester Maddox in his first campaign for governor, Carter took a fateful walk in the woods with his sister, evangelist-healer Ruth Carter Stapleton. That stroll was to become a turning point in his life as a Christian and a turning point in America for the relationship between Christianity and politics. As they talked, Carter realized that his religion had always been secondary in his life, and he began to seek a deeper, more personal kind of faith. The experience was more like a gradual dawning than the zap of a lightning bolt. Deciding to get more involved with the church, the future President volunteered for "mission" work and was assigned, with a fellow peanut farmer from Texas named Milo Pennington, to the godless streets of Pennsylvania and Massachusetts. As Carter later recalled, the two farmers managed to convert between fifteen and twenty families during that first crusade.

During his presidential campaign, Carter, the model evangelical, continued to bear witness. In a speech given at Winston-Salem during the North Carolina primary, he confessed his reliance on divine counsel during troubled times: "I spent more time on my knees the four years I was governor in the seclusion of a little private room off the governor's office than I did in all the rest of my life put together because I felt so heavily on my shoulders the decisions I made might very well affect many, many people. I recognized for the first time that I had lacked something very precious—a complete commitment to Christ, a presence of the Holy Spirit in my life in a more profound and personal way. And since then I've had an inner peace and inner conviction and assurance that transformed my life for the better."

THE USES OF EVANGELICAL CHIC

Despite Carter's frequent reassurances during the campaign that his faith would not jeopardize the separation of church and state, he made such an issue of his religious roots that a fellow evangelical, Republican Senator Mark Hatfield of Oregon, wrote an article for *Sojourners* magazine charging that a little religion went a long way in politics. Said Hatfield, "Most politicians have typically utilized religion much like a woman uses makeup; a little, used discreetly, can improve one's appearance, but too much, used lavishly, can make one look like a clown."

Far from being a liability, however, Carter's ingenuous avowals of faith proved an asset, at least at first. Carter's G-rated confession to a *Playboy* interviewer that he had lusted in his heart brought merriment to an X-rated culture. In 1981, Carter told writer Dotson Rader that his religion had given him a "compensating political advantage" during the early stages of his campaign. Initially there was a boon in "being different. Being Southern. Being Baptist. . . . I undoubtedly got a lot of publicity when I desperately needed it—when nobody knew who I was—that paid off later." Always grateful for a little local color, reporters journeyed into the wilds of Georgia to observe the natives firsthand in their Sunday best. Carter's brother Billy obliged by behaving like the missing link.

If he had not exactly brought everlasting respectability to evangelicals, Jimmy Carter had at least brought them their season in the sun. Although evangelicalism failed to attain the chic status that Garry Wills observed of Catholicism in the sixties, what with its flying and singing nuns, folk masses, radical priests, and the Ecumenical Council, evangelicals attained a special kind of notoriety. As Watergate felons found Christ and Carter's country-boy retinue found power in Washington, born-again became a buzzword that could be applied to anyone who had made a comeback.

Charles Colson's confessional *Born Again* shot to the top of the bestseller charts, and Nixon's former dirty trickster brushed the cobwebs from his eyes, now able to see decay all across the land. Watergate, he felt, had been merely the pustule atop a nation festering with poisonous corruption. To remedy the situation, a roster of famous testifiers, headed by Colson, staked out a kind of celebrity revival circuit, from Christian talk shows to pentecostal pep rallies. Always a big drawing card at these shindigs was Ruth Carter Stapleton, who had been established as a successful freelance faith healer, a kind of minor-league Kathryn Kuhlman, even before her brother became president. With Jimmy Carter's ascendancy, she gained access to more skeptical circles, and sales of *The Gift of Inner Healing,* a therapeutic amalgam of Christian psychodrama, Freudian transference theory, and ritual exorcism, spiraled.

In 1978 a big fund-raising ball was held in Stapleton's honor at Manhattan's Plaza Hotel. A glitzy *People/Women's Wear Daily* crowd, including Diana Vreeland, Norman Mailer, Ahmet Ertegun, and Andrew Young, turned out to dance for the benefit of Holovita, Stapleton's healing retreat near Denton, Texas. A writer from the *Village Voice* reported that, "quite unprepared for evangelical chic," she had attended the event out of curiosity to "witness a Holy Roller meeting in the same room in which Mr. and Mrs. George Zanderer once gave a costume party for their own benefit and called it 'Bal des Saisons.' "

THE GREAT DISILLUSIONMENT

By 1978, however, for many Americans, born-again Christianity had already come to exude the stale odor of redneck religion, as though it had been baptized in Billy Beer. Scandals and rumors of scandals buzzed around Jimmy Carter's handpicked staff like flies at a barbecue. Carter's Christian constituency began to splinter as the fundamentalist fringe became dissatisfied with the President's conciliatory views on moral and military matters. In right-wing fund-raiser Richard Viguerie's words, Carter had "surrounded himself with many people who routinely rejected Biblical principles regarding sexual behavior, family responsibility, abortion, and other key moral issues." For conservative Christians, Carter was not a dyed-in-the-wool Baptist but a liberal in sheepish clothing.

With singer Anita Bryant's 1977 crusade against gays in Dade County, Florida, old prejudices came crawling out of the Ever-glades, and fundamentalism began its greatest comeback since *The Fundamentals* were first issued early in the century by conservative ministers who wanted to set the record straight on biblical iner-rancy. As reporter Perry Deane Young later observed in *God's Bullies,* a searing attack on the new religious right, the Dade County controversy was the first big testing ground for a burgeoning alliance of right-wing political operatives, fundamentalist preachers, and conservative Jews and Catholics. Conservatives from different creeds had found a common cause. Bryant received blessings, advice, and support from the Reverend Jerry Falwell (two years before Moral Majority was chartered); from Senator Jesse Helms's conservative auxiliary, the Congressional Club; from Catholic Arch-bishop Coleman F. Carroll; from the Miami Beach B'nai B'rith; and from H. Edward Rowe of the Christian Leadership Foundation in Washington.

When Bryant and her motley coalition succeeded in overturning the decision by the Miami-Dade council to include homosexuals in the city-county civil rights laws, a star was born. Taking an ax to gay lifestyles, Anita Bryant became the Carrie Nation of the bath-houses. She soon replaced Charles Colson as the Christian celebrity most in demand at conservative gatherings. In January 1978, Bry-ant was invited to address the largely conservative National Reli-gious Broadcasters at their convention in Washington, D.C. Prior to Bryant's appearance, the NRB, which controlled a majority of the nation's religious programming, generally had shied away from political controversy, although individual members always seemed to be keeping the Federal Communications Commission on its toes with controversial crusades or fund-raising schemes.

However, as Bryant opened the convention with a medley of patriotic songs, the TV preachers assembled in the Hilton ballroom experienced both the excitement and the pitfalls of political involvement. A bomb threat was announced by Bryant's husband, Bob Green, who invited those who were frightened to leave. Despite some anxious rustles and coughs in the audience, everyone sat back and prepared for martyrdom. As Bryant was concluding, "This is the time Christians are going to have to start coming out of the closet," a ring of gay protesters who had surrounded the Hilton began to chant, "Anita must go." The war had begun.

THE FUNDAMENTALIST FUROR

As America nodded at the end of the seventies from its liberated binge of sex, drugs, self-discovery, and disco, a motley cluster of short-haired prophets concluded the Me Decade with a flurry of jeremiads. While historians and sociologists were discovering in American civilization such fin-de-siècle symptoms as the culture of narcissism and the twilight of authority, religious conservatives were finding auguries of Armageddon, and political conservatives were foretelling the fall of liberalism. It was a time of strange coincidences and unlikely conversions.

In the autumn of 1979, when the Reverend Jerry Falwell was launching the hastily soldered conservative coalition known as Moral Majority, rock and roll veterans Bob Dylan, Van Morrison, and Arlo Guthrie released portentous religious albums. Shortly after Catholic charismatics braved the Bronx and gathered in the thousands for a tongue-loosing rally in Yankee Stadium, the exiled Dalai Lama arrived in Manhattan to begin his first tour of America with an appearance at St. Patrick's Cathedral, urging peace and simplicity on the mildly curious crowd that turned out to welcome him. And as the Tibetan holy man was humbly greeting millionaires and assorted Buddhists in a heavy Houston downpour, Pope John Paul II was energetically upstaging him in Massachusetts. Hard-nosed newsmen found themselves melting like communion wafers before the hearty charisma of the peripatetic pontiff, until John Paul's beaming pink-cheeked visage was superseded by the pale omnipresent scowl of the Ayatollah Khomeini.

It seemed that America was being held hostage by an alien zealotry, both at home and abroad. The sleek triumphant smile of the

Reverend Falwell began to appear everywhere, like the tacked-up icon of a fundamentalist führer. In the wake of a decade of experiments in moral relativism, the minions of moral absolutism were on the march, using the media to amplify their message and their numbers. In America's heartland, the phantom army of the Moral Majority, whose legions were counted in computerized lists, mounted the attack through the mails and on the airwaves, collating the power of elemental Protestantism. It appeared that a thoroughly modernized machine was being built in order to deliver a very dated message.

Dust flew from pulpits across the country as fundamentalist Christians suddenly found themselves fulminating before a startled secular audience. Old-time religion had awaked to find itself on "Donahue." The religious revival that had been prophesied by George Gallup, Jr., during the afterglow of the misty-eyed patriotic revels of 1976 had come to pass. But the swelling congregations of chastened refugees from secular culture that Gallup had foreseen had spilled out from their pews onto the streets, vowing to sear a path to the seat of government and torch the nation's capital into a burned-over district. In the spring of 1980, a quarter of a million born-again Americans converged on Washington, D.C., to pray for the purification of national politics. Even the sudden penitence of a strayed Southern Baptist president would not have sufficed for a group whose fear of Armageddon had become a kind of fierce longing.

Among fundamentalists, there was talk of a Great Awakening to rival the glorious agitations of the colonial period and the rekindled brushfires of early-nineteenth-century Protestantism. Among others, there was muttering of a Redneck Revival. Images of the Darwin-banning peckerwood pietists ridden out of town on H. L. Mencken's raillery during the 1925 Scopes trial had returned as specters of ancient prejudice and paranoia haunted America. Evolving in isolation, like one of Darwin's marooned species, the fossilized faith of fundamentalism had survived to become an atavistic force in American politics and culture.

Jimmy Carter looked up from his Bible to find that fundamentalism was running amok and he himself had become a false prophet. Carter's election did not usher in an old-fashioned religious revival so much as a new phase in the clash between Christ and culture. It was a clash that not only set millenarian against humanist, pro-lifer against abortionist, and creationist against evolutionist but Christian against Christian, evangelical against evangelical, and preacher against preacher. The fundamentalist war against modern culture was also a war among the churches. Politics was a new front in a long-standing conflict among American Protestants that had culminated with the establishment of fundamentalism during the first part of the twentieth century.

The fundamentalists of the Falwell era, as conservative political strategists recognized, were a subculture in the process of becoming a counterculture. Tutored by conservative political organizers, fundamentalist leaders mastered the grass-roots rallying techniques of the sixties counterculture, including music, marches, and mass gatherings, as well as the sophisticated technology of secular culture. Setting themselves against the Eastern liberal "establishment," whom they felt ruled the nation without the consent of the governed, conservative Christian leaders attempted to smooth over long-standing doctrinal differences and territorial disputes among themselves in order to present a united front—a "Moral Majority," a "disciplined, charging army." They created a new common cause —the family—and identified a new common enemy—secular humanism. As Jerry Falwell described it, fundamentalists had hijacked the jumbo jet of evangelicalism and directed it on a new conservative course.

THE NEW EVANGELICALISM

It was during the public ascension of assorted spiritual potentates during the turbulent autumn of 1979 that I finally began to pay attention to the religious rifts that were slicing up the country, turning single-issue skirmishes and bumper-sticker battles into full-scale ideological warfare. It was not merely the boundaries between church and state that were shifting during this new evangelical revival but the lines between church and culture as well. The missionary impulse to Christianize alien cultures, which had often worked as a kind of spiritual imperialism abroad, had been turned on America itself.

I became obsessed with that old dialectic, Christ and culture: as theologian H. Richard Niebuhr described it, the tension between Christians' religious calling and their social environment. In preparation for this book, I began to follow the progress of that slow train, the juggernaut of evangelicalism, as it chugged through contemporary culture. I found that Christ and culture were meeting in some peculiar places, from punk clubs to Yankee Stadium, from Knott's Berry Farm to the Washington Monument, from drive-in cathedrals to the White House. I pondered such oxymorons as Christian rock and roll and Christian consumerism, such conundrums as why a born-again football team like the Dallas Cowboys relied on computers. I wanted to learn why Billy Graham's *Angels* sold more copies nationwide than Woodward and Bernstein's *Final Days*.

As I made a pilgrimage through the world of evangelicalism, returning to my own Southern Baptist roots in Texas, I found that I had to backtrack across the geographical, cultural, and social boundaries I had crossed when I left home for college and graduate school, eventually moving to the Northeast to join the federation of information dispensers, the dictators of taste, the bastion of secular humanists known as the "new class." As far as the troubleshooters of Moral Majority were concerned, I had become one of the enemy.

I sympathized with a *Village Voice* writer who admitted in a story on the new religious right that she shuddered every time she encountered a fundamentalist preacher. A fire-and-brimstone preacher raging at full steam is a terrifying sight. Nevertheless, during the years I was researching this book, I seldom felt like a bitter apostate; I felt more like an ambivalent émigré. Perhaps that's because I bear no real scars from my own youthful immersion in evangelical zealotry. Mostly I suffer a twinge of embarrassment at the memory of my preteen piety, when I sporadically made a fool of myself by trying to convert the sinners in my neighborhood, including a lively Auntie Mame eccentric who offended my tent-crusader sensibility by drinking beer in her backyard as she listened to rhythm-and-blues albums. (My hypocrisy knew no bounds, since I also took every opportunity to borrow those records to practice my bop technique.) In fact, despite all the tin-horn Savonarolas, the petty "wowsers" of the pulpit, as Mencken called them, that I en-

countered, despite all the scams and absurdities that I discovered in
the rites and practices of contemporary evangelicals, the experience
of working on this book served to strengthen rather than diminish
my own religious faith.

I encountered too many kind, generous churchgoers, witnessed
too many good deeds, listened to too many sincere confessions to
despair of the future of evangelicalism. Sometimes I even found
myself agreeing with angry pompadoured pessimists about the state
of the union—at least about the clouds of doom gathering on the
horizon, about the need for spiritual as well as secular solutions to
the nation's problems. And I could understand if not condone the
hunger for hegemony among conservative Christians who had long
felt themselves to be a beleaguered minority floating in a leaky ark
on a rolling sea of hedonism. Those I could not understand or
condone were the hyperventilating evangelists who rattled the
rusty sabers of Christian militancy or the suave TV Super Savers
who sold their shut-in viewers ever-more-costly plans of salvation.

In the course of my research, I discovered that the world of
evangelicalism was far more diverse than I had ever realized when I
used to wriggle impatiently in the rear pews of my church back
home as our preacher, Brother Johnny, lit into the temptations that
promised deliverance from the dreariness of small-town life. I had
never learned about the radical heritage of evangelicalism in America, about such nineteenth-century prophets of social justice and
emancipation as Charles Grandison Finney and Theodore Dwight
Weld, about strange utopian experiments in holiness carried out on
New England hillsides, Pennsylvania fields, and Southern mead-
ows, about the ferment for social reform that often accompanied
the periods of revivalism that shook the nation once every forty
years or so. And even in the early seventies, I had never encountered the young radical Christian groups who were trying to maintain their Christian faith despite their disillusionment with established churches.

I had been in such a hurry to leave home and church when I went
off to college that I was loath to look back, for fear I might join
Lot's wife as a salt doll. I found myself reborn happily into secular
culture. It was not so much that I had lost my faith or been transformed into a different creature but that I felt I had outgrown the
context in which my faith had been formed.

Although missionaries were always busy carrying the Word around the world, even translating it into Swahili, evangelicalism didn't seem to me then to be a very portable kind of religion—it seemed out of place, certainly, with the new clothes and the new books I had bought for college. Taking my religion with me to the campus and the big city would have been like traveling with a rube relative in a loud plaid jacket who'd try to order a hamburger at a French restaurant. It didn't seem possible to have old-fashioned faith and Fellini too. I assumed that Jesus was inseparable from small-town life and country culture.

Fifteen years later, though, I had learned about other kinds of faith, while fundamentalism had become a force to be reckoned with beyond the boundaries of the backwaters; it had spurred a national evangelical revival, and it had split the Southern Baptist Convention asunder, separating the hawks from the doves, the premillennialists from the postmillennialists, and the ranters from the moderators. I felt like the estranged relative of a quiet, gawky farmer who has suddenly gone on a scythe-swinging rampage in the New York Stock Exchange and become a national media figure.

Fundamentalists were no longer grappling with the demons within but with the humanism without. Instead of peering into their own souls for evidence of guilt, they were looking across town, across the state, across the nation, toward the politicians and purveyors of culture who had invaded their homes, schools, and neighborhoods with unsettling change.

My own church back home, which was now televising its Sunday services, had changed as much as I had. The congregation had moved from a crowded, low-ceilinged meeting hall into a big brick sanctuary. Towering up behind the pulpit was an abstract stained-glass cross that slid up to reveal the baptismal font. New buildings and parking lots had been added, so that the church sprawled into the surrounding neighborhood. Brother Johnny had been succeeded by a series of teachers rather than preachers, and there was less anxious rustling in the pews. The church, with its own cheery fellowship halls, constantly filled with exercise classes, sports contests, and socials, had become the favored church for singles in my town. Brother Johnny occasionally returned for reunion sermons, joking about how he used to spray the front pews with enthusiastic spittle. There was even talk among the deacons about bringing back

Brother Johnny permanently as the dangers of complacency became apparent.

Although conservative evangelicals were trying to cling to an older, simpler world, even as they struggled for success in the larger secular world, their lives had inevitably become more complicated as the Bible Belt merged with the Sun Belt, bringing prosperity, self-consciousness, and outsiders. A few years ago, when a friend told me that no one in her liberal, upscale church had "been there" for her when her daughter was dying of cancer, I thought about my church back home, where one could take that kind of support for granted.

But now I was not so sure. This was the era of televised worship, the "age of the superchurch," as Jerry Falwell had declared. Super Saver preachers and super-duper churches. As one Christian writer complained, excoriating the tackiness as well as the size of these megasanctuaries: "Anyone with semi-civilized taste would have to grimace at most of them: great, looming, sprawling 'plants,' all landscaped and tricked out like suburban office parks. Alack! We perceive millions of dollars' worth of bricks and ersatz-Colonial woodwork . . . announcing, 'Get a load of the size of this operation.' " Some churches had gotten so large that ministers had to resort to mass baptisms rather than individual dippings. Like health-club managers, preachers had to proceed on the assumption that not everyone on the roster would actually show up every Sunday, since otherwise the facilities would get overcrowded.

Perversely, I found myself longing for the old clapboard churches, for the image of the Christian as the poor wayfaring stranger. I thought of the plain white steeples of the old New England meeting houses that bespoke a sensible means of pointing to the heavens, of those churches whose bare-pewed interiors and no-frills services chastened any backsliding longings for the privileged, well-buttressed mysteries of the cathedral.

As I looked back, I realized that, for all its flaws, the church of my childhood had touched my heart and shaped my life in a way that secular culture never could. It had been a meddlesome family, offering a strong system of values and a real community—fellowship for old folks, socializing for harried housewives, visitations for the faltering, prayers for the invalids. If it had shut out other avenues of transcendence, trapping many worshipers in their fears and neuroses, it had at least offered a glimpse of a better life and a better self, and a means of looking beyond the mundane matters of the quotidian. Although during my more class-conscious moments I had longed desperately to be an Episcopalian (it seemed a definite social advantage), I'm not sure I would have been better off without the sense of estrangement from the world I felt in the Southern Baptist cosmos.

However, as evangelical churches grew and prospered, so did their ways of worship. This was a new and brighter evangelicalism, a religion of warm pastels rather than bleak black-and-white. The Easter Sunday principle had predominated over the sackcloth-Sabbath habit. In most conservative evangelical churches, Easter had been a time to dress up in fancy new finery and parade down the aisles, while the rest of the year such conspicuous consumption would have drawn suspicious glances. Spring, resurrection, hope, and new hats all seemed tied up together. And now, for many evangelicals, every Sunday was Easter Sunday. This was a world of semipro choirs and combo accompaniments, of cushioned pews and carpeted cathedrals, of picture-book families and a comic-book culture.

TOWARD AN EVANGELICAL AESTHETIC

Early evangelicals owned no icons of transcendent reality, rehearsed no liturgies to guide them through sacred ceremonies. That function was fulfilled by the pursuit of personal holiness through self-scrutiny. Consequently, the more elemental forms of Protestantism failed to produce a great tradition of high culture in America, and often the war against the flesh became a war against beauty, when the flouting of superstition became the dispelling of mystery. The standard hymn and the sermon were the aesthetic forms of conservative Protestantism, although in rural white churches and in many black churches, where Sacred Harp singing and gospel music flowered, a sense of mystery and grandeur was expressed in a folk culture as radiant as stained glass.

Ironically, the leaders of the Puritan movement in England and

America had never evinced a complete contempt for culture; they themselves had been steeped in the culture of the Renaissance, and their sermons were laced with classical allusions. Artifacts from Puritan New England often display a decorative rather than Spartan sense of design: bold splashes of color leap out like Hester Prynne's scarlet letter from tapestries and samplers stitched by Puritan women. As Max Weber observed, the asceticism that descended like a frost on merry old England and stolid New England was not born of a distrust of learning or beauty but of a deep suspicion of the rites of sacramental salvation, of the lingering practices of magic and superstition that plagued the colony. Science, in fact, was a safe remedy for superstition, aiding the Pilgrim's enlightened discourse with God, while art and other sensuous distractions might sustain the malady.

In the nineteenth century, when science began to challenge the domain of religion, a number of preachers attempted to interpret Christ in the light of new ideas, to formulate a kind of cultural Protestantism. But most conservative ministers, for all their pride in the power of common sense, found that to maintain their belief in the literal truth of the Bible they had to steer clear of modern ways of thinking. Unlike the Puritan divines, the fundamentalists who waged the war on modernism in the twentieth century feared a world contaminated by the cosmology, if not the technological achievements, of science and learning. The ideas and values taught in public schools (inside and outside the classroom) and disseminated in popular culture seemed to challenge the ideas and values taught in church. As evangelist Rex Humbard harrumphed in 1981, "I'd rather be in Heaven learnin' my ABC's than in Hell prayin' in Greek and Latin for some water to cool my tongue." Fundamentalists feared that the beasts in their natures would be given the upper hand by Darwinism and that the voice of faith would be lost in the din of doubt and diversity in the secular world.

For contemporary fundamentalists, the distrust of the idols and icons of superstitious worship expressed by the Puritans had been displaced by a distrust of the empty altar of godless humanism. Yet pressed into competition with secular culture, many of them tried to dress up the familiar ways of worship in new vestments. They gave up the long struggle to uphold the Word over the image and the conscience over the pageant. Despite their iconoclastic tradition, evangelicals had become image-peddlers, and the Word itself became part of a multimedia industry. Though they were convinced that the Second Coming of Christ was imminent, and that they would soon be taken up to the heavens in the Rapture, fundamentalists worked hard to create a culture in their own image, culling themes, techniques, even celebrities from the world of popular culture they despised.

As I made my way through this bright new world of Christianized culture, I sensed a curious air of unreality, of artificiality, about it. The total man had married the total woman in the total Christian wedding in the total Christian church to fulfill the dream of the total Christian family in a total Christian country. Rather than agape, this was agapurgy, as sociologist Ralph Keyes called the synthetic concern generated by the phone counselors, instant encounter groups, and franchised friendships of the technological age. Conservative evangelicals, like love-starved secularists, had adopted the tokens of a mass-produced affection, the illusions of community: bumper-sticker smiles, personalized form letters, televised compassion, published advice.

It seemed that evangelicals were trying to create, amid the secular wasteland of America, a new version of the city on the hill that John Winthrop and his Puritan band envisioned. This new city—or rather, this republic—was to be an artificial paradise on earth, a kind of Christian Disneyland of model families and good clean fun. I was reminded of a time during graduate school when my colleagues and I invented an imaginary theme park called Redemptorama, wherein one could experience the most colorful events of the Bible in Cecil B. DeMille fashion. One could ride the roller coaster of Redemption, career through the Fiery Furnace with Shadrach, Meshach, and Abednego, join Jonah in the whale's-belly tilt-a-whirl.

Subsequently, this notion of a mechanized evangelical utopia was taken to its extreme in *Jesus World,* a satirical novella by evangelical writer Jamie Buckingham that envisioned a computerized gospel-world gone awry. In Buckingham's story, a successful TV preacher convinces a devout financier to construct a high-tech religious theme park near Disney World. The denouement, which involves a laser-and-robot passion play, suggests science fiction. Christian culture, however, is stranger than fiction. In late 1982, as if to fulfill

Buckingham's prophecy, Christian entrepreneur Pierre Bedard announced plans to turn a tract of swampland in Florida into a park called God's World, featuring a Tunnel of God's Love and a daily reenactment of the burning of Sodom and Gomorrah. Said Bedard, the idea had come to him "out of a heavenly cloud . . . in vivid, living color and thundering audio."

Buckingham's televangelist rationalized, as have Pierre Bedard and other such boosters of Super Churches and Christian culture, that such multimedia attractions are necessary if Christianity is to compete for attention in a secular world full of such distractions as pro football, discothèques, skating rinks, TV, and, of course, Disney World itself. Christ, in order to compete with culture, must become a bigger roadside attraction.

Redemptorama, the fantasy world of evangelical culture, was the constricted dream of an America that never really existed. It was the dream of a Christian America that preachers conjured up with images of the *Mayflower,* of feasting Pilgrims, of the Liberty Bell, of the perfect family with Mom and Dad and the kids seated around a cozy fire with their Bibles open to John 3:16. It was the dream of an America they thought they could bring back by such ritual actions as putting prayer back in the schools and by such renewed prohibitions as outlawing abortion. It was a difficult dream to relinquish, and many Christians thought that conservative politicians could save it for them.

VARIATIONS OF CHRIST AND CULTURE

Despite the attempt beginning in the late seventies by conservative evangelical leaders and conservative politicians to present a united front that could sweep presidents in and out of office, overturn judicial decisions, and kill or create constitutional amendments, the extent of political involvement by fundamentalists in America never became as extensive as many liberal leaders feared. To begin with, not all evangelicals were swept up in the fundamentalist crusade; according to most estimates, only a third of the evangelicals in America could be considered hard-shell fundamentalists. Moreover, not all fundamentalists wanted their preachers to get involved in politics. After Watergate, Billy Graham, the most influential evangelical of all, had washed his hands of politics.

I found that the strategies used by evangelicals in their dealings with politics and culture varied greatly in method and intensity. It seemed to me that the stance of evangelicals toward culture reflected variations of the four different attitudes toward modern culture that religious historian George Marsden observed of early fundamentalists and that theologian H. Richard Niebuhr had observed of Christians in general. For purposes of my study, however, I've modified Niebuhr's categories somewhat and expanded those of Marsden to include contemporary conservative factions and strategies. Also, inevitably, there is considerable overlap within these groups. A TV preacher, for example, might be active in the political workings of the Christian counterculture as well as in the cultural endeavors of Christian capitalism.

Separation. At the extreme were the Christ-against-culture separatists who hoped to quarantine themselves completely from the corruptions or distractions of the secular world. At the benign end of the separatist spectrum were the plain people of the Mennonite and Amish communities, with their atavistic beards, bonnets, and horse-drawn carriages, and their patriotism-resistant loyalty to God over country. In the Anabaptist tradition, from which such communities evolved, political and cultural involvements were shunned because it was believed that Satan ruled the age and that his influence extended to the governments of all nations.

At the other end of the spectrum were the doomsayers and survivalists who had set their alarm clocks for a countdown to Armageddon. They eschewed political involvement for different reasons. Certain that the Second Coming was at hand, the more extreme among them retreated to the hills, as Jim Jones and his flock had fled to the jungle, hoarding Bibles and soybeans and, in many cases, guns in anticipation of the End. The most pessimistic of these premillennialists had relinquished the long-cherished Calvinistic/Puritan notion that the destiny of the people of God was to unfold with the progress of a religious/political kingdom—that is, America. Instead of the new Israel, the bright city on the hill envisioned by the Puritans, these folks preferred a well-stocked citadel or a lonely mesa to await the final conflagration.

Recruitment. Most evangelicals, however, rejected that kind of ark-building isolation as a cultist extreme; it smacked of escapism and evaded the missionary duty of all evangelicals to preach the Good News to a fallen world. Protestants have never been comfortable with the Catholic notion of withdrawing from the world, of "cloistered virtue," as Milton expressed it. Most evangelicals advocated a position of Christ *over* culture rather than Christ against culture. In this view, one's duty was not to secede from secular life but, as fundamentalist minister William B. Riley put it, to "strengthen the things that remain." Christians in the holiness/revival tradition simply set out to recruit as many souls as possible. The great revival preachers, from Dwight L. Moody to Billy Graham, carried the torch of conversion in the tradition of the "pulpits aflame with righteousness" that Tocqueville had once found so conspicuous in America.

After the "Great Reversal" in the latter part of the nineteenth century, when many evangelical churches retreated from the tradition of social reform that had sparked the abolitionist movement, involvement by conservative evangelical churches in social, political, and cultural matters did not often venture beyond pronouncements from the pulpit and the establishment of an occasional rescue mission. The focus of reform shifted from the cleansing of public or institutional evils to the scouring of the private lives of individuals.

Civil religion. Prior to the Great Reversal, however, Christ had been regarded as the transformer of culture, and some conservative groups continued to regard him as such. The Puritan vision of America as a Christian nation evolved inevitably into the observance of civil religion: the inflamed patriotism that fuses the cross and the flag. As Robert Bellah has noted, a sense of national calling has always stirred both our preachers and our politicians: "The obligation, both collective and individual, to carry out God's will on earth . . . was the motivating spirit of those who founded America, and it has been present in every generation since." This notion of America's providential destiny has often led in the past to social reform, but it also has led to the planting of burning crosses and the formation of extremist groups who get impatient with the slow course of judicial or legislative action.

Since its founding, when Thomas Jefferson hedged about who it was who had given us our inalienable rights, America has been at once very secular and very religious. The legal separation of church and state mandated by the constitution has presented a challenge to those who would insert God into government. (The consistent use of divine imprimatur on our money is relatively recent, as is the mention of God in the Pledge of Allegiance.) Moral Majority is merely a recent example of societies founded to influence America's institutions of government and learning, from the anti-Catholic Know-Nothings of the 1850s to the antievolution Bible Crusaders of the 1920s to Billy James Hargis's anti-Communist Christian Crusade in the 1960s. Contemporary groups like Moral Majority, however, who acted as a kind of Christian counterculture, became more sophisticated in their methods than their immediate predecessors. Political action committees and computerized mailing lists cued to single-issue politics were an improvement over the covert, hit-and-miss crusades of far-right groups in the fifties and sixties.

Christian capitalism. The attitude of the Christian counterculture was essentially censorious. If thine eye offends thee, pluck it out. If thy neighbor's eye offends thee, block his vision. But the attitude of yet another faction of conservative Christians was considerably more enterprising. If thine eye offends thee, buy Christian bifocals. If thy neighbor's eye offends thee, advise him to tune into a Christian talk show instead of those X-rated cable shows. In this approach, the Christian set out to beat the secular enemy on its own terms—by competing in the marketplace.

In the 1970s, the adventurous entrepreneurial spirit of Christian capitalists leaped over the confines of Puritan separatism. The real business of evangelicalism, after all, was spreading the Word, and that meant more than putting a Bible on every coffee table; it meant the creation of communications industries—television, publishing, radio, recordings. It meant building Christian networks, corporations, and multiministried megachurches. Just as modern culture had blared and published its way into the broad plains and pleasant valleys of middle America, evangelical businessmen would return the favor by flooding the marketplace with their own generic brands of Christian culture.

Christian entrepreneurs began to produce a kind of limited mass culture, turning out sanitized copies of secular products, a season or two behind the times, like discount department store suppliers shaping haute couture into American sizes. If secular business enterprises could market products promising self-improvement, how much better could Christian capitalists promote the religious equivalent. After all, as a number of Christian writers had claimed over the years, Jesus was the greatest salesman of them all. There were Christian self-help books, Christian sex manuals, Christian money guides, Christian quiz shows, Christian athletes, Christian rock stars, Christian T-shirts. In a sense, what these entrepreneurs were creating was not a counterculture but a counterfeit culture.

Of these four basic relationships between evangelicals and culture, I've concerned myself primarily with the latter two, with Christians as the creators of culture and Christians as the transformers of culture, because it is Christian capitalism and political engagement that have transformed the world of evangelicalism and have begun to influence the affairs of the nation.

In the section on Christian culture, I've traced the historical trends that have led to the rift between conservative Christians and secular culture. I've described the growth of Christian capitalism, focusing on the world of TV preachers and the huge multiministried empires being built by powerful churches and preachers around the country. Subsequent chapters deal with two of the stranger creations of Christian culture, the Total Woman and the Christian athlete, who embody in exaggerated form the traditional ideals of feminity and masculinity that conservative Christians consider to be in jeopardy. Further chapters deal with the Christian publishing industry that promotes these conservative ideals and with the Christian music industry, born of the Jesus movement in the late sixties, that has produced the most peculiar hybrid of all in Christian culture: evangelical rock and roll.

In the section on Christian politics, I've begun with the big rally in Washington, D.C., known as Washington for Jesus, the first great political epiphany for fundamentalists, then traced the formation of a conservative Christian counterculture: the Christian liberation front. For the sake of contrast, I've examined the communities of young radical evangelicals whose activism has taken a different direction. Ultimately, I think, it is these groups who provide the most telling commentary on conservative evangelicals and the Christianized culture they've created.

In conclusion, I've evaluated the impact of conservative evangelicals on moderate evangelicals and mainstream Protestants, venturing a prophecy on the church of the center.

PART I

CHRIST AND CULTURE

CHAPTER 1

In Defense of Ignorance:
The Roots of Fundamentalism

I don't know any more about theology than a jack rabbit knows about Ping-Pong, but I'm on my way to glory.

Billy Sunday

Strife, factions, and feuds are inevitable in a religious tradition that emphasizes both an established moral order and the individual free conscience. The Puritan divines who pursued the dual aims of self-reliance and social rectitude sowed the seeds of continuous revolt in American religious life. From the very beginning, when dissenters Anne Hutchinson and Roger Williams were driven from the Massachusetts Bay Colony, Protestantism in America was torn between Calvinistic patriarchs who wanted to establish a strictly governed Christian civilization in the wilderness—a new Israel—and the antinomian free spirits who wanted to wander through that wilderness and find God in their own way.

The Puritan covenant had bound the piety of the individual to the collective good of the community, so that civil and religious duties were inseparable. But Roger Williams, founder of the Baptist church in America, stirred up trouble in the Puritan theocracy by stating that civil magistrates could not enforce church law, thus upholding, in effect, the separation of church and state. After founding his own colony on Narragansett Bay, Williams further undermined the power of the reigning clergy by abolishing infant baptism. He called for a full immersion in baptismal waters, not as a sacrament, but as an act of will by the believer, demonstrating that he or she had gained salvation by faith. In 1644, he issued *The Bloudy Tenent of Persecution,* which declared that "the doctrine of persecution for cause of conscience is proved guilty of all the blood of the souls crying for vengeance under the altar. . . ."

Although the Baptists were condemned by the assemblies of both Massachusetts and Virginia, within a century they had transformed the religious life of the colonies. During the first Great Awakening in America, which spread across the Eastern seaboard during the 1730s, the dour rigidity into which Puritanism had settled was shaken up by "New Light" Baptists who issued a call to emotional conversion. The spirit-rousing style of the revival preacher was born, and Congregationalism was never the same again. Some historians, in fact, have credited the New Light preachers, who traveled widely across the colonies, with creating a sense of unity and common purpose among their congregations that helped to spark the Revolutionary War. Baptists joined the Continental Army en masse.

During the second Great Awakening, which peaked in the 1830s, leaving upper New York state a "burnt-over district" and inspiring reform movements throughout the Northeast, a kind of rivalry began to develop between the established churches of the East and the camp-meeting forms of worship on the frontier that emphasized dramatic conversions and self-reliant theology. For the plain people of Jacksonian democracy, the sedate rituals of Eastern worship reflected the intellectual elitism and spiritual senescence of Eastern city dwellers. And for the Eastern clergy, revivalism was like a brushfire used by a farmer to clear his land. If kept under control, it could hasten the harvest, but if it flamed too high, it could burn down the barn. Lyman Beecher, the eminent Boston Congregationalist, warned of the "extravagance of disorder" and the "semi-barbarism" that could result from the release of pent-up passions in a revival meeting.

Beecher, who feared a variety of evils, founded a proto-Moral Majority group called the Connecticut Society for the Reformation of Morals and Suppression of Vice. Like a number of moral-minded groups of the time that referred to themselves as "benevolent societies," the Connecticut Society specified a source of the nation's problems. The primary targets of Beecher's group were French atheists. Beecher and other New England Congregationalist ministers were incensed by the failure of party politicians to contain the threat of "French infidelism" that they associated with Jeffersonian democracy. Democracy, like revivalism, threatened the stability of the old social order. Beecher warned of the consequences of the "shaking together, in one cauldron of effervescence, all the passions of all the classes of human society."

PRAYING WITH FIRE

Revivalism had been the constant refresher of American Protestantism—the smelling salts, rather than the opium, of the masses. On a small, local scale, preachers whose congregations had fallen into a rut often depended on the temporary aid of revival evangelists to conduct pep rallies of the soul—to increase church membership and fill the offering plates. And on a larger, even national scale, massive revivals occurred regularly during periods of social transition or crisis when established religion had begun to lose its popular appeal. Revivals, it seemed, could relieve both socioeconomic insecurity and spiritual hunger.

Populist piety erupted regularly from the bedrock of American Protestantism. Nevertheless, like the elders of Massachusetts who turned a deaf ear to Anne Hutchinson's claim of a guiding inner voice, leaders of established denominations remained wary of independent evangelists and the emotional excesses of the revival spirit. As Lyman Beecher recognized, revivalism, the euphoric antidote to the sober rationalism of Puritanism and the predictable pieties of mainline denominations, could be disruptive, even anarchistic, in its effects. The Puritans themselves, who set out to achieve a harmony of faith and reason, feared "enthusiasts" like Hutchinson who believed that they could receive all their necessary religious instruction from within. Enthusiasts threatened the unity of life by subordinating reason to the emotions. Likewise, in the nineteenth century, ministers feared the threat to their authority posed by charismatic evangelists with no denominational ties, and they feared the factionalism that could result from the fulminations of independent preachers who invented their own theology as they went along.

THE CULTURE CRISIS

After the Civil War, which divided a number of denominations on the issue of slavery, American evangelicalism was thrown into further turmoil by a series of social and intellectual developments. Industrialization and the influx of immigrants were transforming a culture that had been shaped largely by small-town life and a deeply ingrained Protestant ethic. Revolutionary modes of thought— evolution, higher biblical criticism, new social sciences—were challenging traditional academic disciplines and revising the view of human nature. Liberal ministers, following the lead of Henry Ward Beecher, attempted to accommodate Christ and the idea of progress, while conservative preachers, led by the old guard of Princeton Theological Seminary, looked to the Second Coming rather than to modernism for salvation.

Beecher, the brother of abolitionist Harriet Beecher Stowe, exemplified the "progressive" Yankee evangelical tradition that would come to be identified as liberal. For forty years the pastor of the affluent Plymouth Congregational Church in Brooklyn, Beecher concluded that unless ministers reevaluated traditional faith in the light of modern thought, they would be left behind by "the intelligent part of society." In a speech to Yale divinity students, he warned prophetically, "If ministers do not make their theological systems conform to the facts as they are; if they do not recognize what men are studying, the time will not be far distant when the pulpit will be like a voice crying in the wilderness."

In H. Richard Niebuhr's series of dialectics, Beecher's Christ was the Christ of culture. Beecher and the liberal ministers who followed him served both Christ and culture—a mandate that had been set forth earlier in the century by German theologian Friedrich Schleiermacher. Karl Barth characterized Schleiermacher as "both a Christo-centric theologian and a modern man, participating fully in the work of culture, in the development of science, the maintenance of the state, the cultivation of art, the ennoblement of family life, the advancement of philosophy." Schleiermacher, like Beecher, was "representative of those who accommodate Christ to culture while selecting from culture what conforms most readily to Christ."

The great cultural crisis for Protestant preachers came when new developments in science threatened the long-held optimistic assumption, based on the Baconian tradition of common sense, that the objective investigation of nature would confirm the literal truth of the Bible. A number of clerics refused to follow the liberal resolution of this dilemma, which rendered matters of nature unto science and matters of the soul unto religion. In this accommodating view, science could operate autonomously without threatening religious faith. For conservatives, however, to accept such a dichotomy would deny the eternal verities. The view perpetrated by the influential Princeton Seminary was that the Scriptures were inerrant, whatever scientists might hypothesize about the origin of species: God had provided in his Word only absolute facts that were true for all generations. This view endured well into the Falwell era. Jerry Falwell echoed the old Princetonites when he declared, "The Bible is absolutely infallible, without error in all matters pertaining to faith and practice, as well as in areas such as geography, science, history, etc."

Accompanying the defense by conservative evangelicals of absolute biblical truth was a renewal of interest in prophecy. Conservative theologians stepped up their study of the "end-time" prophecies scattered through the Bible, primarily in the books of Ezekiel, Daniel, and Revelation. The new "dispensation" theology arranged history into a series of seven stages, or dispensations, leading up to the Second Coming of Christ. According to this theory, the world was heading for a cosmic showdown in the valley of Armageddon, which would be preceded by a series of fateful events, including the appearance of the "Antichrist" or "false prophet"—generally taken to be an ecclesiastical tyrant (any resemblance to the Pope was not merely coincidental).

Until the midnineteenth century, most American theologians were "postmillennialists"—that is, they concurred with Jonathan Edwards that the prophecies concerning the Antichrist were already being fulfilled, with America playing a crucial role in leading the way to the golden age of the Millennium. For postmillennialists, social reform and advances in science and culture were steps in spiritual progress that would culminate in the return of Christ. For "premillennialists," however, such optimism about the progress of civilization was unwarranted. They concluded that Christ's kingdom would come about only through supernatural intervention. Instead of welcoming new developments in science and culture as evidence of progress, they saw these developments as signs of increasing secularism and disorder that prefigured the turmoil and torments of the great Tribulation described in the book of Revelation. The duty of a good Christian lay not in social reform or cultural uplift but simply in winning as many souls as possible before it was too late.

FOUNDATIONS OF FUNDAMENTALISM

Premillennial pessimism reinforced conservative antagonism to the spirit of the age. Nearly every denomination in America was affected by the dissension between regional revivalists and Bostonian rationalists, between Bible-embracing conservatives and culture-loving liberals, between last-chance premillennialists and progressive postmillennialists. Evangelical Protestantism was a mosaic of denominations, a very loose, scattered alliance cemented primarily by common beliefs about the Good News of Christ's sacrificial death and resurrection. The conservative movement that came to be known as fundamentalism, which incorporated revivalism, scriptural adamancy, and urgent prophecy, became a stress factor within the mosaic, causing new fractures and realignments within the pattern.

The doctrines of fundamentalism were set forth by conservative Bible teachers and evangelists between 1910 and 1915 in a series of twelve paperback books called *The Fundamentals: A Testimony to the Truth*. Distributed free to ministers across the country, the *Fundamentals* stressed five main doctrines: the divine inspiration of the Bible; the virgin birth of Christ; the substitutionary atonement by Christ for our sins; the resurrection of Christ; and the imminence of his return. The authors stated their case in fairly moderate terms, carefully avoiding specific political or ethical issues. They focused primarily on the integrity of the Bible and the importance of soul-winning. One author even conceded that socialism was not incompatible with Christian faith. Nevertheless, fundamentalism was a frame of mind as well as a creed. It was a state of mind that later came to be labeled as anti-intellectual, paranoid, reactionary; a state of mind, according to some analysts, that was born of such things as social displacement, discontent, despair. Despite its scholarly advocates from accredited seminaries across the country, fundamentalism soon became identified with the backwoods pietists who came to the forefront during the Scopes trial of 1925.

During that sweltering July in a small mountain village in Tennessee, fundamentalism came face to face with modernism and won the battle but lost the war. Young biology teacher John Scopes, accused of breaking Tennessee's new antievolution law by teaching Darwin's theory in the classroom, found himself defended by three eminent lawyers supplied by the American Civil Liberties Union. The team was headed by Clarence Darrow, fresh from the Leopold and Loeb case. Heading the prosecution for the state of Tennessee was the populist and former presidential contender William Jennings Bryan, who regarded the trial as an opportunity to take the stand for the Bible and bear witness against, in H. L. Mencken's words, "the city men who had laughed at him so long." Darrow had taken the case for free, remarking, "For years I've wanted to put Bryan in his place as a bigot."

At one stage of the proceedings, the beleaguered Bryan snapped, "I am perfectly willing that the world shall know that these gentlemen have no other purpose than ridiculing every Christian who believes in the Bible." Retorted Darrow, "We have the purpose of preventing bigots and ignoramuses from controlling the education of the United States and you know it, and that is all."

Darrow made mincemeat of Bryan's biblical literalism, confounding the suspender-slapping orator with the most basic devil's-advocate questions about puzzling episodes and chronologies in the Scriptures. Although Scopes was convicted, the verdict of the press and popular opinion sentenced fundamentalism to a long period of obscurity. As Walter Lippmann later observed, even the best fundamentalist arguments were no longer acceptable to the best educated minds in America.

After 1925, a movement that had once commanded considerable respect began to move completely outside the mainstream of modern intellectual life. Fundamentalism had become synonymous with rural and small-town Protestantism. Worse still, fundamentalism also came to be associated with repressive and extremist groups who operated out of moral zealotry. Bryan's successors founded such antimodernist squads as the Bible Crusaders of America and the Defenders of the Christian Faith. Over the decades various fringe groups, using either Christ or the Bible as a shield, continued to take aim at evolution, modernism, communism, and other manifestations of the devil. Fundamentalists, warned Mencken, "are everywhere where learning is too heavy a burden for mortal minds to carry, even the vague, pathetic learning on tap in the little red schoolhouses. They march with the Klan, with the Christian Endeavor Society, with the Junior Order of United American Mechanics, with the Epworth League, with all the Rococo bands that poor and unhappy folk organize to bring some new light of purpose into their lives."

During the 1930s and 1940s, fundamentalists, having failed to make the leading denominations see the light, began to develop their own separate networks of local congregations, missionary societies, summer conferences, and Bible schools. In 1941, hard-liners led by the Reverend Carl McIntire formed the American Council of Christian Churches, declaring their opposition to the more liberal National Council of Churches, which had been granted a virtual monopoly by the FCC of free broadcast time allotted by local stations to religious groups. Members of the ACCC, who had found radio to be ideally suited to the old-time revival style they practiced, feared they would be shut out of the religious broadcasting business. More moderate conservatives, who also declared their differences from the liberal Protestant denominations, banded together in the National Association of Evangelicals. Members of the NAE wanted to maintain a dialogue with contemporary culture rather than withdraw from it, as the ACCC threatened. Evangelical leaders like Carl F. H. Henry were concerned by the isolation of conservative Christians from the mainstream of social and intellectual life. By the 1970s, the long-standing "war of the churches," as Martin Marty has called the conflict between conservative and liberal denominations, spread to the nation at large, and one wondered if the moderate evangelical center could hold.

BATTLES OF THE BOOKS

As Richard Hofstadter observed, the defensive, antimodernist views of the fundamentalist right hardened into political paranoia and a rabid anti-intellectualism. Most fundamentalists would have agreed with William Jennings Bryan that "It is better to trust in the Rock of Ages, than to know the age of the rocks; it is better for one to know that he is close to the Heavenly Father, than to know how far the stars in the heavens are apart." In fundamentalist epistemology, the Bible was all one knew of truth, and all one needed to know.

It was in the classroom where conservative Christians were most vulnerable, where contemporary culture could make its most direct attacks on their values. Consequently, most of the key issues for fundamentalists involved education. During the 1950s and 1960s, feeding on cold-war paranoia, fundamentalist groups began their public comeback with assaults on the deficiencies of public education. Carl McIntire's Twentieth Century Reformation and Billy James Hargis's Christian Crusade campaigned to restore Bible-reading in the schools, stop federal aid to education, abolish busing, and put an end to the teaching of the new math, sex education, and sensitivity training in the classroom. Dr. Gordon Drake of the Christian Crusade struck the first blow against sex education in June 1968 by proclaiming over the Crusade radio network that SIECUS (the Sex Information and Education Council of the United States) and the NEA (National Education Association) were promoting a bestial view of sex. In a pamphlet titled *Is the Schoolhouse the Proper Place to Teach Raw Sex?*, Drake claimed that sex education was a direct attack on traditional Christian values. Sex education would usher in a Communist takeover, argued Drake, using the familiar fundamentalist equation of socialism and riotous sensuality.

With the Supreme Court's ban on school prayers, fundamentalists marked the beginning of yet another phase of decadence. The banishment of God from the classroom, according to Bill Bright of the Campus Crusade for Christ, led directly to crime, racial conflict, drug abuse, political assassinations, the Vietnam War, sexual promiscuity, and the demise of American family life.

In reality, the 1962 Supreme Court decision meant the beginning of the end of Christian cultural hegemony in America. Banning official school prayers was a blow to civil religion, to the Puritan-inspired image of America as a Christian commonwealth, a nation whose institutions operate with divine sanction. During the 1960s, the antiwar movement, the civil rights movement, the sexual revolution, and the women's movement began to challenge the assumption that as long as God was in His heaven, all was right with America.

During the seventies and eighties, the conservative Christian strategy toward public education reflected two classic Christian responses to noxious stimuli: censorship and separatism. The first strategy involved banning offensive books from libraries, replacing textbooks, abolishing sex education, and juxtaposing the theory of evolution with the biblical story of creation; the second involved the establishment of Christian schools wherein biblical values would not be challenged.

Initially, the leaders in the book-banning crusade were not preachers or right-wing demagogues but parents. Across the country, hundreds of such organizations as Young Parents Alert, People Concerned with Education, and Guardians of Education pressured local school boards to remove books that their members found objectionable from reading lists and libraries. In Gretna, Virginia, the high school parent-teacher committee voted to black out the pages in *The Treasury of American Poetry* containing Allen Ginsberg's "Howl." In French Lick, Indiana, *Death of a Salesman* was banned from a high school English class. The famous *Pico* v. *Island Trees* case involved a ban by a Long Island school board of nine books, including Bernard Malamud's *The Fixer* and Kurt Vonnegut, Jr.'s *Slaughterhouse Five*. In the two years following Ronald Reagan's election, such attempts to raid library shelves rose by over 300 percent, according to Judith Krug of the American Library Association.

Although book-banning efforts often seemed mere random attacks on individual books, purging an obscenity here and a bawdy poem there, parental groups were beginning to assault the very nature of public education. Instead of talking about atheism, communism, or sexual free-for-alls, these groups began using a term popularized by conservative preachers to account for the nation's decline in morality. At the heart of most classroom instruction, and indeed of contemporary culture, conservatives said, was the philosophy of "secular humanism," which established man rather than God at the center of the universe and encouraged free inquiry without establishing a system of moral guidance.

Secular humanism, in fact, was a fairly new addition to the conservative Christian's catalog of pulpit epithets. In 1978, Alexander Solzhenitsyn had warned a complacent America of the dangers of "rationalistic humanism," the "prevailing view of the world which was first born during the Renaissance and found its political expression from the period of the Enlightenment." Also during that year, an article by constitutional lawyer John W. Whitehead and former congressman John Conlan of Arizona had appeared in the *Texas Tech Law Review* claiming that the Supreme Court had virtually eliminated theism from public schools and supplanted it, by default, with secular humanism.

In 1980, the Reverend Tim LaHaye, a founder of Moral Majority, identified humanism in his influential *The Battle for the Mind* as a man-centered movement that had sneaked into America by way of such rationalist thinkers as Voltaire and had now become a full-fledged religion that threatened to displace Christianity as the national creed. Humanism, claimed LaHaye, had made America safe for the United Nations, big government, test-tube babies, Hollywood celebrities other than John Wayne, the NAACP, the ACLU, the NEA, NOW, the labor unions, and Jimmy Carter.

Humanists, insisted fundamentalist crusaders, were trying to unfetter the beast within human nature; they failed to recognize man's inherent sinfulness. The humanistic trend in psychology—the "human potential movement" celebrated by peak-seekers Abraham Maslow and Fritz Perls—had begun to counter the gloomy determinism of classical psychoanalysis with the sunnier views and speedier methods of Gestalt psychology and Transactional Analysis. The new psychology proposed a more upbeat model of the psyche, based on the assumption that the impulses of human beings are good. In this view, there was no original sin, no inevitable, tragic collision between desire and civilization.

Casting off the burdens of conformity, the self-actualized human was to follow the imperatives of growth over responsibility, of spontaneity over duty. However, to conservative evangelicals, as well as to a number of skeptical Freudians, the hot-tub baptisms offered by California humanism were no better than a dip into hedonism. To fundamentalists, permissiveness and the pursuit of pleasure were not the solutions but the problem. The relaxing of sanctions on human behavior would simply make it easier to sin.

In the classroom, secular humanism translated into the teaching of "situation ethics" rather than right and wrong, of moral and cultural relativism rather than the Judeo-Christian code. Even a subject like the new math, which taught that there were no absolutes, contained the "seeds of cultural disintegration." Conservatives found that the humanistic bias was particularly evident in science, history, health, and social-science textbooks.

There was just too much "negativism" in most of America's new textbooks, argued Mel and Norma Gabler, founders of Education Research Analysts, a textbook-screening service that they operated out of their modest home in Longview, Texas. The Gablers believed, as they told Rice University sociologist William Martin, that the purpose of education was "the imparting of factual knowledge, basic skills and cultural heritage," and that education was best accomplished in schools that emphasized "a traditional curriculum of reading, math, and grammar, as well as patriotism, high moral standards, dress codes, and strict discipline, with respect and courtesy demanded from all students." That ideal education, they felt, did not include such reversals of traditional priorities as the honoring of Crispus Attucks and Abigail Adams over Paul Revere and Benjamin Franklin. And it didn't include aberrations from New Right positions on defense, capital punishment, gun control, civil rights, Taiwan, the Panama Canal, or women's liberation.

The Gablers worked as a virtual nationwide clearinghouse for textbooks, focusing their energies on the annual textbook adoption proceedings of the Texas Board of Education. Because the state of Texas was the nation's largest single purchaser of textbooks, it acted as a national bellwether on textbook selection. Citizens of the state who objected to textbooks being considered for adoption were invited to submit "bills of particulars" listing their objections and to testify at the state adoption hearings. Over the years, the Gablers perfected their nitpicking techniques, sometimes overwhelming the adoption committee with the sheer bulk and detail of their testimony. It was difficult to determine the actual success rate of their endeavors, since many of the books they objected to might have been dropped in any case. But a number of publishers began to modify their texts in anticipation of attacks by the Gablers and other groups.

Conservative groups were not concerned merely with sins of commission but with those of omission as well. They felt that conservative Christian values had been effectively censored out of the nation's classrooms. It was not a difficult case to prove. As *Nation* writer Curtis Selzer discovered during the textbook protests in Kanawha County, West Virginia, textbooks did not always reflect the values of the community in which they were taught. When Selzer examined the books adopted by the local board that angry parents had complained about and, it was rumored, burned, he discovered that the white, working-class protesters from the coal fields and mountains of Appalachia had grounds for complaint. Wrote Selzer, "The editing reflects a value system that runs counter to most of what they cherish." The books tended to "play out the alienation felt by urban intellectuals and university militants of the 1960s, who seem to the protestors to have taken over the publishing houses in New York."

As objectionable to parents as the inclusion in the books of unpatriotic and sacrilegious selections "was the almost total exclusion of people like themselves from the 'multi-cultural' texts. The editors had not thought that coal miners, or country folk, or Appalachians or working people were either distinguishable groups or important enough to include. Paradoxically, the board's attempt to broaden the English curriculum had shifted the spectrum away from the majority of citizens in the county."

DARWIN REDUX

The claims by the citizens of Kanawha County and other regions of editorial bias in textbooks were as valid as complaints by women and minority groups during the sixties and seventies that they were being treated unfairly or ignored in the nation's textbooks. It was little wonder that conservative Christians felt they were being shut out of mainstream culture. However, it was their obsession with one particular classroom issue that ensured that they would never be taken seriously by leaders in the centers of learning. For fundamentalists, the chief sin of omission in the classroom was the neglect of the biblical story of creation.

In 1981, the nation experienced a sense of déjà vu as the Reverend Jerry Falwell set up TV cameras where William Jennings Bryan had made his last stand in the old Dayton, Tennessee, courthouse. Falwell launched a nationwide appeal for funds to defend antievolution laws that were under consideration in twenty states and that had been passed in two. Chief on the docket was a statute passed by the Arkansas legislature requiring the "creator" theory of origins to be given equal time in the classroom whenever the subject of evolution was raised. One could imagine an instructor walking up to the blackboard and drawing a lightning bolt alongside a dinosaur.

In order to avoid charges of injecting religion into the classroom, fundamentalists stuffed the book of Genesis into a test tube and called it "creation science" or "creationism," granting it the scientific status accorded the theory of evolution. In keeping with their propensity for appropriating the forms and language of secular culture, they established creation-science research centers that attempted to muster scientific evidence in support of instantaneous creation and the catastrophic flood that only Noah, his family, and his menagerie had survived. (Unfortunately, no research papers supporting the creationist theory had been published in reputable science journals.)

The Arkansas law (Act 590), originally drawn up by the Institute for Creation Science in San Diego, posited: "(1) Sudden creation of the universe, energy, and life from nothing; (2) The insufficiency of mutation and natural selection in bringing about development of all living kinds from a single organism; (3) Changes only within fixed limits of originally created kinds of plants and animals; (4) Separate ancestry for man and apes; (5) Explanation of the earth's geology by catastrophism, including the occurrence of a worldwide flood; and (6) A relatively recent inception of the earth and living kinds."

The attitude of creationists toward evolution theory was best expressed by the cover of a popular book on creationism called *What's All This Monkey Business?* written by Phyllis and Monty Kester, a Baytown, Texas, couple who rivaled the Gablers in their textbook vigilance. On the front jacket was a dopey-looking ape with wings and halo, holding a stone tablet inscribed "We've Got Our Rights!"

William Jennings Bryan's moldering teeth must have rattled as the ACLU yet again mounted a defense for the teaching of the theory of evolution and yet again prepared an assault on the biblical story of creation. However, this time the confrontation was not simply science vs. religion; it was an extension of the war of the churches. The plaintiffs seeking the overturning of the law included Southern Baptist, Presbyterian, and Methodist ministers as well as Roman Catholic, Episcopal, and Methodist bishops. And this time it was the book of Genesis rather than evolution that was actually on trial.

The role of Clarence Darrow was taken by a number of clerics and scientists. The clerics testified that creationism was a religious doctrine, and scientists testified that by no means could it be considered a science. Michael E. Ruse, philosopher of science from the University of Guelph, in Ontario, Canada, asserted that creation science could not be considered scientific because the theory did not rely on natural law; could not be tested for truth; and was so rigid that its adherents would not revise it even when scientific evidence was found to contradict it.

The case for creationism was so poorly presented that fundamentalist leaders themselves sensed that they had been embarrassed almost beyond redemption. The series of dubiously credentialed academics who took the stand for creationism found their case seriously undercut by various digressions, including the assertion by Dr. Norman Geisler of the Dallas Theological Seminary that he believed UFOs were "a satanic manifestation in the world for the purpose of deception." It was little wonder that Judge William Ray Overton ruled against the creationists. Overturning the law, he found that creation science "has no scientific merit or educational value." Said Overton, "Since creation science is not science, the conclusion is inescapable that the only real effect of Act 590 is the advancement of religion."

BIBLE SCHOOLS

Actually, many fundamentalists would have concurred with Judge Overton's latter point; they would not only *have* agreed, but seconded the notion that classroom teaching should further the Christian cause. However, many fundamentalists turned their energies from attempting to reform public education to establishing a private Christian alternative. As Catholic parents had been doing for generations, conservative evangelicals began to support separate Christian schools that would shield their children from alien ideas and habits. At the end of the seventies, over a million children were attending Christian (i.e., evangelical or fundamentalist) schools. And by the early eighties, Christian schools were multiplying at the rate of hamburger franchises. Every seven hours, a new Christian operation opened its doors.

Some of the schools apparently were established to avoid court-ordered integration. Beginning in 1970, the IRS had revoked the tax exemptions of a number of schools, including North Carolina's pious, teetotaling Bob Jones University, because of their segregationist admission policies. But most Christian schools had been established with another priority in mind: the teaching of Christian culture. In a Christian curriculum, reading, writing, and arithmetic were lessons in Christian values. Those values applied to black as well as white students; all students were welcome who did not present discipline problems.

More than two thirds of Christian primary and secondary schools used a standardized curriculum packaged by an outfit called Accelerated Christian Education based in Lewisville, Texas. ACE was the Burger King of Christian education. For a fee of $5,000, ACE could set up any fundamentalist preacher as the principal of his own private school. ACE supplied workbooks, texts, and tests for the first grade through the second year of college; trained classroom supervisors (there were no "teachers" in the ACE program); and for additional fees would provide red-white-and-blue uniforms, desks, and various supplies. Christian schools could completely avoid transactions with secular businesses, experts, and authorities.

The ACE logo featured an eagle holding an American flag over an open Bible; it was a perfect emblem for civil religion. In addition to heavy-duty Bible study, ACE placed special emphasis on the concepts of free enterprise and individual initiative. Accordingly, ACE schools used a peculiar combination of little-red-schoolhouse discipline and Summerhill self-motivation. Each student was assigned a separate study carrel and given a series of twelve booklets designed for his or her grade level. Calling on supervisors only when they needed assistance, students could progress from level to level at their own pace, grading their own tests except for the final. (Each test was prefaced with the suggestion, "Ask Jesus to help you.") Both the workbooks and the tests combined sacred and secular material, often in the same sentence. Students at the third level learned, for example, that "God made the Earth to travel through space around the sun" and that the study of history was important because it taught that "when people did right, God blessed them." Twelfth-level students learned that "the free market economy diminishes rather than increases the amount of inequality in society."

ACE fitted perfectly the plan for Christian education that Jerry Falwell had outlined in his book *Listen, America!*: "In Christian schools, education begins with God. The objectives are based on Biblical principles, with God as the center of every subject. The philosophies taught stand as witness to society, as the ultimate goal, not as a reflection of man's sinful nature. In science the student learns God's laws for the universe; in history, God's plan for the ages; and in civics, God's requirement of loyalty and support for the government He has ordained."

Although proponents of ACE claimed that students who completed the program were academically a step ahead of students in public schools, such claims were hard to verify. ACE schools were generally unaccredited, and ACE students usually avoided testing their mettle in secular competition, choosing instead to attend Christian colleges which were also unaccredited. In many states, secular school officials were not convinced of the quality of separate Christian education. In Nebraska, after years of legal battles between state authorities and sponsors of religious schools, a sheriff in the town of Louisville was finally ordered to padlock the door on Faith Baptist School, which had been operating without accredited teachers in the basement of Faith Baptist Church. The church pastor, who had acted as director of the school, was jailed at one point in the controversy, and he continued to conduct classes in a bus parked in front of the padlocked church.

Taking his "Old Time Gospel Hour" to Louisville to broadcast a rally in support of Christian schools like Faith Baptist, Jerry Falwell claimed that the padlocking "smacked of Moscow and Peking." Nevertheless, other conservative Christian leaders had their doubts about the effectiveness of ACE and other separatist curricula. The principal of the Christian school in my hometown, for instance, who measured several ACE students on the California Assessment Program Test, found that their skills fell below their professed grade levels.

Christian education prepared students to progress successfully within a closed Christian community; whether it prepared them to live in a modern world of multicultural, multiethnic communities was another question. As Frances Fitzgerald observed in a story on Jerry Falwell, Christian education "is not a moral and intellectual quest that involves struggle and uncertainty. It is simply the process of learning, or teaching, the right answers."

I want you to know that the children, the students, don't have any vote on what's right or wrong around here. We tell them what to do, what time to get up, what time to go to bed, and they say "yes sir" and "no sir" and they wear what we tell them to wear. And the boys have one head of hair, and the gals dress like young ladies, and I want you to know that the kids who come through these schools know what life is all about.

Jerry Falwell

When I was growing up, there had been no need in my town for a separate Christian school; there was no chasm between the Christian boosterism I learned at church and the patriotic values I absorbed in civics class or the rugged individualism I cheered at football games. The worst vice I could have succumbed to by consorting with my nonreligious peers was chugging a six-pack of beer in the church parking lot. But now, students at the school I had attended were a tougher sort. Drugs, delinquency, and sexual promiscuity had invaded my quiet little town. It was not difficult to understand why so many parents now supported a private Christian school where kids could grow up the old-fashioned way: slowly.

Yet public school had always been the main link between fundamentalists and a larger world. It was difficult for me to imagine growing up without the constant tension between the simple goodness one was taught at church and the more complex, contradictory values one learned at school and on the street. To burn with virtue on Sunday and yearn to fall on Monday may have been confusing but ultimately, I think, it built character.

Surely children who grew up in a totally antiseptic environment would be susceptible to any number of germs once they left quarantine. And surely they would suffer from the lack of intellectual exercise that came from jumping back and forth between the worldly and the sacred, between culture and Christ. Surely they would be limited even in their spiritual quests, never knowing the fear and trembling of doubt. For the most part, Christian schools were cloisters without windows. As the basis of a new Christian culture, they offered a singularly dark and narrow vision of the future.

CHAPTER 2

The Lord Has Many Mansions: Multifaceted Ministries and the Super Churches

There was once a wayward salesman named Earl Bigg, who traveled the edges of the Electronic Kingdom selling miraculous kitchen appliances. One day he heeded the call of the Lord to become a drummer of men instead of vegematics. He took correspondence courses in the Lord's business, and he began dropping in on radio stations along his route, where he prayed on the air for a new puree of faith. As he himself prospered, he began to preach the gospel of success through positive blending. His followers multiplied, and Earl Bigg became Brother Bigg, a preacher with his own TV studio set in a scenic pine grove by the sea and a syndicated show called "Praying for Dollars." Brother Bigg worked many miracles over the airwaves, and before long he controlled his own satellite dish, his own PFD network, and his Plexiglas prayer tower shaped like a food processor.

The notion of a separate Christian culture, boosted by the secular ideals of "bigger and better," led a number of evangelicals to run their religious endeavors like a corporation. Political involvement by fundamentalist preachers during the Falwell era diverted attention from a much more permanent crusade going on in America: the establishment of Christian capitalism.

By the beginning of the eighties, the Lord's business had become big business. Evangelists had become entrepreneurs, and entrepreneurs had become evangelists. The phantom congregations of the nation's TV preachers had become rooted in elaborate institutions, and ordinary churches had grown into Super Churches.

Every preacher, it seemed, aspired to his own Total Image Center, as TV talk-show host Jim Bakker named his new layout of Christian buildings in Charlotte, North Carolina. The evangelicals who presided over this era of Christian boosterism had become builders of church complexes as well as congregations. They had become promoters of products as well as prayers, sellers of image as well as substance. They had become architects of what the Reverend Bill Sharp of Las Vegas called the "multifaceted ministry."

Sharp, who had been raising money to construct a Christian nightclub atop a 230-foot space needle, described his multimedia vision to writers Robert G. Kaiser and Jon Lowell: "See, there are a lot of Christian people who would like to come to Las Vegas, but they don't have a reason. We're going to give them a reason. Our Christian nightclub. Having a Christian breakfast on radio every Monday morning from that nightclub in the sky. The hotel, the Bible college, the network, the television, the crisis center. What I'm trying to say, in essence, is we're trying to put together a spiritual shopping center in a city."

Sharp's vision of a space-age revival tent, an unwitting parody of the tawdriest elements of both Las Vegas and evangelism, revealed the measure of accommodation Christ had made to culture in the era of casinos and shopping malls. Christians were enticed into churches as tourists or customers, and TV viewers built monuments to the charisma of their favorite ministers. The business of bearing witness in the technological age seemed to operate according to the Reverend Robert Schuller's principle of possibility-thinking: ministry expanded according to the size of the minister's vision and the rate of donations received.

Typical of this rapid expansion of ministries was Anita Bryant's

moral crusade. After her successful 1977 campaign to repeal a
Dade County, Florida, ordinance that banned job and housing discrimination against homosexuals, Bryant broadened her approach
to promoting Christian values in American life. Following the counsel of conservative advisers and playing down her role as persecutor
of gays, Bryant, with her husband Bob Green, founded Anita Bryant Ministries to "bring America back to God and rebuild the
moral fiber in our nation." Bryant was chairman of the board and
Green the president.

In a promotional brochure, the former Miss America runner-up
and promoter of Florida's citrus bounty vowed to "go beyond addressing the surface symptoms of such problems as homosexuality,
abortion, ERA, pornography, etc. and rebuild a foundation to deal
with the root of the problem i.e. the disintegration of the American
family." Proceeding in the usual pattern of the multimedia ministry, Anita Bryant Ministries planned a diversified crusade: a series
of "sacred concerts" by Bryant; a five-day-a-week radio show
hosted by Bryant and Green; a television special starring, among
others, Pat Boone and General William Westmoreland; a packaged
Design for Successful Living Seminar; and a research and education
department with a "special interest in analyzing the impact of federal government policy on American family life."

Preachers, both ordained and self-annointed, became more and
more ingenious at the business of promoting themselves and their
congregations. Even the sky was no limit. Lloyd J. Tomer, pastor of
the Benton, Illinois, Church of God, reportedly tried to convince
his congregation to purchase two jets once owned by Elvis Presley.
Couples could tour the "museums with wings," promised Tomer,
and listen to music by Presley's former backup group, the Stamps
Quartet, all for only $300, which would go toward the construction
of a new auditorium for the church.

Carrying out the Lord's work had become a matter of supply-side
spirituality. Building more and better Christian facilities would
stimulate the demand for Christian services. Sometimes, however,
those services were a matter of luxury rather than necessity. When
Christian businessman Howard "Bud" Fisher and musical producer
David Van Koevering met and founded Masters Marketing, the
two men felt their partnership had been ordained of God. Fisher
had long been interested in Guy Lombardo's lavish Tierra Verde

Hotel, located on an island off the west coast of Florida, and Van Koevering agreed that the hotel should be claimed by God's people as a Christian convention and conference center.

In January 1980, the men announced their plans for converting Tierra Verde into a nightclub to be used for television productions, a "Hall of Faith" rotunda displaying artifacts of Christianity's "Major Ministries," an Olympic-sized swimming pool, a sixty-seven–slip marina, and a bait shop: "Just as men of science are launching missiles from the East Coast of Florida, a place is now available to men of faith to launch His TRUTH from the West Coast of Florida. . . . Jesus loved the water. He spent great periods of time on the Sea of Galilee. Masters Marketing is providing that same restful atmosphere for the use of God's people."

THE SUPER SANCTUARIES

Every time a group of Christians have moved from the catacombs to a brush arbor . . . to a wooden-frame building . . . to a brick structure . . . along the way it has lost something. It gave up something it believed about Jesus and never seemed to get it back.

Will Campbell

Contentment with the status quo was not a common evangelical trait. Like insecure shepherds, preachers were always counting their sheep, as well as their blessings, boasting about the size of their flocks. Conservative evangelicals, having felt themselves in the minority so long, took particular pride in tallying their triumphs. And the multiministried Super Church was a matter for particular pride. As Falwell himself proclaimed in an introduction to *The Fundamentalist Phenomenon*, "the age of the superchurch" saw fundamentalist churches grow to "mammoth proportions." These humongous churches, still growing, "ministered to thousands of people and developed large professional staffs." Falwell's own Lynchburg Baptist Church became one of these mammoth-proportioned Super Churches, its membership comprising, according to Falwell's claim, a fourth of the population of Lynchburg.

Perhaps the proudest Super Church of all, though, was the First

Baptist Church of Dallas, the starship of the Southern Baptist fleet, piloted by Pastor W. A. Criswell. Criswell's congregation, to hear him tell it, was composed of winners. Dallas Cowboy place-kicker Rafael Septien, overcoming the initial suspicion aroused by his foreign soccer style of addressing the ball, became the 20,000th member of the church. By 1983, the church counted some 23,000 members on its rolls, making it the largest Southern Baptist congregation in America.

The church itself was well equipped for fitness-building, with its own Nautilus machines, sauna, twin gymnasiums, skating rink, bowling alleys, and racquetball courts. Those who prayed together played together. According to William Martin, the multitudinous ministries of the church included "21 choirs, a mission center, an academy with a kindergarten-through-twelfth-grade enrollment of over six hundred, the Criswell Center for Biblical Studies with over 275 students pursuing two degrees of religious certitude, an FM radio station, and a Fellowship of Christian Truckers whose members minister at truck stops and terminals in Dallas County." The annual budget of the church is $8 million.

W. A. Criswell had reason to indulge in a little pride and apotheosis: "This place in the eye of God is more favored than any other. It is from here, from our dear church, that we are all going to heaven." Criswell's confidence had even made a believer out of billionaire reprobate H. L. Hunt, who was baptized at the church in 1960. Hunt had been so captivated with Criswell's rhetoric that he printed some 200,000 copies of an anti-Catholic Criswell sermon attacking John F. Kennedy during the 1960 presidential campaign.

For conservative evangelicals, when it came to churches and egos, bigger was better. In a zero-sum theology, one more convert for Christ and conservatism meant one less recruit for the devil and humanism. As evangelical congregations grew and prospered during the multidenominational church boom in the fifties and even during the sixties when mainstream Protestant churches began to shrink, church growth became a new theological discipline within evangelicalism. The "church growth movement" began officially in 1955, with the publication of *The Bridges of God* by Donald McGavran, founder of the Fuller Theological Seminary School of World Mission and Institute of Church Growth. At Fuller, the new intellectual center of evangelicalism, scholars discovered that church growth was based on the simple "birds-of-a-feather" principle: congregations flocked together and flourished when they were composed of the like-minded.

The secret of success for TV evangelists was their ability to create a sense of common identity and mission among armchair worshipers, and the secret of success for evangelical churches was their aura of homogeneity—the firm congregational feeling of neighborhood, family, doctrinal, or even racial identity. One knew what kind of worship to expect from conservative churches, just as one knew what kind of burger to expect from McDonald's. Evangelicals had largely resisted the demands for "relevance" in the sixties, even as more liberal churches were allowing Sufi-dancing in the aisles. The accommodations that evangelicals had begun to make to modernism were less obvious and less threatening to upwardly mobile congregations.

When liberal denominations cited such contextual factors as changes in family income or the national population shift to the Sun Belt in order to account for their own congregational decline, conservative analysts claimed that such institutional variables as theological conservatism and a unitary set of beliefs were the basis for their own church growth. And as evangelicals set out systematically to account for their success, the causes of church growth became their own rationale; expansionism and homogeneity became ends in themselves. Meanwhile the Super Savers set out to bring all of America into the fold—an America shorn of its shaggy and tangled pluralism.

Behind the growth of the Super Churches and the Electronic Kingdom were two different spiritual mandates drawn from the Bible: the cultural and evangelistic. The key scriptural sanction for the business of evangelism and church growth was taken from Matthew 28:19–20. Christ's directive to his disciples—his Great Commission —was interpreted by electronic preachers as a mandate for super-salesmanship of the spirit—a command to broadcast their ministry far and wide: "Go ye therefore, and teach all nations, baptizing them in the name of the Father, and of the Son, and of the Holy Ghost: Teaching them to observe all things whatsoever I have commanded you."

It was these verses that the Reverend Freddie Stone (played by

Ned Beatty) quoted to the disenchanted Tom McPherson (John Ritter) in ABC's 1982 made-for-TV movie *Pray TV*. When Mc-Pherson, an ingenuous young missionary hired by Stone, discovered that boxes bound for Brazil from the Divinity Broadcasting Network were full of satellite components instead of missionary supplies, he reacted as Donald Sutherland did upon discovering a truckload of pods in *Invasion of the Body Snatchers*. For McPherson, satellite beams were no substitute for in-the-flesh witnessing. Stone responded by pointing out the greater evangelistic efficiency of immediate telecasting over trudging missionaries.

The Super Savers found safety of conscience, as well as status, in numbers. But the growth of the multifaceted ministry had been defined by the cultural mandate as well as the Great Commission. The sanction for the worldly concerns of churches and clerics was found in Genesis 1:28, when God bade Adam and Eve: "Be fruitful, and multiply, and replenish the earth, and subdue it: and have dominion over the fish of the sea, and over the fowl of the air, and over every living thing that moveth upon the earth." These duties of worldly stewardship, as defined by church-growth advocate C. Peter Wagner, concerned such "global responsibilities" as "distribution of wealth, the balance of nature, marriage and the family, human government, keeping the peace, cultural integrity, liberation of the oppressed."

While the cultural mandate became for many evangelicals in the nineteenth century the basis for the Social Gospel and the call to massive reform, for many others the extent of the social mission of the church was emergency rescue. And for conservative evangelicals, always suspicious of the siren calls of secular culture, the primary concern had traditionally been Bibles before butter. Until conservative evangelicals themselves became politically active, following the cultural mandate had been primarily the prerogative of mainline Protestant denominations.

Complaining of the emphasis by United Methodist church leaders of social concerns over winning souls in the sixties, a conservative evangelical charged that Methodists had become "keepers of the aquarium" rather than "fishers of men." In fact, leaders of the church-growth movement pointed out that it was the denominations emphasizing cultural over evangelistic concerns whose congregations had begun to decline in the sixties. As Jeffrey Hadden observed in *The Gathering Storm in the Churches,* the social concerns of many Protestant church leaders during the sixties tended to out-strip those of their congregations. And although conservative evan-gelical leaders themselves risked creating such a rift at the end of the seventies when they began to seek political solutions to their moral imperatives, they tended to hew more closely to the consen-sus of their congregations.

THE MINISTRY OF NUMBERS

The Super Savers of evangelicalism discovered that the key to spreading the Good News and increasing the size of their congre-gations was to blend the evangelistic and cultural mandates into the imperatives of Christian capitalism: Find a need and fill it; find a hurt and heal it. Or, as in Jerry Falwell's case, find a fear and sear it; find a hate and inflate it.

As Falwell knew, the key ministry in the multiministried Super Churches was the ministry of numbers, and it was the Super Savers who ventured into the Electronic Kingdom who rang up the great-est scores for the Great Commission. With the advent of televangel-ism, the lives of many enterprising evangelists came to resemble rags-to-tabernacles parables. The rise of Jerry Falwell, the son of an alcoholic wastrel who began his preaching career in an abandoned Donald Duck bottling plant, was the paradigm of the man-with-a-mission stories so common in the world of evangelicalism.

"Something *good* is going to happen to *you,*" veteran broadcaster Oral Roberts promised his viewers every week. Certainly some-thing good had happened to *him,* and to other traveling evangelists who had forseen the miraculous properties of the electronic media. There was no need to become a circuit rider with bus lag when one could ride the electronic circuits.

With the reverence of a prophet describing his first glimpse of the promised land, pioneering televangelist Rex Humbard de-scribed to the 1982 convocation of National Religious Broadcasters his fateful discovery of the drawing power of TV. During the fif-ties, when he was still traveling with the Humbard Family Singers as part of his father's tent-revival show, he had spotted a crowd of people gathered before a TV set in the window of O'Neil's Department Store in Akron, Ohio, and he knew then that he would find a way to preach over the airwaves. In just eight years, after beginning his ministry in a movie theater purchased for $65, he had built his own Cathedral of Tomorrow in Akron, designed specifically for broadcasting the Word. The "Rex Humbard Hour" was carried by over two hundred TV stations in America and over four hundred radio and TV stations worldwide.

Oral Roberts himself, once a backwoods tubercular stutterer, had parlayed a portable revival tent and a hot healing hand into a television ministry, a college with a winning basketball team, and a City of Faith complex with a hospital as tall as the 900-foot Jesus who appeared to the evangelist one night in a dream-vision.

LETTING THE SUN SHINE IN

Although Roberts acknowledged the miracles of modern technology when he filled his towering new hospital with the latest equipment, he also continued to faith-heal the old-fashioned way—with the heel of his hand. But other Super Savers preferred to use their persuasive powers in more subtle ways. On the brighter side of evangelicalism were the positive thinkers, the apostles of Norman Vincent Peale, who preached the gilded gospel of success. Chief among them was Robert Schuller, who began preaching atop the refreshment stand of an Orange County drive-in to a congregation of cars and wound up advising thousands of viewers from the cheery sunlit pulpit of the Crystal Cathedral.

Whereas Peale had prescribed mental exercises to supercharge the hidden powers of the subconscious, with God acting as a kind of divine dynamo, Schuller threw open the shutters and let the Southern California sun shine in on the psyche. As the pale, wounded ego basked in the warm glow of optimism, the world became a paradise of possibilities. The cross became a plus sign rather than an emblem of sacrifice. Speaking in alchemical aphorisms, Schuller bade his listeners, viewers, and readers to draw a pension from their tension, to turn their scars into stars. He practiced as well as preached the Possibility Thinker's Creed: "When faced with a mountain, I will not quit. I will keep on striving until I climb over, pass through, tunnel underneath—or simply stay and turn the mountain into a gold mine, with God's help."

Schuller, who could turn cars into pews, lawns into churches, pledges into bricks, and slogans into books, was a genius at fusing Christ and culture, at adapting the Message to any medium. He succeeded by sanctifying the icons of California culture—sunshine and the automobile—as he conducted an outdoor ministry to the congregation of drivers and passengers parked at the old Orange Drive-In Theater. "Come as you are in the family car" was the first of his famous mottoes. As his congregation grew, he commissioned architect Richard Neutra in 1961 to design a modest chapel in Garden Grove, from which he could still preach to an overflow crowd of families parked in concentric rows of cars. In 1968 came the Tower of Hope, a fourteen-story carillon housing the Chapel in the Sky and numerous offices needed to accommodate the everyday business of the Garden Grove Community Church.

By 1975, five years after he began televising his services, he was possibility-thinking about a monumental sanctuary that would rival the great cathedrals of Europe. Except, as he instructed architect Philip Johnson, this cathedral would not be like "the gloomy cathedrals of Christendom which are based on the Roman catacombs. We will worship under God's great sun and moon and stars." The cost would be great, he predicted, but "it will be a work of art and so useful and long-lived that it will be a super-bargain for everyone."

Schuller, who had maintained an affiliation with the Reformed Church of America—formerly the Dutch Reformed church, the oldest Protestant denomination with a continuous ministry in the United States—had in mind a bright new jewel of Protestant architecture to outshine the crumbling seats of Catholic splendor in the Old World. From the pure austerity of little white churches in New England to modern prayer towers and broadcast towers pointing upward amid Sun Belt Babels, evangelical architecture had evolved into the American vernacular of overreaching.

And so, only a stone's throw from Disneyland, the see-through Crystal Cathedral of Orange County arose like a mirage of faith, an edifice of mirrors, a California epiphany, a trompe-l'oeil of light. When Beverly Sills sang at the grand opening in May 1980, the

only trepidation was that her high C might shatter Schuller's handi-
work. Shaped like a four-pointed star, the sanctuary's glass-clad
skeleton of grids and trusses shimmered on its foundation like a
high-tech miracle. And unlike Gothic cathedrals, whose cleresto-
ries, spires, and stained glass subdued the sun into an interior light
as elusive and mysterious as the spirit, the light and space of the
Crystal Cathedral became a glorious open book. The translucent
panes of silver-coated glass created what Philip Johnson called
"sub-aqueous" light—light filtered through water. No flying but-
tresses here, whose supportive strength was invisible from the interior; the lacy white gridwork of Schuller's structure did its buttress-
ing in sight of the congregation.

With the sunlight bouncing off the cathedral as though from a
huge semiprecious outcrop, the Garden Grove Community Church
epitomized the glittering ambitions of the multifaceted ministry.
The rationale for constructing this highly conspicuous symbol of
success was not the establishment of visible proof of divine election
but the creation of a giant lure for potential positive-thinkers. In
1974, when Schuller's most flamboyant gimmick was the set of
fountains that sprayed on cue, he had declared, "We are trying to
make a big, beautiful impression upon the affluent non-religious
American who is riding by on this busy freeway."

The cathedral itself appeared to be an unreal media icon—the
cathedral of the cathode ray. But the church bureaucracy that toiled
nearby oversaw a full complement of activities for its local congregation and for visitors lured in off the freeways. Schuller was not a
dictator or a demagogue but a "motivator." The Garden Grove
offered so many programs to its ever-growing, upward-of-10,000
membership that they did not need to look elsewhere for a social or
athletic life. For "positive Christian singles," the church issued a
monthly "motivator Calendar of Events" that included, in a typical
month, an ice-cream social, an "oldies and goodies" dance, a luau, a
bicycle outing and picnic, and numerous "afterglow" sessions following the evening service.

THE BODY SNATCHERS

If this California version of the evangelical Super Church seemed all sweetness and light, other Super Churches, in other regions, grew by proffering gloom and doom along with their recreation programs. The Reverend Jack Hyles, the Super Saver of the Midwest, author of *How to Boost Your Church Attendance* and *Let's Go Soul Winning,* presided with a pulpit-pounding fist over the 56,000-member congregation of the First Baptist Church of Hammond, Indiana, proclaimed as the "World's Largest Sunday School" and the "Fastest Growing Church in America." Hyles also presided over a church complex that included a cavernous no-frills sanctuary, twelve buildings and parcels in downtown Hammond, a fifty-three-acre Bible camp in Illinois, and Baptist City, a campus that held a grammar school, high school, and the Hyles-Anderson College for aspiring preachers. If the schools were unaccredited, and if much of Hyles's ministry took place in dilapidated buildings along a seedy, once-thriving street in a seedy, once-thriving town, Hammond First Baptist could take pride in the sheer volume of its business.

For Hyles, such success with superlatives in a humble setting was a triumph of the will. Unlike most Super Savers, he did not have much of a media presence. He wore nerdy glasses, spoke in a monotone, and constantly cleared his throat as he preached. But if he was not able to transmit his ministry to the multitudes via television, he had found another way to conquer phlegm and reach the masses. Hyles, like Robert Schuller, turned America's worship of wheeled transport to his advantage. The secret of his ever-swelling congregation was "The World's Largest Bus Ministry." Every Sunday morning some two hundred buses pulled into Hammond from Chicago and its environs, crowded with the crippled, the deaf, and the retarded, with displaced Southerners, with Spanish-speaking immigrants, with chattering children from ghettos and barrios, with homesick sailors from the Great Lakes Naval Training Center. Like the painted-van ministries of the West Coast Jesus movement, Hyles's bus flotilla acted as a kind of body-roundup service.

Hyles targeted the homes of the poor, the isolated, the lonely:

housing projects, apartment houses, trailer courts, country roads.
The door-to-door solicitor and the bus drivers, according to Hyles's
church manual, were to look "for houses where the windows are
not all in and there is a cardboard over a broken pane, where the
front glass of the door has been broken out and a piece of linoleum
has been tacked in its place. . . . You are looking for a place
where there is a preeminence of junk in the yard, possibly an old
car or two up on blocks, and lots of children. . . . Any place
where there is a great concentration of populace is the best place
for a bus ministry . . . particularly the lower-class and lower financial sections of town."

Once the poor, the young, and the meek had been rounded up
and delivered, many just going along for the ride or for a promised
souvenir, they were separated according to age, race, and handicap.
Black and Hispanic children had their own Sunday school building,
while Hispanic adults gathered at the Spanish Bible School. Yet
another building was set aside for the blind and the retarded. The
core congregation was composed of whites who, for the most part,
approved of busing black children fifty miles for Christ but disap-
proved of busing them across town for school integration—a common attitude for fundamentalists who had never reconciled their
missionary zeal with their separatist impulses.

A CHRISTIAN EXCLUSIVE

The Great Commission presented homogeneous Super Churches
with a difficult conundrum: how to save souls without getting contaminated by the unsaved. It also presented Christian businessmen
with the dilemma of how to drum up business without attracting
the wrong kind of customers. The notion of the church as multiministried industry led ultimately to the vision of a new Christian
metropolis: a cross between Calvin's Geneva and a shopping mall.
As R. H. Tawney described the heroic age of Calvinism: "The
essence of the system was not preaching or propaganda, though it
was prolific of both, but the attempt to crystallize a moral idea in
the daily life of a visible society, which should be at once a Church

and a State. Having overthrown monasticism, its aim was to turn the secular world into a gigantic monastery. . . ."

Inevitably, perhaps, it was California Christians who popularized the ultimate means of evangelical exclusivity: the *Christian Yellow Pages*. In Orange County, one of the chosen places of evangelicalism, it was possible to dwell in a total Christian environment. Letting their fingers do the walking through the *Christian Yellow Pages,* evangelicals could buy a car from a born-again dealer, get their taxes prepared by a devout CPA, get their necks uncricked by Christian chiropractors, consult Christian lawyers for Christian divorces, purchase their fashions from a Revelation outlet, get their carpets cleaned by a Christian-operated hydro steam unit, have their coiffures trimmed at Hair After, have their pools cleaned by New Life Pool Maintenance, have their drains unclogged by Agape Plumbing, and get their pests fumigated by Golden Exterminators, Inc.

When two Jewish businessmen sued the directory after they were told they could not advertise in its pages, the lawyer for the publication, David Llewellyn, explained that its purpose was to "permit born-again Christians to associate with other born-again Christians in a metropolitan area." Said Llewellyn, responding to a Los Angeles judge's ruling that the publisher of the directory could not limit advertising to born-again Christians, "There is no question that a Christian who uses the *Christian Yellow Pages* and goes to someone and discovers that he is dealing with a Scientologist, a Moonie, a Hare Krishna or an atheist will be stunned, very offended and feel misled, and the whole purpose of the *Christian Yellow Pages* will have failed."

CHAPTER 3

The Total Woman vs.
the Whole Woman:
Christian Brides
and Evangelical Feminists

Who can find a total woman? for her price is far above rubies.

The dominance of her husband doth safely trust in her, so that he shall have need of spoiling her.

She seeketh romance, and reward, and worketh willingly with her hands.

She riseth also while it is yet night, and lighteth the candle of her husband.

She girdeth her loins with Saran Wrap, and prepareth herself for whoopee.

She perceiveth that her merchandise is good.

She openeth her mouth with the babble of bimbos: and in her tongue is the law of flattery.

Although most of the leaders of the growing Christian/industrial complex were men, women were the principal consumers of Christian culture as well as the mainstays of most congregations. Men may have pounded the pulpits and passed the collection plates in conservative churches, but women were the angels in the pews, the keepers of the church, who made the world of evangelicalism work. Evangelical women taught Sunday school classes, watched Christian soap operas, bought inspirational books, visited the sick, baked cakes and casseroles for church fund-raisers. In the big multiministried churches, where every day was Sunday, women could find sanctuary all week long, studying macramé or self-defense as well as the book of Revelation.

Nevertheless, the new books, magazines, classes, and programs designed for Christian wives and mothers were beginning to acknowledge a certain restiveness among women long accustomed to traditional supporting roles at home and at church. Women received mixed messages from Christian counselors, some of whom advocated the patience of Griselda, some of whom advised the resourcefulness of Scarlett O'Hara—but all of whom recognized that money, peace of mind, and good men were getting hard to find.

Today's Christian Woman, a publication designed for evangelical housewives, typically contained tips for job interviews and money management rather than strudel recipes and crochet patterns. By contrast, *Happiness Is Homemaking,* a guide to joyous old-fashioned domesticity by radio talk-show host Ella May Miller, began with a bit of plain talk and morale-boosting: "It is popular for the modern woman to resent being a housewife, to feel it is a second-rate profession. This need not be the case. Homemaking can be enjoyable, when you join hands with God." Miller's solution, a variation of the standard evangelical exhortation to women, was a bigger dose of selflessness: "Aren't we focusing on wrong values—on purely selfish goals? Somehow we have failed to emphasize woman's role as helper to man (not his boss or competitor). . . . Real happiness comes in forgetting self. You forget self as you get interested in Jesus Christ."

Virtue was not enough, however, for most women; virtue wouldn't hold a straying husband. Putting Jesus first wouldn't pay the mortgage or fill an empty day. Social and financial needs were driving wives out of their exemplary kitchens to seek jobs or therapy rather than self-denial or repentance. For many evangelical women, the bubble had burst. They had grown frustrated by indifferent husbands, distracted preachers, rebellious children, the dull daily round. It would take a miracle, it seemed, to keep a family together amid the economic insecurities and multiple temptations of the postsuburban age. After much soul-searching, some evangelical women, finding fault in the system, became feminists; some, finding fault in themselves, set out on courses of self-improvement; and some, finding fault in secular humanism, enlisted in the new campaign for moral vigilance.

PEIGNOIRS AND PATRIOTISM

If Marabel Morgan and Phyllis Schlafly hadn't existed, conservative leaders would have been hard put to invent them. Who could have envisioned a headstrong former beauty queen who would combine the Bible with *Cosmopolitan* magazine and come up with *The Total Woman,* the best-selling book of 1974? And who could have predicted that a prim Catholic hawk would almost single-handedly defeat the Equal Rights Amendment and become the sweetheart of Moral Majority? Yet Morgan, a Miami housewife and mother of two, and Schlafly, Illinois lawyer and mother of six, became theorists of a women's submission movement that acted as an effective backlash to the women's liberation movement. It was Morgan who brought the sexual revolution into the ken of evangelical housewives, and it was Schlafly's rhetoric that defined conservative policy toward women's issues.

As feminism entered its "second wave" in the seventies, conservative Christians endeavored to hold back the tide by reviving the feminine mystique. Just as the pseudoscience of creationism was hoisted up as a shield against the subversive doctrine of Darwinism, the vision of the happy housewife was dusted off to serve as a rallying point amid the hordes of swinging singles, women's libbers, and gay hedonists who were threatening to invade the inner sanctum of the family room. If the traditional family was in trouble, it was up to women to put the zip back into married life and the starch back into their husbands' collars. The standard line was that if men were having a hard time being men, it was probably because women were not at home acting like women. During an era of endangered sex roles, the old models of male and female had to be outfitted like Captain and Mrs. America; this was no time for cross-dressing. (A revival preacher I heard inveighing against women in pantsuits came up with the sartorial maxim that men at least had a reason for the zipper in their pants.)

Since too much assertiveness might scare their husbands right out of the driver's seat and send a marriage on a collision course, women were advised to use submissiveness to keep their breadwinners on the straight and narrow. And how might this be accomplished in Christian fashion? Because simply keeping a family together was the supreme Christian duty, nearly any means justified the end. Theology thus took a backseat to psychology. For Marabel Morgan, a self-taught scholar in these matters, the best method was that better known to Playmates than to Sunday school teachers: sex. A smart wife relied on a warm, candle-lit atmosphere to loosen up a selfish husband's libido and his checkbook. For Phyllis Schlafly, who came at the problem fresh from the frozen tundra of the Far Right, the answer was even better known to preachers than to politicians: sanctions. A woman's security depended on a harsh moral climate to stiffen a weak husband's conscience or enforce his sense of duty.

Morgan's approach, of course, was more fun for husbands. A man married to a Total Woman wouldn't know whether he'd be coming home after work to Lolita or Bathsheba. *The Total Woman,* first published in 1973, added the ingredient of blatant seductiveness to the arsenal of coy wifely strategies that already had been advocated in Helen Andelin's popular *Fascinating Womanhood* (1965). Andelin, a doctor's wife of Mormon background whose book sold nearly half a million copies, had advised women to pump up their husbands' egos by acting helpless. The Fascinating Woman, according to Andelin, was actually a little girl in disguise: "Childlikeness will make a man feel bigger, manlier, and more like the superior male." In designing her wardrobe, the Fascinating Woman emulated the styles of the playroom: "jumpers, pleated skirts, and baby doll yokes and lots of petticoats and pantaloons. . . . Ribbons and flowers add girlishness to hair styles, as do barrettes and bands."

Even frustration was a permutation of pertness for the Fascinating

Woman: "There is no better school for learning childlike anger than watching the antics of little children, especially little girls who have been spoiled by too much loving." Andelin's scenario of womanhood was all too literally set in a doll's house. One could conjure up a grotesque vision of Alice-in-Blunderland: a mature homemaker resembling Lucille Ball takes a bite of a Hostess cupcake and finds herself shrunk down to kindergarten size, cavorting about her toy kitchen in a pinafore and throwing a tantrum when the Toll House cookies burn.

Morgan, however, led the evangelical woman out of the romper room and into the bedroom. When her own dream of marriage as the "all-American Cinderella story" crumbled, and she found herself stuck with a grouchy husband who daily walked into the house after work under "a cloud of gloom," she set out on a salvage mission: "I bought all the marriage books I could find. I read until I felt cross-eyed at night. I took self-improvement courses. I studied books on psychology. I studied the Bible." Like so many pre-Falwell evangelicals, who looked for the source of their misfortunes in their own shortcomings, Morgan set out on a program of self-uplift. And like so many religious women, who found the sin in themselves rather than in the social system, she sought a personal rather than a political solution to her problems.

Morgan devised a 4-A program of submitting-for-success: Acceptance, Admiration, Adaptation, and Appreciation. The Total Woman was born. She was to bite her tongue and Accept her husband, since "nagging him over trivia will only drive him up the wall or out the door." She would find something to Admire about her laconic hubby and compliment him on his body, however odiferous or flabby, "by an act of will." She would Adapt to his wishes, however inconvenient or silly, using submissiveness as the "biblical remedy for marital conflict." And finally, she would Appreciate her husband, however surly or stingy, by constantly checking her "gratitude meter."

The real key, however, to becoming a Total Woman was versatility: "A Total Woman caters to her man's quirks, whether it be in salad, sex, or sports." Homework assignments for a Total Woman course included taking long bubble baths and dreaming up costumes with which to surprise one's husband after a long day at the office. One woman "welcomed her husband home in black mesh stockings, high heels, and an apron. That's all. He took one look and shouted, 'Praise the Lord!' " As feminist writer Andrea Dworkin later expressed it, Morgan taught Christian wives "how to cater to male pornographic fantasies in the name of Jesus Christ."

Considering whether this pliant attitude placed a woman on a "slave-master basis with her husband," Morgan concluded, "A Total Woman is not a slave. She graciously chooses to adapt to her husband's way, even though at times she desperately may not want to." Morgan had articulated the American variation of Jeanne Moreau's Gallic feminism: the liberated woman is free to choose the man to whom she will enslave herself. And according to Morgan, her husband in turn "will gratefully respond by trying to make it up to her and grant her desires. He may even want to spoil her with goodies."

Like so many other Christian self-help programs, *The Total Woman* offered a payoff in the here and now. The Total Woman could look forward to substantial rewards for her creative docility. Testified a graduate of the Total Woman school of gratitude: "The Total Woman is in heaven—a beautiful suite overlooking the Atlantic Ocean in the heart of San Juan—new, gorgeous luggage in my closet, with the sweetest guy in the world as my companion." And in addition to those surprises after work, husbands themselves could expect other benefits. One of Morgan's first and most successful Total Woman classes was held for the wives of Miami Dolphin football players. Recounted Morgan, "The girls listened well and really tackled their assignments. . . . By the way, it is interesting to note that their team won every game that next season, and became the first undefeated team in the history of professional football, including play-off games and the Super Bowl." (In fact, in 1975 I happened to interview an alumna of that famous class who was traveling around the country spreading word of the Total Woman miracle.)

FAITHFUL TO THE END

For many love-starved or bored women who had opted for homemaking over careers and who, like Morgan, had found that their "moonlight and roses had turned to daylight and dishes," the Total Woman concept was the answer to their prayers. Disillusioned by the collapse of their dreams, yet threatened by the rhetoric of the women's movement, they welcomed a plan that would enable them to take the initiative in some way and turn their lives around—a plan that challenged the sanctity neither of the family nor of the Bible but that allowed them to reap the benefits of the sexual revolution. Morgan, like Ella May Miller and other righteous advice-peddlers, advocated traditional subordination for women. But Morgan's method promised fantasy and frivolity in addition to the practical reward of a faithful and generous—and game-winning—husband. After a day of chauffering the kids around in the station wagon, a Total Woman could drive home to *la dolce vita*.

As Barbara Grizzuti Harrison has written, Morgan and her sisters in bondage acted as "happiness merchants who teach us not to confront our human pain and suffering directly, but to learn, through self-deception, to rejoice in our bonds and fetters, and thus to escape the travail and confusion that are an inescapable part of the human condition." Thus while many housewives across the country were learning in consciousness-raising sessions how to air their discontent, groups of conservative evangelical women were learning in seminars spun off from *The Total Woman* or *Fascinating Womanhood* how to make the best of what they had. Regional variations of the Christian womanhood curriculum flourished. In California, the Patricia French Charm School franchises focused primarily on poise and makeup. In Texas, according to *Texas Monthly's* Greg Curtis, a course devised by Dallas housewife Susan Key called Eve Reborn drew thousands of women, many of them wealthy and socially prominent. For Key, however, the doctrine of submission had more to do with the spiritual well-being of one's spouse than the eliciting of "goodies." According to Key, God gave women "a unique capacity for submission and obedience and when this capacity is thwarted by rebellion and deceit, it becomes a capacity to destroy which begins to work within her heart and then sulks out to her intimate relationships, widens to her acquaintances, to society, and then into history."

Key's approach was considerably less frivolous than Morgan's. Other books by fundamentalist women made the pleasure principle advocated by Morgan a kind of grim duty. Judith M. Miles, author of *The Feminine Principle: A Woman's Discovery of the Key to Total Fulfillment,* wrote that when a baby girl is born, "a new incarnate picture of the human soul and of the human race is begun." If the child grew up properly submissive, she would symbolize the bride of Christ, but if she sought her own selfish fulfillment, she would symbolize "the harlot of Babylon." Miles said of her own marriage that she was "stunned into a new kind of submission" after reading St. Paul's injunction: "Wives, be subject to your husbands, as to the Lord" (Ephesians 5:22). Miles concluded that she "was to treat my human husband as though he were the Lord, resident in our humble home. This was truly revelatory to me. . . . Would I suggest to Jesus that he finish some task around the house? . . . Would I ever be in judgment over my Lord, over His taste, His opinions, or His actions?"

In the sequel to *The Total Woman* called *Total Joy* (1976), Morgan, too, made the connection between submitting to God's will and to the wishes of one's husband. Even though the acceptance of arbitrary authority clearly went against the grain, Morgan insisted on a biblical literalism, adhering to the same verse that had stunned Miles. Said Morgan, through clenched teeth, "I believe the Bible is truth, and I know that my strength, my joy, and direction come from reading that Book daily. Therefore, I can't ignore the principle of adapting, even though at times I could scream rather than live it."

THE TRANSFIGURATION OF THE MASTER

For fundamentalists, as for generations of theologians before them, Paul's hierarchical analogy—"For the husband is the head of the wife, even as Christ is the head of the church"—seemed to set forth for all time the lordly rights of husbands. When a woman disobeyed her husband, she disrupted the chain of command that emanated from God to man. A breakdown of distinctions between male and female, like the breakdown of distinctions between man and animal implied in Darwinism, meant a disturbance of the God-given order of things. And for an evangelical woman, the notion of

submission had a double impact. As a born-again Christian, she was
to surrender her life to Jesus ("Have thine own way, Lord"), and as
a woman, she was to submit to the will of her husband ("love,
honor, and obey").

For the willful woman, submitting, like riding a bicycle, could be
learned. Yielding to Jesus made it easier to yield to her spouse. In
her own book on submissiveness, Anita Bryant (a Total Woman
alumna) described the battle to control her feelings of rebellion
against a demanding, controlling husband: "Only as I practice
yielding to Jesus can I learn to submit, as the Bible instructs me, to
the loving leadership of my husband. Only the power of Christ can
enable a woman like me to become submissive in the Lord." Eventually, however, the price for conjugal peace became too high. In
May 1980, when Bryant filed for divorce, she complained that her
husband, who apparently had pressured Bryant into an ever-greater
public role in the pro-family crusade, had "violated my most precious asset—my conscience." A woman who submitted blindly to
her husband, then, was in danger of divided loyalties, particularly if
her husband did not share her faith or her virtue.

Morgan and Miles took Paul's analogy a step further than mere
submissiveness. In a strange and desperate process of transfiguration, the gloomy husband who walked in the door after work assumed the aura of Christ. The figures of the heavenly Lord and
earthly master—transubstantial and consubstantial husbands—had
become merged. In a sense, Jesus was not only taking on the sins of
the unruly wife, he was also taking on the sins of the inadequate or
domineering husband. The evangelical woman, who typically had
experienced a deep, personal feeling of salvation, believed that
Christ had taken all her sins upon himself and atoned for them
through his death and resurrection. And it should not be difficult
for her to envision Jesus sitting across from her at the dinner table,
his unconditional love shining through the fretful glance of a tired
husband. Despite the implied idolatry, such an act of imagination
was a mystical transference not unlike that described by Mother
Teresa, who has said that she sees the face of Christ in the faces of
the poor and dying in Calcutta.

Healer Ruth Carter Stapleton had used a variation of that act of
transference as the basis of her revisionist therapy for troubled
Christians. As a young wife she herself had experienced the sense

of inadequacy and frustration described by Morgan and Bryant. She became "gripped with the illusion" that she was "a hopeless failure —as a wife, as a mother, as a person." Isolated in a lonely North Carolina suburb, feeling trapped by marriage and motherhood, she drove her car into a power pole, jumping out only at the last minute. In her book *The Gift of Inner Healing* she recounted the advice offered by a male religious mentor: to let Jesus "walk into the graveyard of my past pains, where I had buried alive so many experiences." This process of recuperation involved a faith-healing of the psyche, a "healing of the memories," in which the sufferer began "cutting out the old sick memories and replacing them with new rich images in our deep mind."

Stapleton's method, which resembled the "guided fantasy" technique used in humanistic psychology, was to pinpoint the pain and relive the hurtful scenarios, allowing Jesus to become the substitute father or husband. She counseled a young woman named Mary Ann, whose father had ignored her on the occasion of her first date, to imagine that Jesus had been there in the same room. Jesus, unlike the preoccupied father, noticed Mary Ann's new dress and told her how beautiful she looked.

After Mary Ann forgave her father in absentia, Stapleton moved on to the current dilemma of an unhappy marriage. Stapleton told Mary Ann to "spend a little time each day visualizing Jesus coming in the door from work. Then see yourself walking up to him, embracing him. Say to Jesus, 'It's good to have you home, Nick.' " In this way, Stapleton told Mary Ann, "you will condition yourself to respond to Nick as you would respond to Jesus." Stapleton's approach, like that of Morgan, involved a surrender to—even an embrace of—the status quo. One aimed for an inner glow rather than a change in one's external circumstances.

Yet because Stapleton approached healing "holistically," and simply because she was a woman evangelist, she was assailed by a number of fundamentalist leaders. She had been branded a witch by a minister in Alabama in 1970, and when conservative Christians began to turn against her brother after the presidential election in 1976, they began to try to discredit her as well. Stapleton later told writers Flo Conway and Jim Siegelman that she had been targeted by preachers in a direct-mail campaign and singled out in a defamatory book. The few times I saw her at public appearances, she did not seem to be feeling well, and she made jokes about the inability of the healer to cure herself. Sadly, in April 1983, Stapleton was diagnosed as having cancer of the pancreas. Refusing medical treatment, she said she would rely on God to help her. Despite a program of prayer, meditation, special diet, and exercise, she was dead within six months.

STAND BY YOUR MAN

In some cases, the sacrifices made by evangelical women for the sake of their faith neared martyrdom. These acts went far beyond Morgan's remedies for the suburban blahs. For most "obedient" women, there were no "goodies" as a reward—simply the satisfaction of following God's will or, perhaps, the blessed release from the fears and insecurities involved with independence. Such was the case with beautiful country singer Jeannie C. Riley, whose commitment to Jesus also meant cleaving unto a drunken redneck husband. Following her overnight success with the nationwide hit "Harper Valley PTA," Riley was tempted to change her lifestyle—and her man. Feeling she had outgrown her husband, Mickey, a beer-guzzling, jug-eared grumbler who ran a gas station, she divorced him. But she began to feel guilty regrets during the courtship of her new suitor, Roger, a sweet-talking sophisticate who knew how to wine and dine a woman. Although Roger seemed to fit in better with her new Cadillacs-and-miniskirts image, Mickey, after all, was the father of her child.

In her autobiography, *From Harper Valley to the Mountain Top,* written with Jamie Buckingham, Riley told of her struggle to choose between Mickey and Roger: "Roger and I shared the 'beautiful' things of life together—poetry, music, and beautiful scenery. Mickey wasn't interested in things like that. He was a West Texas cowboy with blue jeans and grease under his fingernails. He worked at a greasy old service station and talked about cows and pigs. He had never asked me to sit in the den at night, sunk deep into a shag carpet, cuddling in front of a crackling fire while sandalwood and vanilla candles burned on special holders, listening to sad guitar music from a stereo and talking in whispers about things romantic."

Riley complained that "it didn't seem fair to have to give up such an interesting person as Roger and be cast into the prison cell of marriage to Mickey." She fought against her destiny. But she found that she was fighting against God's will: "God wanted me to return in humility, submit myself to him [Mickey] despite the unattractive circumstances and say, 'Here I am, Mr. Drunk, ready to become Mrs. Drunk if that is what God wants.'" But that, of course, was not what God intended: "He wanted to restore us in proper, divine order. He wanted to give Mickey a new, husbandly authority. And he wanted me to be willing to submit to Mickey's wise counsel and loving protection—which became evident almost instantly the minute I came down off my throne and allowed God to place my husband on the throne of our home." Riley, like other reborn Eves, had learned the wisdom of submission.

FROM REVIVALISM TO REVOLT

Although such a resolute abdication of independence may seem atavistic to career women who dress for success rather than surrender, yielding the right of way has been a common occurrence among religious women in America. Historian Martha Tomhave Blauvelt has described the overpowering sense of resignation felt by nineteenth-century women whose weddings coincided with their conversions: "The renunciation of past sinfulness, recognition of one's powerlessness in matters of salvation, and acceptance of God's sovereignty that characterized the Calvinist conversion paralleled the renunciation of youthful frivolities, acceptance of a drastic loss in independence, and recognition of man's superior authority which women experienced as they made the transition from carefree single girl to stolid matron. In this regard, conversion was the means through which women adapted to their culture's demands that they submit to both God and man."

Nevertheless, the conversion experience can also bring an infusion of hope and an overwhelming feeling of worth in the eyes of God. For many women, as for many blacks, the evangelical church in the nineteenth century seemed a portal to a new life. Conversion brought women a sense of release from everyday concerns, and the church brought a new dimension to their lives. In church, women found companionship and community as they shared emotional experiences with other women; they found a sphere of their own. Taking to heart the evangelical ideal of self-improvement and self-scrutiny, they thought about themselves in new ways and examined their lives with new awareness, keeping records of daily progress in memoirs, diaries, and letters.

All of our studies, surveys, and polls support this fact: women are more religious than men, hold their beliefs more firmly, practice their faith more consistently, and work more vigorously for the church.

George Gallup, Jr.

Without women, evangelicalism would have withered on the vine. Even the sternest of preachers relied on women for sustenance and moral support. Although they might blame women for that first forbidden bite from the apple, ministers who looked out from their pulpits every Sunday onto a sea of bonnets bowed in prayer had to acknowledge the importance of women in keeping the fire going. Church membership records show, for example, that women comprised two thirds of the worshipers who joined the New Jersey Presbyterian, New England Congregationalist, and Southern evangelical churches during the Second Awakening (1795–1830).

A number of preachers encouraged women to play a more participatory role in church and in social reform. Charles Grandison Finney, commonly regarded as the greatest revival preacher of the nineteenth century, allowed women to lead prayers in "mixed" congregations. Inspired by Finney and other such progressive evangelical leaders, women became very active in reform movements that involved not only women's rights but abolitionism, education, and professional social work. Abolitionism, in fact, became a breeding ground for feminism as women argued for greater freedom in working for reform. As abolitionist/feminist Angelina Grimké argued, moral reformations are "bound together in a circle like the sciences; they blend with each other like the colors of the rainbow;

they are the parts only of our glorious whole and that whole is Christianity, pure *practical* Christianity."

Many newly converted women wanted to share their experience with others in an even more direct way—as preachers. In the eighteenth century, a number of women preachers emerged from New Light Baptist congregations, and in the nineteenth century, during the "Holiness" movement that swept the Methodist denomination, a number of women began to act as public evangelists. In 1869, popular evangelist Margaret Newton Van Cott became the first woman licensed to preach in the Methodist Episcopal church. (The license was revoked in 1880 as more and more women sought ordination and the church elders became wary.) Most women, however, did not play so public a role in their evangelical activities. Confining their efforts to their homes and their immediate social circles, they made converts among their own sex, thus assuring, in Martha Blauvelt's words, that "evangelical religion would remain Women's domain throughout the nineteenth century."

You are the devil's gateway. You are the unsealer of that forbidden tree. You are the first deserter of the divine law.

Tertullian

Despite women's numerical dominance of evangelical denominations, evangelical concern for women's rights diminished rapidly after the Great Reversal during the late nineteenth century that shifted Christian priorities from social reform to soul-winning. Preachers kept harping on the evidence of Eve's secondary position in creation and her primary place in original sin. This was the apple-and-rib recipe for Sunday morning misogyny. They kept opening their Bibles to those admonishments in the letters of St. Paul that have "stunned" Christian women into submission over the centuries.

Nevertheless, during the 1970s, as the secular women's movement gained momentum, more and more evangelical women began to redefine their roles in the church. They began to reexamine the biblical texts that preachers used as the loci classici for male superiority, finding evidence in the New Testament that it was culture rather than Christ that had mandated a patriarchal system of worship. And it was culture that now mandated a less subordinate role for women. The same quest for control of their lives that drove some women into Total Woman seminars drove others into the Evangelical Women's Caucus or even out of the church.

The EWC, whose members initially tended to be drawn from the academic community, was concerned with establishing the equality of men and women without abandoning basic evangelical beliefs about Christ and salvation. In its official "Statement of Faith," the EWC declared that "the Bible, when properly understood, supports the fundamental equality of the sexes." Equality, however, had been subverted rather than supported by the church: "We see much injustice toward women in our society. The church especially has encouraged men to prideful domination and women to irresponsible passivity."

Yet if it ever came down to choosing between Christ and contemporary culture, between the church and secular feminism, most members of the EWC would choose the church. The question for devout women who were conservative by tradition was how to choose both. Those who became feminists did so in spite of St. Paul and his various expounders. As evangelicals, they could not simply jettison the Bible. Consequently, in order to justify their position in evangelical terms, they used the techniques of modern biblical scholarship in order to reinterpret troublesome texts. Wrote Phyllis Trible, professor of Old Testament Studies at Union Theological Seminary, "Much as the ancient housekeeper of the New Testament, while possessing nine coins, searched for the tenth which she had lost, so we too, while acknowledging the dominance of male language in scripture, have lit a lamp, swept the house, and sought diligently for that which was lost."

Generally, evangelical feminists dealt with the misogynistic bias of Paul's domestic code in three ways: they placed his ideas about women's subordination within the cultural context in which they were issued, identifying them as a prejudice of the times; they pointed to other passages in which Paul talked about the ultimate equality of being one with Christ ("there is not any Jew or Greek, not any slave or free, not any male and female; for ye are all one with Christ"); and they posed the alternative of "mutual" submission of husband and wife rather than the idolatrous, one-sided submission of the wife to the husband.

In the ground-breaking *All We're Meant to Be: A Biblical Approach to Women's Liberation* (1974), writers Letha Scanzoni and Nancy Hardesty used basic hermeneutic and etymological approaches to discover the origin of key words and texts, often finding that original meanings had been distorted by inadequate translations or interpretations. Perhaps most significant was their gloss on the word "head" as it was used by Paul to describe the relationship between Christ and the church and the relationship between husband and wife. The original Greek word, *kephalē,* Scanzoni and Hardesty indicated, had nothing to do with thinking or decision-making—with functions associated with the brain. It was used, rather, in the sense of fountainhead or source: " 'Head,' as used metaphorically in the New Testament, points overwhelmingly, *not* to a corporate organizational chart, but to a dynamic, organic, living unity—a 'one flesh' relationship, if you will."

Feminist scholars pointed out that the women described in the Scriptures who came into contact with Jesus managed to transcend the social or domestic conventions of the time. Mary of Bethany dared to sit with the other disciples discussing theology with Jesus instead of puttering around in the kitchen with her sister Martha. Martha reproached her, asking Jesus, "Lord, dost thou not care that my sister hath left me to serve alone? Bid her therefore that she may help me." Jesus responded, "Martha, Martha, thou art careful and troubled about many things: But one thing is needed; and Mary hath chosen that good part. . . ." Mary Magdalen (whom some scholars take to be the same person as Mary of Bethany), who offended the male disciples by the extravagance of her devotion to Jesus, witnessed the crucifixion while the disciples, fearful for their lives, went into hiding. She helped to place the body of Jesus in the tomb, and she was the first among the faithful to see him after he had risen.

For evangelical feminists, the Total Woman concept of submissiveness denied the full humanity that Christ offered to all those who believed in him—master or slave, Jew or Greek, man or woman. In a book called *The Complete Woman: Living Beyond Total Womanhood at Home, on the Job, and All by Yourself,* evangelical writer Patricia Gundry offered the Whole Woman as an alternative to the Total Woman. Wrote Gundry of such books as *Fascinating Womanhood* and *The Total Woman,* "I don't blame the women who wrote these books for telling their fellow women to limit themselves and get what they want by manipulation." But Morgan's philosophy of creative meekness would not suffice for long: "As long as women believe that being less than they really are is the way to find whatever it is they are missing, they will still be seeking."

Going still further, in *Sexism and God-Talk: Toward a Feminist Theology,* Rosemary Radford Ruether, professor of applied theology at Garrett-Evangelical Theological Seminary, used the "full humanity" of women as the basis of a feminist theology: "The critical principle of feminist theology is the promotion of the full humanity of women. Whatever denies, diminishes, or distorts the full humanity of women is, therefore, appraised as not redemptive." According to Ruether, because Jesus called for a reversal of the traditional social and religious order—"the last shall be first"—he was instituting a "new reality" in which hierarchy and dominance were done away with as principles of social relationships. Said Ruether, "Once the mythology about Jesus as Messiah or divine *logos,* with its traditional masculine imagery, is stripped off . . . Jesus . . . can be recognized as a figure remarkably compatible with feminism. This is not to say, in an anachronistic sense, that 'Jesus was a feminist,' but rather that the criticism of religious and social hierarchy characteristic of the early portrait of Jesus is remarkably parallel to feminist criticism."

Unlike radical feminist Mary Daly, an ex-Catholic who found it necessary to reject the entire Judeo-Christian tradition in favor of a worldview based entirely on women's experiences, Ruether found much that was valid in that tradition. In place of traditional Christianity, with its power-wielding clerics and patriarchs, Ruether called for a more inclusive spirituality, a concept of the divine that acknowledged the importance of *Shekinah,* the female principle of wisdom.

SEX BEGINS AT THE ALTAR

Marabel Morgan's neoromantic Total Woman, a cross between Marilyn Monroe in *Diamonds Are a Girl's Best Friend* and the Old Testament character of Jezebel, should have been anathema to conservative Christians as well as to evangelical feminists. But like the best of the multiministried preachers, Morgan was able to justify the worldliest of behavior in biblical terms. Moreover, Morgan's gleeful bedroom games reflected a basic shift in the attitudes of conservative Christians toward sex.

Despite all the subliminal excitement that had enlivened worship services in America since New Light Baptist preachers began to arouse their congregations during the first Great Awakening, most nonprohibitive clerical pronouncements on sexuality had focused on dutiful procreation. Adam's lapse into uxoriousness was still a dire precedent. But theological misogyny had been tempered over the centuries by practical considerations. Echoing Paul's prescription of married love as a remedy for concupiscence ("better to marry than to burn"), Martin Luther had regarded the role of wives as therapeutic—to provide a safe outlet for otherwise shameful desire. Said Luther of woman: she is "an antidote and medicine; we can hardly speak of her without a feeling of shame." And though historical revisionists have demonstrated that the Puritans were not as puritanical about sex as legend would have it, women's sexuality, when it was admitted to, was regarded as a necessary evil in the fulfillment of her role as helpmeet. John Calvin himself had grudgingly admitted to the importance of companionship in a wife; Eve was created in order for Adam to recognize himself "as in a mirror"; Adam "saw himself complete in his wife, where he was only one half formerly."

In the perfectionist view of feminity that flourished in the nineteenth century, the woman's role was that of Goethe's "eternal feminine"—to draw man upward. The mildest female spirit could tame even the wildest masculine spirit. A literature of domesticity charged women with the guardianship of spiritual values in the home as well as in the church. Wives were to tidy up the carnal clutter of their husbands' souls. Girls were taught modesty and piety as a kind of initiation into the cult of True Womanhood. In 1841, Catherine Beecher, in her widely read *Treatise on Domestic Economy,* urged women to exercise their "exalted privilege" to renovate degraded man and "clothe all climes with beauty."

During this "feminization of culture," when women became the principal focus and principal consumers of popular literature, moral discourse was directed primarily at women as the keepers of conscience in the family. The exalting of women's virtue and the idealizing of the Christian home gave women a valued role in society. But those attitudes also had the effect of keeping her there. Women's success as homemakers was measured by the moral character as well as the worldly success of their husbands and children. In her 1842 book, *The Claims of the Country on American Females,* Margaret Coxe set forth the ethical obligations of motherhood: "To American mothers . . . is then committed, in a special manner, the solemn responsibility of watching over the hearts and minds of our youthful citizens who are soon to take their places on the public arena, and to give form and individuality to our national character."

Though the round-heeled Total Woman would seem an unlikely descendant of the high-minded True Woman, the distance was not as great as it might seem from the corseted angel of the Victorian age to the negligeed siren of the new evangelical era. If, for Morgan, virtue was no longer its own reward, the role of the Christian woman, even though she might be bedecked in Frederick's-of-Hollywood finery, was to be domestic, submissive, and therapeutic. If the kind of therapy Morgan advocated was more than Luther had bargained for, it was a matter of adapting to the times. During a time of devalued masculinity, a woman was doing her part for God and country just by reminding her husband he was a man.

Not only had sex—conjugal sex, that is—been added to the list of approved pleasures for the Christian couple; it had become a weapon in the battle for the family. Christians hoped to wrest the joys of sex, like the powers of TV, from the exclusive possession of secular humanists. Sex, then, would not prove an allurement to the godless life but an antidote, an antidote that wives should know how to administer.

The popularity of family seminars and Christian sex manuals during the seventies and early eighties indicated that conjugal love was no longer a furtive duty but a practiced pleasure. In a book called *Sex Begins in the Kitchen,* Christian psychologist (and part-time comedian) Kevin Leman advised, "Sex is beautiful, sex is good, it is a God-given capability each of us has to enjoy." Because so many Christians, he observed, had been "brought up in homes where it was conveyed that sex is bad," he spent a good deal of time with his patients "undoing—particularly with married women—what well-meaning parents did to them when they were young kids, giving them tremendous hang-ups about sex."

In order to be effective, the antidote sometimes had to taste as strong as the poison. Seminars on family life directed by conservative evangelical counselors that stressed discipline for children and obedience for wives often advocated assertiveness for women in the bedroom. Some stressed the spiritual rather than the physical dynamics of marital satisfaction, but others dared to be frank. Some, like popular writer and pastoral counselor Charlie Shedd, combed the Scriptures for relevant verses, giving biblical literalism a new meaning. Generally, the license for pleasure was taken from the Old Testament rather than from the New, while the imperative for male "headship" was taken from the pronouncements of St. Paul. Shedd's playful guide to married bliss, co-written with his wife Martha, called *Celebration in the Bedroom,* took its cue from the sensual raptures of the Song of Solomon, as did Shedd's Fun Marriage Forums held for evangelical couples.

In a more serious and more explicit vein was *The Act of Marriage: The Beauty of Sexual Love* (1976), written by Tim LaHaye and his wife Beverly, which had sold over a million copies and was into its thirty-first printing by 1981. LaHaye, the versatile Moral Majority spokesman, was also president of Family Life Seminars, traveling over 100,000 miles annually to conduct his counseling sessions for married couples. The tone of the LaHayes' book ranged from matter-of-fact to feverish. Sex for a woman was described as a "hygienically relaxing experience on the marriage bed," while, for a man, "The titanic emotional and physical explosion that culminates the act of marriage is easily the most exciting experience he ever enjoys."

Applying the Christian ethic of competition to sex, the LaHayes noted that Christians not only enjoyed sex, they enjoyed it more than did nonreligious couples. Proudly they cited *Redbook*'s survey of sexuality among 100,000 women which concluded "sexual satisfaction is related significantly to religious belief. With notable consistency, the greater the intensity of a woman's religious convictions, the likelier she is to be highly satisfied with the sexual pleasure of marriage." Said the LaHayes, "We believe that even though Spirit-filled Christians do not have an obsession with sex, do not corrupt their minds with warped distortions of it, and do not speak of it incessantly, they enjoy it more on a permanent lifetime basis than any other group of people." Their theory for this Christian capacity for satisfaction: "When a person's sins are forgiven, his conscience is freed, thus removing a common cause of orgasmic malfunction." In fact, one of the rewards for conversion was better sex. One young man informed LaHaye, "Pastor, I never dreamed when I accepted Christ that He would invade our sex life, but we had never been able to make my wife's bells ring until after we were converted. Now she has a climax most of the time."

The key to the wife's sexuality was surrender. LaHaye quoted Dr. Marie Robinson's clinical pronouncement on the subject from her 1962 treatise called *The Power of Sexual Surrender:* "The ability to achieve normal orgasm can be called the physical counterpart of psychological surrender. In most cases of true frigidity it follows on a woman's surrender of her rebellious and infantile attitudes as the day the night. It is the sign that she has given up the last vestige of resistance to her nature and has embraced womanhood with soul *and* body."

Drawing on a quasi-medieval theory of personality, LaHaye categorized the woman who refused to submit as "choleric." The choleric woman liked "to lead, make decisions, and dominate everything." Such a woman disrupted the cosmic chain of command from God to husband to wife to children. She threatened her marriage, promoted humanistic values, and risked raising homosexual children. Worse still, the aggressive woman caused her husband's sex drive to flag: "We look for this problem to increase as the woman's lib philosophy creates more conflict in the home and continues to assault the male ego."

The only place, then, for female assertiveness was in the bedroom. The good Christian wife acted submissive until the lights went out—and then it was time to take matters into her own hands. Clearly the woman's duty was no longer the Victorian imperative of taming the rampaging male; it was up to the wife to turn her pussycat of a husband into a tiger. She was guardian not merely of his virtue but of his virility. Expressing it in athletic terms, LaHaye declared: "For most of their marriage, a woman has expected her husband to 'carry the ball'; now it is time for her to hurry onto the playing field and call some of the plays." Specifically, the spirit-filled woman should exercise those lax vaginal muscles: "When she develops those otherwise lazy muscles to such a point that she can crimp down on his penis once he is inside, she will greatly contribute toward keeping that organ hard."

THE POWER OF THE REACTIONARY WOMAN

Despite the growing catalog of Christian erotica, conservative Christian men were less concerned about their endangered libidos than about their endangered prerogatives. Reforms advocated by members of the religious right promoted the near-divine rights of husbands. Conservative legislators proposed bills that would restore America to the golden age of patriarchy, before the federal government stepped in to protect the rights of wives, children, and homosexuals. The Family Protection Act, the omnibus pro-family bill originally introduced (unsuccessfully) into Congress by Republican Senator Paul Laxalt of Nevada and supported by Jerry Falwell's legions, forbade federal attempts to change state statutes on child abuse. Federal funds for operation of a child-abuse program without authorization from the state legislature were prohibited. On the issue of spouse abuse, state statutes regarding family relationships were to be protected from federal interference. Private associations to care for victims of domestic violence were encouraged. In a later version, the bill proposed the withdrawal of federal funding from those agencies that supported battered-wife shelters.

Since getting the federal government off her back was hardly the top priority of the average Christian homemaker, the social programs of the New Right would seem to offer few incentives to women. However, there were practical benefits for wives whose husbands practiced what they preached. Presumably a husband who had pledged to support the traditional family would be more likely than a swinging secularist to bring home the bacon and less likely to take a jab at his wife. As any churchgoing wife could tell you, a good Christian husband would be less likely to fool around, get drunk, or gamble away his paycheck than would a seize-the-day humanist. But it was Phyllis Schlafly, the nemesis of the ERA, who best knew how to turn an apprehensive housewife into a pamphleteering zealot.

Schlafly enlisted in her Stop ERA a regiment of wives who were convinced that the real threat to their marital happiness and security was posed by members of their own sex—by feminists as well as floozies. Like Schlafly, some of the principal pro-family activists, such as Connaught (Connie) Marshner, chairman of the Pro-Family Coalition, and Onalee McGraw of the Heritage Foundation, had long-time ties to right-wing political groups. But most of the conservative Christian women who fought such issues as ERA and abortion were single-issue recruits. They weren't simply killjoys who wanted to restore old-time morality in order to take the jiggle out of "Charlie's Angels" and the casual pleasures out of promiscuous sex. They were frightened wives who regarded their very way of life as threatened. As they saw it, abortion devalued the sacred process of reproduction, the principal basis of their status as women, and the ERA undermined the male breadwinner ethic, the basis of their social and financial security.

In a section devoted to the feminist movement in his book *Listen, America!* Jerry Falwell had deferred to the wisdom of Mrs. Schlafly on the consequences of the ERA. Characterizing the leaders of the women's movement as a "minority core of women who were once bored with life, whose real problems are spiritual problems," he summarized an anti-ERA presentation made by Schlafly during services at the Thomas Road Baptist Church. Schlafly, like Falwell, had preached directly to her constituents' sense of vulnerability. The ERA, she had avowed, was "antifamily"—it "would take away the marvelous legal rights of a woman to be a full time wife and mother in the home supported by her husband." If men and women were treated equally by the federal government and the courts, the "benign discrimination" that had preserved the rights of women as wives and mothers would cease: "Wives have traditionally had in this country a variety of extensive rights based on their marital status, as a result of our public policy to respect the family as the basic unit of society; and as a statutory and common-law balance to the biological fact that only women have babies."

Any threat to the status of the housewife was also a threat to the American way of life. In *The Power of the Positive Woman*, Schlafly had described the ideal wife not merely as a happy homemaker but a "patriot and defender of our Judeo-Christian civilization." Echoing Margaret Coxe and other nineteenth-century proponents of True Womanhood, Schlafly declared, "It is the task of the Positive Woman to keep America good."

The Positive Woman was not motivated merely by altruism, however. She was also motivated by fear. Schlafly predicted that the ERA would cut all the ties that bind, creating anarchy at home, at work, at school, even at boot camp. ERA activists, according to Schlafly, would use the federal government as a bludgeon to "eliminate the eternal differences and the roles that God has ordained between men and women," resulting ultimately in the spectacle of G.I. Josephines hurling grenades in combat as feebly as they threw baseballs on the playing field. Schlafly quoted the poetic pronouncement of retired Brigadier General Andrew J. Gatsis on the horrors of hoydens on the battlefield: "Are we really ready to have them face the cold, steel bayonet of the male enemy soldier. . . . Think of the young eighteen-year-old moist-eyed girl with homesickness, looking at the faded twilight; she believes the sky is lost forever."

However, even more terrifying than the looming menace of national anarchy were the familiar specters of the footloose husband and the abandoned housewife, the dual casualties of secular living. Without a wife dependent on his support, a husband would collapse, leaving him an emasculated wreck or driving him to brutish behavior. Without her husband's protection and support, a housewife could be turned out into the economic marketplace, where she would have neither the skills nor the attractions to compete. For Schlafly, the ERA would lead not to the liberation of women but to the liberation of men—from the necessity of supporting their wives.

As Barbara Ehrenreich has observed in her book, *The Hearts of Men: American Dreams and the Flight from Commitment,* the distrust of men and the fear of feminists were inseparable in the ideology of Schlafly and the New Right. Unlike Marabel Morgan, who believed in the possibility of rekindling the romance in a marriage, Schlafly dashed a bucket of cold water on the housewife's illusions about love. Dismissing the argument made by some ERA proponents that "husbands support their wives only because of love, not because of the law," Schlafly explained that love "is not apt to survive all those years for better or worse, for richer or poorer, in sickness and in health, till death we do part." If love were the only basis for a man's financial support of his wife, a husband could "stop supporting his faithful wife of twenty or thirty years by the simple expedient of saying, 'I do not love her anymore; I love a younger woman.' "

It was not love that lasted, then, but duty—duty enforced by law as well as convention. What Schlafly and other conservative Christians hoped to establish was a set of consequences—legal, social, and even medical—for those who deviated from the mold of the traditional family. Without the bonds of authority, tradition, and duty, there was no firm foundation for a Christian society.

CHAPTER 4

The Spirit of Winning: Sports and the Total Man

Upon the fields of friendly strife are sown the seeds that, upon other fields, on other days, will bear the fruits of victory.

Douglas MacArthur

If Jesus Christ were alive today, he would be at the Super Bowl.

Norman Vincent Peale

The militant trumpet blares of masculine superiority that periodically have announced the resurgence of conservative Christianity in America have not managed to obscure the uneasiness men have felt about the influence of women and about their own roles in the church. During the late nineteenth century, for example, the preponderance of women in the church pews and at the cash registers of popular culture caused a backlash. As historians Ann Douglas, Jackson Lears, and others have suggested, the apparent collusion of women and liberal ministers in appropriating the subject of morality created a hostile defensiveness and a muscle-flexing bravado among men who felt excluded or alienated from the sentimental pieties of the church—and of popular culture as well. One could not have Little Eva and hunting trophies too. As one scholar put it, "In its very success, middle class culture had come to seem stifling, enervating, effeminate, devoid of opportunities for manly heroism." Conservative preachers as well as restless spirits like Teddy Roosevelt hailed the virtues of the martial spirit, the cleansing power of muscular Christianity. In this view, the feminine influence might be uplifting, but too much of it was dangerous.

Traditionally, women simply have been more at home in church than men. For one thing, they seem to get along better with preachers. Even the homeliest preachers have had a better way with women than with men—always a cause for suspicion in the mind of a jealous husband. In the nineteenth century, when revival fervor was causing such stirring in the pews, there were a number of cases of preachers being shot or tarred and feathered by husbands who did not share their wives' uninhibited piety. In his autobiography, frontier Methodist evangelist Peter Cartwright recounted the fury of a wealthy man whose wife and two daughters Cartwright had converted: "He not only threatened to whip me, but to kill me. He said I must be a very bad man, for all the women in the country were falling in love with me; and that I moved on their passions and took them into the church with bad intentions."

Eventually Cartwright managed to win the man over. But an episode related by historian Donald G. Mathews in his fine book *Religion in the Old South* did not end so happily. A preacher named John Tanner "once baptized a woman who had for a long time wanted to join the church, but whose husband—a 'great persecutor,' one clergyman called him—had persistently and stubbornly refused to allow it. Finally, during a revival, she gathered up her courage, related her experience of grace to the church, asked to be admitted into the community of faithful people, and was baptized. Her husband's fury was so intense that months later he deliberately intercepted Tanner on the way to meeting and shot him in the thigh with a horse pistol.''

Jealousy, however, was not the most troubling emotion that men associated with preachers. Worse still was guilt. Traditionally, most of the vices put on parade from the pulpit were those that tended to lure husbands rather than wives away from respectability: drinking, gambling, whoring, cursing, immoral conduct. If a man didn't feel the watchful eye of God upon him as he struggled against tempta-tion, he could certainly sense the accusing eyes and hear the wag-ging tongues of his fellow church members. Shirley Abbott, the author of *Womenfolks: Growing Up Down South,* has suggested that men in the frontier era may even have welcomed that peer pressure to remain virtuous: "For their part, perhaps the sinful males, strug-gling with wild animals and Indian attacks and rocky homesteads and trying not to consume the entire produce of their still under the circumstances, did not mind having a place to go for confession and a little help from friends in controlling self-destructive impulses.''

Even for men who welcomed the moral constraints offered by the church, there were other emotional difficulties to overcome. There has always been something of the spiritual panderer in the revival specialist who acts as go-between urging the union of Christ and soul. The great evangelists of the sawdust trail, and the Super Savers who succeeded them, used the pulpit as a cosmic stage, upon which they stalked and sweated, working their congregations to the burning edge of agony and surrender. While women could swoon or weep, joyously weak-kneed, during the sermon, guilt-wracked men knelt grim-lipped, their wills bent like birches in the wind, ready to snap back upright after the service. Even in the livelier pentecostal sects, except for the snake-handlers, women were more demonstrative in their worship, trembling and shrieking unashamedly when possessed by the Holy Ghost.

The central evangelical experience of yielding to a superior be-ing was a humbling experience for a man; how could he surrender himself emotionally without losing his manhood? It was the genius of evangelical preachers to make the born-again experience seem a masculine rite of passage. Christianity was like a team, an army, into which one was initiated, with Jesus as the commander. That was a kind of subordination men could understand. For women, Jesus could be a comfort and a constant companion, but for men he was more like a boss. Or a coach.

THE GOD SQUADS

Sports were an inevitable addition to male-dominated multiministried churches. During the rise of Moral Majority, when it seemed that there were fewer and fewer arenas in which men could assert their manhood without women trying to muscle in on the action, it was crucial for men to maintain control of the churches as a preserve of masculine power.

If the model fundamentalist woman of the Falwell era was a positive-thinking housewife kneeling in a negligee at the altar of masculinity, the ideal evangelical man was a tireless athlete who exerted his competitive spirit for God, country, and business. While the aspiring Total Woman studied to weaken her will, the total Christian male practiced getting tough for Jesus. It was time for tough love for one's family and tough luck for one's competitors. The paradigm for the Christian life was no longer the pilgrimage but the game, played by the rules of St. Paul and Vince Lombardi. St. Paul: "Know ye not that they which run in a race run all, but one receiveth the prize? So run, that ye may obtain" (1 Corinthians 9:24). Vince Lombardi: "Winning isn't everything; it's the only thing."

The resurgence of evangelicalism in America had brought with it a revival of muscular Christianity and a return to the social Darwinism of the athletic arena. Jesus the teacher had become Christ the competitor, as in the film version of *Elmer Gantry*, when Burt Lancaster avowed to a barroom full of backsliders that Christ was the greatest quarterback who ever lived. From the pulpit, preachers prayed for winning seasons, sprinkling their sermons with so much athletic symbolism that they sometimes sounded like color commentators on TV sports broadcasts. Straining for sinewy images, they fused athletic and religious symbolism in crude metaphysical conceits reminiscent of country singer Bobby Bare's mock-sincere rendition of "Drop-Kick Me, Jesus, Through the Goalposts of Life."

The character-building benefits of sports could be obtained by spectating as well as participating. Rather than trying to lure the more fervent fans in the congregation away from the worship of their sports idols, the wilier preachers managed to merge the altar with the scoreboard, so that Jesus was never the loser. Many churches were virtual cheering squads for their local teams. The pastor of the Second Baptist Church of Houston, for example, knew better than to force his congregation to choose between the pew and the bleachers. During the football season, the most devout Oiler fanatics could attend the special "Oiler Service" at 8:30 A.M. so they wouldn't be late for the kickoff at the Astrodome. No less accommodating was the Reverend W. A. Criswell of the First Baptist Church of Dallas. One year, when the Dallas Cowboys were scheduled to play in the Super Bowl at a time that overlapped with the regular Sunday service, the church elders considered delaying the service. Instead, they taped the game on a Betamax, and the congregation adjourned to the cavernous church basement after the sermon to watch the playback.

Participating in sports was not only good, clean American fun; it was a means of firming up one's fortitude to do battle with the moral flabbiness and easy physical gratifications associated with contemporary culture. There was no room for gender doubt or socialist anarchy on the football field. Infusing the pep talks of preachers and high school coaches alike was the credo that one could effect a moral regeneration of school, church, community, and country by going all out to win football games, track meets, golf tournaments, and the game of life itself. Implicit, too, in the evangelical enthusiasm for sports was an ambivalence about the growing prosperity and physical comforts of churches and individuals alike. There was always the danger of growing "soft" in one's complacency when church pews and hardships were cushioned. Sports represented a return to an older ascetic/martial ideal of harsh conscience, selfless duty, and strict discipline.

Although a few hardy souls pointed out that athletes now hied to the highest bidder, and pro clubhouses were corporate countinghouses, it was difficult to argue that sports were a pagan endeavor. Many of the biggest gladiators were Christians. By 1980, there were almost as many chapters, "huddles," and local fellowships of the nationwide Fellowship of Christian Athletes (FCA) as there were pro, college, and high school football teams. Devout players had organized specialized prayer groups within every professional sport, and on many teams the Bible-toters outnumbered the infidels. Baseball players could attend Baseball Chapel meetings, while bodybuilders could join the International Fellowship of Christian Iron Men, and golfers could pray together during Professional Tour Chapel. Secular humanism seemed to be as rare on the gridiron, the green, and the baseball diamond as on the battlefield.

This boom in Christian athleticism was promoted by such evangelical enthusiasts as Tom Skinner, the rabble-rousing black evangelist who had inspired the Washington Redskins and the New York Yankees; "Doc" Eshleman, the ex officio NFL chaplain whose hobby of ministering to pro athletes landed him in a different NFL city each week during the football season; and Dr. Louis Evans, the Presbyterian minister-at-large who founded the FCA in 1955 with this motto: "Until a person knows where the spiritual home plate is, how can he get the ball over?"

Such devotion above and beyond the call of duty was the inspiration for the character of Dr. Tom Bennett in Peter Gent's novel *North Dallas Forty.* Bennett had "set out to fulfill the bargain he had made with the Lord. In an even swap with God for salvation and its Puritan ethic ramifications, Doctor Tom swore an oath to the Lord Almighty on the blood of the crucified Christ that he would carry the mantle of Christianity without recompense to a congregation that desperately needed his divine guidance. He chose the National Football League."

> *God loathes mediocrity.*
>
> Gary Player

I was neither shocked nor baffled by the notion of a double ministry to body and soul, since my own conversion experience at the age of nine had been inspired by an all-pro lineman named Bill Glass who was touring the Texas revival circuit during his off-season. Glass, a part-time seminarian who was then a starter on the Detroit Lions, had appeared as valiant as Samson to a dreamy young girl in a small town where pep rallies weren't much different in spirit from worship services and football players were pampered like gods. As the biggest celebrity to hit town that year, Glass had an immediate edge over the local pastor, Brother Johnny, whose red-faced fervor was considered excessive by the younger members of the congregation. Glass's huge body, its heroic massiveness looming over the pulpit, had seemed a bulwark against doubt and pain. As he described the sweat and blood of the crucifixion, the supreme sacrifice, his shoulders hunched as if in anticipation of the snap of the ball from center, he seemed strong enough to have borne the agonies of Golgotha, strong enough to have deflected a legion of Romans. Glass merged with my Sunday school image of a mild and merciful Jesus, and I saw an invincible redeemer who not only understood my weaknesses but who could fight my battles for me.

> *I ran on, and as I ran, I made a prayer; it wasn't theological either, I tell you that. I said, "God, if you ever helped mortal man, help me to get that ball!"*

> Billy Sunday

Glass, in fact, was a latter-day proselyte of the cult of the Christian athlete that peaked early in the century with the career of William A. "Billy" Sunday, the baseball-player-turned-evangelist. As his biographer William T. Ellis described him, Sunday "was a man's man. His tabernacle audiences resembled baseball crowds in the proportion of men present. . . . Sunday talked religion as he talked baseball. His words smacked of the streetcorners, the shop, the athletic field, the crowd of men." Rescuing the Bible from women and overly refined preachers, Sunday restored the masculine aura to Christ and delivered Christianity to the businessmen and bully pulpits of the land.

For social critic Thorstein Veblen, who regarded both the sporting and the religious temperaments as predatory, the Christian athlete had represented a juncture of two kinds of barbarism. But for conservative Christians, the cult of the arduous life was a means of resolving the old Puritan squeamishness about sports; it was a way to embrace both asceticism and sheer physicality. As he strived mightily, the muscular Christian did not have to doubt either his masculinity or his faith.

Originally, the Puritan ethos had precluded any sort of games. A code called The Book of Sports, which promoted games on Sunday, was made into law by James I and Charles I as a means of counteracting Puritan influence. Play-hating Puritans in Massachusetts and Connecticut banned dice, cards, quoits, bowls, ninepins, "or any other unlawful game in house, yard, garden, or backside," singling out for censure "the Game called Shuffle Board, in houses of Common Interteinment, whereby much precious time is spent unfruitfully." But as the character ethic evolved from the Puritan work ethic, competition became a kind of test to weed out the weaklings from the ranks of the elect. Competition built character, and winning, like wealth, was evidence of God's blessing.

Not long after Sunday's career began to decline, legendary Notre Dame coach Knute Rockne took up the banner of Christian competitiveness. Like Sunday, he spent countless afternoons addressing business-luncheon audiences about the need for strenuous competition in a world going soft. A late convert to Catholicism, he brought a plain Protestant pragmatism to his pep talks. He had a patented "fight talk" that he delivered in his high, rasping voice to Studebaker salesmen, emphasizing that the "trouble in American life today in business as well as sports is that too many people are afraid of competition. They are unwilling to make the sacrifice that means achievement and success." One had to bite the bullet and win one for God, the Gipper, and the GNP.

In this rather grim, utilitarian view of athletics, competing in sports, like soldiering, seemed a matter of duty. In some cases, however, Christian coaches held out other incentives to their athletes. A case in point was Oral Roberts University, a school that, like its founder, had yet to establish national credibility. When evangelist Oral Roberts wanted to put his new university in south Tulsa on the map, he realized that it would take time and a good faculty to establish a reputation for excellence, so he settled on a souped-up athletic program as a shortcut to prestige. And since it would have been foolish to try to build a football team to compete with the Oklahoma University Sooners, Roberts focused on basketball. He hired coach Ken Trickey from Middle Tennessee State

University to develop a fast-break style known as "runnin' and gun-nin' " and financed a flashy school band.

Roberts did much of the recruiting himself. Realizing that few top players would have been attracted to a school that forbade smoking and drinking and required chapel attendance, the evange-list ordered a luxury dorm for athletes to be constructed. Within five years the Oral Roberts team made the NCAA play-offs and the National Invitational Tournament in New York.

When the ORU team traveled to Madison Square Garden in December 1971 to participate in a double-header, Roberts sent thousands of letters to his followers in the area, pleading with them to attend the game: "Like everything else at Oral Roberts, athletics is part of our Christian witness. The players on our basketball team are all Christian boys. When we received this invitation to play in Madison Square Garden, we felt led to the Lord to make it an opportunity to witness." After the team defeated Hofstra Univer-sity, Roberts assembled his followers under the Garden rotunda and assured them, "This was a victory for God, not for basketball."

ORU's string of victories for God came to halt, however, in Janu-ary 1980, when the school was put on a one-year probation by the NCAA. Violations listed by the NCAA included the gifts of cash and plane tickets from coaches to players, as well as the payment of inflated salaries to athletes for summer jobs. Apparently faith was not enough for either the coaches or players of ORU.

SANCTIFIED SWEAT

For many Christians, athleticism was itself becoming a kind of reli-gion, with its own kind of grace. By the 1970s, self-fulfillment, along with fame and money, had supplanted sportsmanship and self-sacrifice as the supreme values of athletic diversion. Catholic author Michael Novak argued in his book *The Joy of Sports* that sports were "natural religions," with baseball, football, and basket-ball a kind of "holy trinity." One could imagine the Pittsburgh Steeler fullback ricocheting toward eternity near the goal line, just as the Jicarilla Apache had run between the circles of the sun and the moon in the desert and the Athenian youth had raced for

Apollo in the stadium above the sacred way at Delphi. According to Novak, American sports fans ought to have recognized that they were performing a kind of sacrament, for sports brought to men's lives—whether they were players or spectators—the kind of experiences once provided mainly by religion. Sport, like religious transport, was a means of transformation that brought the Christian into contact with the ultimate. "Church and stadium alike are places of renewal, recreation, and sanctity," opined Charles Prebish, associate professor of religious studies at Penn State University.

> . . . [W]rite the vision . . . that he may run that readeth it.
>
> Habakkuk 2:2

The notion of running one's way to glory received a big boost in 1981 with the movie *Chariots of Fire,* choreographed to the transcendent pounding of composer Vangelis's synthesized score. In the Oscar-winning film, Eric Liddell, that other great Christian athlete of the early twentieth century, was portrayed reverently by actor Ian Charleson as the first proponent of the runner's high. Liddell, a bandy-legged little Scotsman who won the 400-meters competition in the 1924 Olympics, ran like a mad priest, his head flung back in blind volition, feeling God's pleasure.

Liddell found no contradiction between running fast and witnessing for Christ. In the film, he tells his doubtful sister, who wants to drag him off to missionary work in China, "God made me for a purpose. He also made me fast. Not to run would be to hold him in contempt." Yet Liddell ultimately obeyed a higher calling and became a missionary. Shortly after his triumph in the Olympics, he left for China, where he died a few years later in prison.

Despite the valiant Scot's example, few Christian athletes have stopped competing before age dictated a change in vocation. (An exception was boxer George Foreman, who had a vision of Christ in 1977 after losing a bout to Jimmy Young on St. Patrick's Day. Subsequently he put his gloves away and founded his own church in Houston.) Born-again athletes have tended to use sports as their pulpit, applying the principles of sportsmanship to the Christian life. Particularly effective for many years in winning converts were the Athletes in Action, who began operating as a branch of the

Campus Crusade for Christ, competing as a kind of paraprofessional league but usually managing to score a high percentage of wins against secular teams who deigned to play them. However, their effectiveness in converting teenagers seemed dependent on their ability to deliver points. Said an AIA basketball player, "It's important for us to win, not because God wants winners, but because Americans do." Players for the AIA, he said, were out to prove that Christians were not "Casper Milquetoasts."

Born-again athletes who remained on pro teams had even stronger incentives to bolster the image of Christians as tough customers. In the early years of the FCA, pro football players were cast in the mold of pagan Goliaths rather than God-fearing gladiators. Backs were glamorous playboys, and linemen were mean renegades in whom the quality of mercy was not trained. The body was not a temple but a juggernaut. Football memoirs like Jerry Kramer's *Instant Replay* and Joe Namath's *I Can't Wait Until Tomorrow ('Cause I Get Better-Looking Every Day)* tended to be odes to pain or paeans to hedonism. Pregame prayers were routine, but Christian players were considered oddball goddy-goodies by their teammates. In the film based on Peter Gent's *North Dallas Forty,* the pious second-string quarterback (whom some people took to be a thinly disguised Roger Staubach) was portrayed as a sniveling hypocrite, and the team's sanctimonious chaplain bumbled around the locker room, an oblivious missionary surrounded by bloodthirsty savages in pads and bandages.

That skeptical attitude toward pious players survived even as Christians on many teams began to outnumber the secularists. Baltimore Orioles manager Earl Weaver reportedly once queried a born-again player caught snoozing on first base what the Bible had to say about base-running. And in 1978, the San Francisco Giants were nicknamed the God Squad when pitcher Bob Knepper was said to have attributed a game-losing home run scored against him to God's will.

New York *Times* sportswriter George Vecsey interviewed a number of Giants players who had become concerned about the potential complacency of their born-again teammates, but most expressed grudging admiration for their Christian colleagues. Fritz Peterson, a member of Baseball Chapel in the Chicago area, heatedly denied the placidity sometimes attributed to devout players, claiming that

82920

"if Jesus Christ was sliding into second base, he would knock the second baseman into left field to break up the double play. Christ might not throw a spitball but he would play hard within the rules."

So many of the hardest hitting, meanest swinging, longest strid-ing, and straightest shooting superstars in pro sports were born-again testifiers that any lingering notions of the pacifying effect of prayer should have been dispelled. Included on the roster of de-vout Christians were then-Yankee Tommy John, marathoner Al-berto Salazar, '76er Julius Erving, Steeler Terry Bradshaw, Oiler Earl Campbell, and Patriot John Hannah. Hannah, who had been dubbed the greatest lineman in the history of the NFL by *Sports Illustrated,* gained a certain notoriety when he passed out New Tes-taments instead of cigars to Pro Bowl players when his child was born.

THE FAITH FACTOR

When one considered the factors of demographics, stress, and peer pressure at work in the lives of athletes, it seemed inevitable rather than strange that pro players were converting in such numbers. Athletes tended to come from the same geographic and economic sectors that produced the greatest proportion of evangelicals in America. Growing up in a lower-middle-class family in a small town in the South, Southwest, or Midwest increased the odds that one would become either an athlete or an evangelical, or both. And born-again experiences in the general population tended to occur during times of duress or "identity crisis," often during adoles-cence or middle age. (Jimmy Carter's conversion experience after losing the governor's race in Georgia was a case in point.) For athletes, who lived through a prolonged adolescence and then faced retirement at thirty, those vulnerable times of passage were compressed and intensified.

Players who neglected their educations for workouts, who had been primed for physical prowess like prize bulls, tended to have limited intellectual and emotional resources and little real-world experience to draw on when they could no longer cut the mustard. When troubled, rather than making visits to the psychiatrist's couch or taking mystical journeys to the East, they were more likely to choose the source of relief closest to home.

According to evangelical writer Bob Hill, who interviewed dozens of born-again players for his book, *The Making of a Super Pro,* many players, suffering from boredom and loneliness, tried every avenue to oblivion and returned to the religion they knew as kids because it offered more permanence. For some players, it seemed, Christ was the ultimate placebo. They called on Jesus as the perfect coach with the perfect game plan, the valiant lineman who could block out a path for them, the omniscient spectator whose love and enthusiasm never faltered. A sentiment I could well understand, from my own brief vision of Jesus as hulking rescuer.

Most players, in fact, found their religiosity to be an asset rather than a liability. Faith helped them to conquer fear, weariness, slumps, and negative attitudes. In his book *The Power of Positive Thinking,* Norman Vincent Peale recounted the time major league pitcher Frank Hiller restored his strength during a game on a blisteringly hot day by repeating Isaiah 40:31 over and over again: "But they that wait upon the Lord shall renew their strength; they shall mount up with wings as eagles; they shall run, and not be weary; they shall walk, and not faint."

Peale's recipe for success was based on an adage by William James: "Our belief at the beginning of a doubtful undertaking is the one thing that insures the successful outcome of our venture." Positive thinking, as applied to sports, seemed to be a variation of the Dumbo's-feather principle. In the Walt Disney animated film, the little flop-eared elephant could not fly without his magic fetish. Just so, many players could not perform without their own sacred confidence-builders. As an example of the power of positive expectation, Peale described an obscure bat-blessing incident in Depression-era Texas, when a faith healer named Schlater was asked by the manager of the San Antonio club in the Texas baseball league to pray over the team bats. The team won their next game and then went on to win the league championship. For years, players preferred to face opposing pitchers with a "Schlater" bat.

Ultimately an athlete's ability to produce those wondrous moments of deliverance in a game was as much a mystery as his inability to do so. There was a certain fatalism involved in fondling a favorite bat or praying for relief from a slump like a farmer praying for rain. Although practice, technique, and strategy obviously affected probability in a game, winning often seemed a gift of grace, a power that could come and go like a deity's whim.

Apparently, there were many kinds of fortitude to be gained from one's faith. For John Hannah, it was consistency. Hannah related: "When I have a right relationship with Christ, I have found that I can play the game more relaxed and make fewer mistakes." A born-again bodybuilder used Christ to muster his motivation: "I didn't feel like working out today. But I felt the Lord's will come over me and I knew I had to come to the gym." Golfer Larry Nelson used Christ to calm his nerves: "I went into the final round of the Inverrary Classic in Florida with a three-shot lead. I could have worried about losing, but for the first time as I went into a situation of this type, I felt buoyed up with God's peace. No longer looking over my shoulder, I went on to win my first tournament on the PGA tour."

Some athletes sought not only peace but perfection from their Bible studies. Former athlete Wes Neal, who worked for several years with the athletic-ministry branch of the Campus Crusade for Christ, founded the Institute for Athletic Perfection with the premise that biblical principles were the ideal foundation for athletic training. Neal, who had been traveling the country with an evangelistic weightlifting team, found himself asking, "How do I lift weights the way God wants me to lift them?" Turning to the Bible, he found that there were specific answers to such questions. He compiled in a training manual a list of Bible verses that seemed to apply directly to various dilemmas in the life of an athlete, including anger, depression, money, and team spirit. Under the section for contract negotiations, he referred the athlete to Luke 3:14: "And the soldiers likewise demanded of him, saying, And what shall we do? And he said unto them, Do violence to no man, neither accuse *any* falsely; and be content with your wages."

This blunt directive was seldom followed, of course, in the NFL or in any other league, for that matter. An exception was Steve Largent, a receiver for the Seattle Seahawks, who announced during the summer of 1982 that he felt obligated to honor his contract with the Seattle club even if the NFL Players Association called a preseason strike. "God's word calls a contract a vow," said Largent.

"I've made a vow with the Seahawks that I will play football with them for three more years."

Dietrich Bonhoeffer, a German Christian hanged for his resistance to the Nazis, said, "When Christ bids a man come and follow him he bids him come and die." To be a Christian means giving up a comfortable position on the sidelines and getting in the game.

Bill Glass, *Don't Blame the Game*

Wes Neal was not the only contemporary ex-athlete to devise a precise formula for a winning attitude. One of the best-known motivators in the business was Bill Glass, my erstwhile hero. Glass now worked as a freelance chaplain (he was never formally ordained), operating various crusades from his headquarters in a shopping mall in Midlothian, Texas, about sixty miles southwest of Dallas. He was in constant demand as an inspirational speaker for prison groups, Baseball Chapel, and various NFL clubs. He often spoke to the Dallas Cowboys before their games, and once he was asked by both the Cowboys and the Los Angeles Rams to speak in chapel before an important game. He had written a number of books, including a volume called *Expect to Win,* in which he offered a specialized variation of Peale's positive-thinking strategy, a kind of mind-over-muscle mental judo adapted to the needs of the Christian athlete/achiever.

Anxious to meet Glass again so many years after succumbing to his testimony, I arranged an interview at his Midlothian headquarters. When he strode into his small suite of offices on a warm autumn morning, he was genial but distracted. His daughter was sick, and he had to depart shortly for a board of directors meeting for Baseball Chapel. He was almost as big as I remembered him, the shoulders and mouth as broad, the hands as huge. When I reminded him of that long-ago crusade at the then-small Baptist church in my hometown, he smiled wrily. "How could I forget Brother Johnny," said Glass. "I used to make fun of him. I'd imitate him, the way he used to say 'Beloved' "—Glass pursed his lips and stretched out the syllables. "But he was no dummy," Glass added quickly in response to my startled look. "If his message was simplistic, it was because the congregation expected it."

Had that pulpit-pounding approach gone out of style, then?

"Maybe, but I still don't have much use for unemotional preachers. The churches that have the ministers who *believe* the gospel are growing—it doesn't have anything to do with education or intelligence. I'm more stimulated myself by a sophisticated approach, but the preachers who choose an intellectual method are from churches that are dying. When it comes to pro ball, most of the players are college graduates. But the theoretical, abstract preacher—they don't want to hear it. They say, 'Tell me about something that's real to *you* or don't waste my time.' "

How did he himself preach to athletes?

"When I speak to a team before a game, I find that I'm talking a Christian line, but I'm also talking motivation. I know that most players aren't into a heavy spiritual content, so you don't preach a sermon like you would in church. I talk about how I used to get myself ready before a game; it's the Christian power of positive thinking. I have a computer-like subconscious that's going to operate the way I program it. I can't say I'm gonna ask God to bless me professionally unless I'm willing to do the preparation."

In addition to its practical value, then, for pregame psyching up, what did Christianity have to do with sports—why, in his opinion, were so many athletes professing born-again experiences and joining groups like the FCA and Baseball Chapel?

"When I first started going to seminary, there wasn't much interest on the team in chapel, but there were a number of players who grew up in Christian homes. The groundwork was there. By the time I retired, there were twenty to twenty-five players who would come to chapel regularly. It's the same with other teams.

"I think sports have gotten tied into religion because with sports everything is more stark, more dramatic than in everyday life. Are you going to make it, or aren't you? You might get the snot knocked out of you at any time. It's a very existential experience, right out there on the edge, being tested every week, when you're only as good as your last game. You get it every week—three different film angles on everything you do, right there on the instant replay; you can't fake it. It's a highly pressurized existence. Our society is drawn into sharp contrast: if you're pagan, you're very pagan. It's either 'I'm gonna be a committed Christian' or 'I'm gonna overdose.' A player gets to feeling he can't handle it, and he finds God, sex, or drugs.''

How did he apply his theories to his own life?

"When my son Bobby developed a hip infection that kept him out of sports for two years, I told him, 'You can either say you're gonna learn from this and let it be a source of strength, or you can nurse, rehearse, and curse the problem.' It's like Rafer Johnson, who was born with a club foot. You can't read a biography about a famous person that they didn't have a problem to overcome; momentum makes you an achiever. I never pushed my boys—I didn't want them to play in Little League, where the coaches all play Vince Lombardi—but it's in the Scripture that whatever you do, you do it with all your heart. The bottom line is that Bobby is now playing for Baylor, and my oldest son made the cut for the Cincinnati Bengals.''

Christian and pagan athletes alike had long sought some form of grace under pressure. Glass seemed to be suggesting that Christian faith offered, in practical terms, a detachment from anxiety that allowed the athlete to perform at his peak. Choosing Christ over sex and drugs, then, was a matter of choosing the better opiate—or at least the better bromide. Faith acted as both an upper and a downer, as a spur to achievement and a painkiller for failure. For Glass, however, faith seemed primarily a stimulant for success.

When it comes to religion, I am not a scrambler. As an athlete I have gone somewhat against the grain. . . . I have been tabbed a gambler on the field. . . . But I pray to God I will never gamble with my immortal soul.

Roger Staubach,
First Down, Lifetime to Go

If ever a team had been an arm—or army, perhaps—of Christian boosterism, it was the Dallas Cowboys in the seventies, with Roger Staubach's Hail-Mary passes, Tom Landry's computerized sense of calling, and the First Baptist Church's team spirit. Shortly after I spoke with Bill Glass, I drove to Dallas to ask Staubach and Landry about the connection between Christ and victory. Although Dallas was not generally known for the kind of rabid rooting that characterized the Luv-Ya-Blue boosters of Houston, the entire city was bestirring itself to pay tribute to Staubach with a gala in Texas Stadium that very week. As I listened to radio announcements of the event, which was to be hosted by Bob Hope and Suzanne Somers, I felt as though I had secured an audience with Captain America, the avatar of lost American ideals.

Although Staubach had descended to the realm of lesser mortals since his retirement by selling land, investing in fried-chicken franchises, advertising cheap slacks and Rolaids, and campaigning for Ronald Reagan, I was still a little apprehensive about meeting him. As I waited in his new real estate office in a sleek, smoky-glass building in north Dallas, I was surrounded by the evidence of America's approval. Next to the huge "NFL Player of the Year" gladiatorial bronzes on his desk was a fan's football to be signed, a stack of fan mail to be answered. On the walls were permaplaqued awards, corporate testimonials, an engraved Optimists Creed. On a shelf was a still-cellophaned set of *Conflicts of the Ages* from Pacific Publishing. On a coffee table were back issues of *Texas Realtor* magazine. It seemed that here was a man who had it all—his faith, the adoration of millions of fans, an old-fashioned family, a heroic career completed while he was still in his prime, a lucrative new career and elegant office in a woodsy plaza only minutes away from the Cowboys' headquarters.

It was all too perfect. It was easy to see why fans in other cities resented the Cowboys. Washington writer George Gildea had exhibited that admiring rancor in the September 1980 *D* (Dallas's city magazine): ". . . it's not simply that the Cowboys are good. It's that they seem to be above the battle. It's the shift in the shotgun and then a cute double reverse to avoid the grimy doings at the line of scrimmage. It's a preoccupation with excessive display, like picking up 30 yards at a clip and not even getting their uniforms mussed. Those beautiful uniforms. Those beautiful cheerleaders. Those beautiful computers . . . America's team. Disgusting. . . ."

I had seldom cheered for the Cowboys, for reasons along those lines, but I had watched their games whenever I could, even after I left Texas, and often found myself anticipating Staubach's last-minute rescues. His ability to deliver two-minute-warning miracles seemed a mystical deviance from the Cowboys' programmed game plan—he seemed the spirit in the machine. A fervent Catholic, a gambler with an utter reverence for authority, he had adapted to the Cowboys' computerized Protestant ethos without losing his faith in intercession. He was the obedient officer who executed orders like an automaton and then found it within himself to lead an unbidden kamikaze charge. His autobiography, *First Down, Lifetime to Go,* published by Word, Inc., in 1974, was the account of a dutiful son, dutiful husband and father, dutiful soldier, dutiful Catholic, and dutiful quarterback—constantly driven, almost despite himself, by a competitive urge.

Staubach arrived at his office in a dark pin-striped suit, offering a polite apology for being late and a firm handshake, despite the dangling, useless pinky on his passing hand, one of the stigmata from his NFL career. But it didn't take long to place him on the defensive. Although he knew that I had come to talk about religion, Staubach seemed eager to dispel his super-Christian image. I asked him what he thought about the film version of *North Dallas Forty* and the character of the Bible-gripping quarterback. "What bothered me," he said irritably, "was the hypocrisy of the character. I wasn't the type to bring a Bible into the locker room—I would have been laughed out of there. I'm a very fierce competitor—I've been known to play hurt—and they had the guy in the movie crying. I never was a pansy they made that guy out to be."

Had his religious faith frequently caused him to be misunderstood?

"I really get bored with that goody-two-shoes image people have of me, like that *Sports Illustrated* story leading off with me in the confessional. I don't want be tabbed that way—life isn't all gloom and doom if you're a Christian."

Why, then, had he just rewritten his autobiography for Word, Inc., a religious publishing house?

"Word wanted to redo the book because of the good seasons I'd had since the first one. But I didn't want to write just a Christian book, with my faith as a cross or shield in front of me—I wanted non-Christians to read it, too. The new book will make me more of a three-dimensional person; it talks about some of the unpleasant things in my career, like the fistfights I had with Clint Longley."

How did he relate his religious beliefs to things like money, competition, and success?

"Even if I was a non-Christian, I'd be a competitor. I had it inside me when I was growing up. But I'm not a knockdown competitor in business. I recently went to a Christian conference on how to handle money—I do think it's okay to have money. I know there are people starving while I'm sitting here, and we could live on less than we do. But as long as money doesn't become the bottom line. I never had an agent, for instance. And even the apostles weren't perfect—they were fickle. We don't have the opportunity ourselves to stick our hands into the wounds."

What did he think about players who regarded their win-loss records as a matter of divine intervention?

"I'm not into that, into saying that everything is God's will. Let's say that there's thirty Christians on a bus, and it goes over a cliff. The two that survive say 'Thank the Lord.' Or there are people who say 'When I found the Lord we won the district championship.' I don't think it works that way. You have to look at the permanence of Christianity and not get too literal or fundamental. But then there are things you can't explain, like Cheryl Prewitt, Miss America, whose leg grew two inches to make it normal."

What about allegations that the Cowboys put pressure on players to conform to an all-American Christian image?

"It comes down to skills. If you can produce, they don't care what you are. If you try, the management will work hard for you. It's a bunch of———that Thomas (Hollywood) Henderson was cut because he didn't fit the image. Look what happened to him at San Francisco after he left the Cowboys. If he had been cut for that reason, I would have been the first to object. Landry would keep an atheist on the team who mouthed off every Sunday as long as he produced."

The team itself is a fiction and playing for B.A. made it all the more obvious to me. Team success to B.A. meant personal success. But it wasn't winning that B.A. cared about; or football, or God; it was how those things combined to make him successful.

Peter Gent,
North Dallas Forty

I spoke to Tom Landry himself at Cowboy headquarters only a few minutes after I left Staubach's office. Although it was the day before a big game with the Redskins, he seemed relaxed, even avuncular. Landry indoors, minus all-weather hat and earphones, was taller, huskier, and friendlier than I anticipated after watching him on television. He carried himself like a five-star general on holiday. I felt as though I must be hallucinating the kindly twinkle in his eye. Yet it was easy to imagine powerful and tender egos alike being battered into obedience against that granitic self-confidence.

Landry, a Methodist, was always willing to talk about faith and fortitude. He spent a good deal of his spare time with the FCA. "I talk to high school and junior high school audiences," he said, "trying to relate athletic qualities with spiritual qualities—the similarities between being a Christian and being an athlete. I think our country is in trouble—we're too soft. If you avoid disciplining a youngster, he'll never have character; he'll turn to escapism to handle adversity. St. Paul himself was a sports spectator; he used athletic terms. I talk about the four points of faith, of training, of goals, and commitment, about being a champion on the field and a champion for God.

"Most of us fail to fulfill our potential because of our own doubts and anxieties—a Christian is relieved of a lot of the anxieties that hold back an athlete. The champions don't fail in those difficult moments. I think Roger Staubach's faith enabled him to do what he did in the two-minute period; he knew he could handle it whether he won or lost."

Did some players use their faith simply as a good-luck charm or as good PR?

"We're all guilty of using our faith as a crutch. Sometimes it's because of lack of maturity. But it all comes down to performance. I've had to cut some great Christian players, and it hurts, but I can't go by my personal feelings."

How did he reconcile his faith with the competitiveness and violence of sports?

"Christ ran the money changers out of the temple, and he showed strength in adversity, as well as gentleness. A contest is a learning and a teaching experience. If you go out and win, you're teaching the opposition something. If you say you can't play within the rules and play a tough, punishing type of game, you can't play as a Christian. We try to eliminate the vicious side of the game, but you have to punish the opposition."

Did he have a conversion experience, and did it change him radically?

"I had studied management and industrial engineering before I became a Christian—I'm very method-oriented, and that hasn't changed. But all my life I thought all I had to do was be a great athlete and a great coach. I was a churchgoer, but I wasn't really a Christian. I was never really committed to Christ until I was thirty-three. I went to a Bible-study group because some friends had invited me, and I was ripe for it. It wasn't as though I was down and out, because I had just had a great season. I came to it as a winner. A calmness and a peace came over me rapidly.

"I hope I can be an example. My ambition is to bring people to Christ. It's the only thing. Even the Super Bowl is a platform for that."

In 1924, illustrator Warner E. Sallman was asked by Dean Sellers of the Chicago Art Institute to create a "virile, manly Christ." Sallman's portrait of a robust, strong-jawed Jesus, minus halo, which first appeared as a charcoal drawing in an issue of the Covenant Companion, *became the prototype for pinup icons of Jesus. "No pale, anemic Christ is this," Sellers is reported to have said.*

Landry's reference to the "softness" in the American character was familiar. Like Billy Sunday and Knute Rockne, he was speaking in the standard rhetoric of the character ethic. The fear of softness was a common sentiment among American leaders, from coaches to presidents. Even John F. Kennedy resorted to such a rationale when he promoted "vigah" and created the President's Council on Physical Fitness. The assumption was that a nation's very spirit, its strength and stamina, could be tested through the speed of its sprinters, the heft of its shoulders.

But for many conservative Christians, sports were the showing forth of a system of social Darwinism that decreed the survival of the fittest on the field, on the job, in the marketplace. As these Christians pursued more aggressive policies in every arena, there was little opportunity for turning the other cheek or celebrating the meek. Bill Glass admitted in his book *Don't Blame the Game* that he had felt a twinge of concern when he blindsided a rookie quarterback and knocked him cold, yet he concluded, "The weak shouldn't play in the first place. . . . Being rough, tough and aggressive doesn't mean you don't care about your opponent as a human being."

The bottom line for Tom Landry, as for any nonreligious coach, was winning, not testing character. Despite Landry's avowal that competing built character, self-reliance, and sound judgment, he seldom let Staubach call his own plays. Like a cautious business executive, he relied on statistics to reduce the element of chance in every game. Moreover, Landry wasn't averse to a little non-Methodist hocus-pocus in pregame preparation if it gave his team any sort of edge. The Cowboys frequently found themselves guinea pigs for a variety of performance-enhancing techniques, including being dunked in sensory-deprivation tanks and being conditioned by instant-replay reinforcement.

Landry's authoritarian approach seemed to give new credence to the neo-Marxist critics who had argued in the sixties that athletes were pawns in the hands of a power structure composed of retired athletes and businessmen, and that sports helped to socialize fans and players alike into accepting the rules of the game and the system, upon which they had no influence. Certainly, athletics had consistently been in the service of conservative ideology in America. Sports appealed to fans from nearly every social class or political persuasion, but as James Michener admitted in *Sports in America,* "The athlete and his coach move in a world of conservative values and are surrounded by conservative types. Very few Democrats among the alumni have private jets, or good jobs to dispense, or the spare cash to endow athletic scholarships."

During the Vietnam War, sports events were often the occasion for patriotic gestures. While flags were burning on campuses, they were being waved on football fields. Former pro Dave Meggyesy charged in his exposé, *Out of Their League,* that "A military aura surrounds football. Not only in obvious things like football stars visiting troops in Vietnam, but in the language of the game— 'throwing a bomb,' being a 'field general,' etc., and the players' obligation to duty. The game has been wrapped in red, white, and blue."

For we wrestle not against flesh and blood, but against principalities,
against powers, against the rulers of the darkness of this world,
against wickedness in high places.

St. Paul

Although Tom Landry admitted to me that he doubted whether
God actually took sides in a football game, Christian athletes, like
the legions of Moral Majority that were besieging Congress and the
courts, seemed confident that the best defense of the faith was the
offense. They seemed to have lost sight of the clear lines of battle
laid down in the very Scriptures they cited so often. St. Paul was
indeed fond of athletic images. But he always tempered his rather
Roman enthusiasm for contests of will with the Christian reminder
that worldly victories were fleeting and laurel leaves withered. The
real battle was against the weaknesses of one's own flesh, not that of
one's competitors or even of one's enemies.

The savior Bill Glass used to talk about in revival meetings resisted the temptations of worldly success: power, money, renown.
The savior Glass described in those simpler days understood failure; he was the champion of the poor and the powerless, of those
who had never won, at least in worldly terms. Yet it seemed that
Christian athletes, like the new evangelical activists and the new
Christian capitalists, were not prepared to wrestle against the
principalities and powers; they were too eager to bear the banners
and wear the uniforms of success.

CHAPTER 5

God and Money: The Gospel of Christian Capitalism

He that loveth silver shall not be satisfied with silver; nor he that loveth abundance with increase: this is also vanity.

Ecclesiastes 3:10

God bless free enterprise,
System divine.
Stand beside her, don't deride her,
Just so long as the profits are mine.

from a YAF song booklet

As evangelicals and their churches prospered, it seemed that success was next to godliness. And for the Super Savers, the Horatio Algers of the pulpit, the preachers of the Bible and the bootstrap, who had themselves turned down-at-the-heels ministries into thriving enterprises, Christianity was the faith of champions—the faith of captains of industry, of football teams, of armies. Christianity meant power and prosperity. As the chaplains of a military-industrial Christianity, the Super Savers preached the old-time gospel of *Geld und Geist.* Their belief in the no-holds-barred spirit of free enterprise linked the Super Savers with conservative businessmen and political strategists for whom laissez-faire was the golden rule. Super Savers, in fact, regarded generous millionaires and born-again businessmen as patrons, acolytes, and exemplars.

Since the prayer meeting revival of 1857–58, known as the Businessmen's Revival, America's popular evangelists have tended to preach business boosterism along with their call to conversion. Complained Rollo Ogden in *The Nation* in 1886: "Indeed, so far has the church caught the spirit of the age, so far has it become a business enterprise, that the chief test of ministerial success is now the ability to 'build up' a church. Executive, managerial abilities are now more in demand than those which used to be considered the highest in a clergyman." Businessmen, similarly, have tended to boost a conservative form of Christianity. In 1910, it was a California oil millionaire named Lyman Stewart who financed the publication of the twelve-volume series of *Fundamentals* that set forth the precepts of conservative evangelicalism.

Max Weber's observation that the Protestant ethic was good for business has continued to hold true in the particular as well as in the abstract. Although, as R. H. Tawney and others have pointed out, Weber placed too narrow an emphasis on the Calvinistic notion of the "calling" (one's chosen enterprise in life, apart from one's spiritual strivings), there is little doubt that commerce, after being baptized in the icy waters of Calvinistic theology, was no longer, as it had been for medieval theologians, an activity perilous to the soul. Greed became less of a danger to one's virtue than sloth.

The exercise of Protestant piety seemed inevitably to increase one's prosperity, a cause-and-effect sequence that John Wesley himself had described: "For religion must necessarily produce both industry and frugality, and these cannot but produce riches." As Tawney put it: "So far from there being an inevitable conflict between money-making and piety, they are natural allies, for the virtues incumbent on the elect—diligence, thrift, sobriety, prudence—are the most reliable passport to commercial prosperity."

In the new evangelical age that began in the late 1970s, the bond between faith and fortune was continually strengthened. Evangelicals of the booming Sun Belt were achieving success on a personal, corporate, and denominational level. However, it was up to the Super Savers to capitalize on such unprecedented prosperity and teach evangelicals to get rid of their inferiority complexes. Accordingly, Robert Schuller's 1982 manifesto, *Self-Esteem: The New Reformation,* set out to "erase the notion that Christianity is supposed to promote false humility and fear of success."

Yet Wesley had also foreseen a paradox in the worldly boon gained by religious fervor: "But as riches increase, so will pride, anger, and love of the world in all of its branches." So as worship produced riches, riches undermined worship: "Whereas riches have increased, the essence of religion has decreased in the same proportion." In Weber's analysis, the practical idealism associated with the business pursuits of the bourgeoisie ultimately dissolved into an orgy of materialism—a denouement that conservative as well as radical thinkers have attempted to contend with. Wasn't it inevitable that capitalism should be undermined by its own success, that its very abundance should produce decay and corruption, that the constant change it generates should erode the traditional values on which it has depended?

Wesley's paradox was resolved in the traditional inspirational literature of success by championing the concepts of stewardship and the character ethic. Building one's character and one's fortune were synonymous in the great gospels of success, from Benjamin Franklin's *The Way to Wealth* to Horatio Alger's *Bound to Rise.* One had to get ahead in order to get right with God and country. Wealth became a measure of worth, both social and spiritual. The pious, self-made tycoon whose hard work was blessed by riches was America's answer to the European aristocrat. Affirming the made-in-America values of liberty, opportunity, enterprise, ingenuity, and capital, the businessman obeyed his calling by building a fortune and then giving it away during his dotage—the American version of noblesse oblige.

In the Gilded Age gospel of wealth, the concentration of money in the hands of a competitive few was, in industrialist Andrew Carnegie's words, "not only beneficial, but essential for the future progress of the race." Carnegie's own career had been a perfect example of social Darwinism—the theory that unrestrained economic competition would lead to material abundance and social harmony. An immigrant who started out as a bobbin boy, Carnegie exercised his right to maximize his private economic good, and thereby created an industry that produced cheap steel for the nation's railroads as well as thousands of jobs for American workers.

At the turn of the century, when the dark side of industrialism was becoming ever more apparent, muckraking journalists attacked the abuses of big business, and novelists turned to naturalism to lay bare the traits of greed and selfishness in human nature. Yet optimistic Protestant ministers continued to expound the virtues of capitalism. The Reverend Lyman Abbott, who had preached in Brooklyn's Plymouth Congregational Church, the old stomping grounds of the Reverend Henry Ward Beecher, brought the ethical teachings of Jesus to bear on the capitalist system, concluding that the ambition to succeed was "the mainspring of activity; the driving-wheel of industry; the spur to intellectual and moral progress. It gives the individual energy; the nation push." Establishing a foundation for capitalism in a theory of biblical economics, he claimed that "Jesus Christ was one of the men who think that it is right to be rich. He did not condemn wealth. On the contrary, he approved of wealth; he approved of the accumulation of wealth, and he approved of the use of accumulated wealth to accumulate more wealth."

As the dour rigors of the character ethic merged with the pragmatic imperatives of popular evangelism, some preachers even asserted that getting right with God was a means of getting ahead in business. The order of the old formula had been reversed. God had become more a means than an end.

Dwight L. Moody, the first great Super Saver, a former shoe salesman from a small New England village who rose to evangelical prominence in the wake of the great depression of 1873, set forth the Christian solution to the nation's economic troubles: "It is a wonderful fact that men and women saved by the blood of Jesus rarely remain subjects of charity, but rise at once to comfort and respectability. . . . I never saw the man who put Christ first in his life that wasn't successful."

Moody's own urban revival meetings, the prototype of Billy Graham's stadium crusades, brought a kind of middle-class respectability to the sawdust trail. Wrote the Reverend Lyman Abbott, in tribute to Moody, "As he stood on the platform, he looked like a business man; he dressed like a business man; he took the meeting in hand as a business man would. . . ." And like a good businessman, Moody employed modern sales and marketing techniques, sending out advance men and hiring publicity agents to swell the turnout for his revivals.

Moody's techniques were adopted and expanded by the next great Super Saver, Billy Sunday. Sunday, who larded his sermons with tall tales from his baseball career, used to refer to his revival meetings as business campaigns. Before he arrived in a city to win his standard quota of souls, a special tabernacle was constructed, and the city was blanketed block by block by local volunteers who organized prayer groups from which the massive revival audiences would be drawn. Thus Sunday was always guaranteed a full and receptive house.

Sunday, who was raised by his widowed mother in a proverbial two-room log cabin in Ames, Iowa, and who spent part of his adolescence in an orphanage, was another Alger paragon. As Sunday liked to recall, "I have crept and crawled out from the university of poverty and hard knocks, and have taken post-graduate courses." Campaigning more like a high-powered pitchman than an anxious-seat exhorter, convincing his listeners of his point-by-point system for social and spiritual success, Sunday managed to save more than 300,000 souls during his career. Riding the crest of pre-Depression business boosterism, Sunday thrived on such slogans as "It pays to serve God" and "I never saw a Christian who was a hobo."

It was during the flush of Christian economic optimism before the crash of 1929 that the ministry of positive thinking was born. Positive thinkers had no use for the gloomy pieties of their Calvinistic forefathers. The Puritan devotion to self-improvement—the notion of *mécanisme dans l'âme,* as a skeptical French engineer called it—had developed into a practical program for achieving health and wealth. For the positive-thinking precursors of Norman Vincent Peale and Robert Schuller, who churned out prescriptions for success in the twenties, meditating on money and well-being became a new mode of prayer. In this way of thinking, Christ was not merely merged with culture; he was submerged in business. In 1925, advertising whiz Bruce Barton combined Christ and corporate man in his best-selling *The Man Nobody Knows,* characterizing Jesus as the First Great Executive, the First Great Advertising Man, the Founder of Modern Business.

Peale himself dabbled for a time in the polemics of Christian economics. During the thirties, forties, and early fifties he supported a number of groups that advocated a return to laissez-faire, including Frank Gannett's Committee for Constitutional Government, H. L. Hunt's Facts Forum, and the Christian Freedom Foundation. In order to illustrate his positive-thinking principles, Peale filled his books with parables about successful businessmen. Typical was Peale's eulogy to the late Harlowe B. Andrews of Syracuse, New York, "one of the best businessmen and competent spiritual experts" he had ever known. Andrews, according to Peale, believed that "the trouble with most prayers is that they aren't big enough. 'To get anywhere with faith,' said he, 'learn to pray big prayers. God will rate you according to the size of your prayers.' "

THE SPIRIT OF FREE ENTERPRISE

During the conservative revival at the end of the seventies, as the new evangelical right merged its legions with other conservative forces, the defense of free enterprise became as celebrated a cause as the Panama Canal. Fundamentalists who assailed evolution with one breath upheld social Darwinism with the next. Christian economists like Gary North and Elgin Groseclose cranked out dozens of books, pamphlets, and newsletters specifying the sins of the Federal Reserve System or arguing for the godliness of the gold standard. North established the Christian Enterprise Institute, a sort of religious mail-order version of the Washington-based American Enterprise Institute. Dallas billionaire Nelson Bunker Hunt, who inherited his father H. L.'s proclivity for crackpot causes, tried to corner the market on the world's silver supply because he believed that the

price ratio of gold to silver would eventually return to its ratio in
Biblical times of five to one.

There were plenty of latter-day Lyman Abbotts to celebrate the
virtues of capitalism on spiritual as well as pragmatic grounds. In his
book *Wealth and Poverty,* conservative writer George Gilder attempted to correct the intellectual consensus that capitalism, at its
heart, was morally vacant, driven, as R. H. Tawney said, by the
"vulgar itch of acquisitiveness." Gilder wrote disparagingly of cyn-
ics who hesitated to "believe in capitalism: in the enriching mysteries of inequality, the inexhaustible mines of the division of labor,
the multiplying miracles of market economics, the compounding
gains from trade and property." For Gilder, capitalists were not
motivated, as Adam Smith had posited, by greed and self-interest
but by higher aims: "Capitalism begins with giving. Not from
greed, avarice, or even self-love can one expect the rewards of
commerce, but from a spirit closely akin to altruism, a regard for
the needs of others, a benevolent, outgoing, and courageous tem-
per of mind." Social Darwinism had been anointed with the sacred
unguents of venture capital.

The capitalist was a votive figure whose risk-taking ventures were
acts of faith in a providential universe. In Gilder's mystical view of
mammon, the original sin was welfare, which deprived the poor of
the chance to gamble with their fates: "The attempt of the welfare
state to deny, suppress, and plan away the dangers or uncertainties
of our lives, to domesticate the inevitable unknown—violates not
only the spirit of capitalism but also the nature of man." Gilder
assailed the hypocrisy of secular humanists who would "discharge
their repressed spirituality in millennial programs for the restructur-
ing of all human life." Unlike the capitalists who discharged that
spirituality in investments, Gilder failed to acknowledge that his
own misty-eyed celebration of human economic enterprise, merg-
ing the spiritual yearnings of the capitalist with his utilitarian activities, was itself a kind of cryptohumanism.

Catholic writer Michael Novak, who had merged his own spiritual and economic yearnings by joining the American Enterprise
Institute, also brought a sacral aura to the activities of commerce.
For Novak, the greatest spiritual rationale for the system of democratic capitalism was a pragmatic one: it was the most efficient of all
economic systems at creating wealth. Taking Catholic theologians

to task for their naïveté in economic matters, he attributed the relative prosperity and success of the United States to its Protestant work ethic and the relative poverty and backwardness of Latin American nations to their mystical, otherworldly Catholic orientation. Unlike Gilder, however, he did not place a religious icon at the center of capitalism; for Novak, the secret of democratic capitalism was the empty altar: "Respect for the transcendence of God and for full freedom of conscience—respect for the common human wandering in darkness—is better served, however, even in Christian and Jewish terms, by the reverential emptiness at the heart of pluralism than by a socially imposed vision of good."

Both Gilder and Novak seemed to be employing an inverted form of Hegelian/Marxian phenomenology, with the notion of spiritual destiny unfolding in an economically determined history. However, other apologists of capitalism who inspired the Super Savers and the muscle-flexing religious right were less grand in their arguments. Harold Lindsell, editor emeritus of *Christianity Today* and author of the *Lindsell Study Bible,* acknowledged the element of greed in human nature. And like Adam Smith, he concluded that the best economic system was that which worked to channel individual greed for the benefit of the whole of society. In a book titled *Free Enterprise: A Judeo-Christian Defense,* he asserted that in the system of free enterprise the consumers themselves became limiters of corporate power, the invisible hand directing the economy: "Under free enterprise the people who purchase commodities are kings and queens of the marketplace."

Turning to the New Testament, Lindsell found, as had Lyman Abbott, that Christ did not indict wealth per se but merely the hoarding of wealth. James's savage incrimination of the rich—"Go to now, ye rich men, weep and howl for your miseries that shall come upon you"—Lindsell found to be a warning against the *misuse* of wealth, not the simple possession of it. But Lindsell, unlike Gilder or Novak, did acknowledge the serpent in the garden of commerce. Where capitalism sometimes went wrong, argued Lindsell, was in its abandonment of the charitable principle of stewardship. Capitalism, then, was not inherently altruistic, as Gilder had claimed: "The biblical stewardship mandate gives free enterprise a human face and governs the innate selfishness of men by requiring of them an altruism which fits the second table of the law, that we are to love our neighbors as we love ourselves." For Lindsell, as for most conservative Christians, the strongest virtue of capitalism was relative rather than absolute; it was better than godless socialism, in which one's altruism was enforced by government rather than by conscience.

A number of Super Savers turned to the books of Simon and Friedman rather than the books of James and John in bolstering their defense of the American way. Former treasury secretary William E. Simon's *A Time for Truth* celebrated the "capitalist miracle" that had "occurred in the United States, the politically freest nation in the world." For Simon, the free enterprise system was synonymous with the identity of America: "America was born a capitalist nation, was created a capitalist nation by the intent of its founders and the Constitution, and developed a culture and a civilization that were capitalist to the core. . . . An American who is hostile to individualism, to the work ethic, to free enterprise . . . is in some profound sense advocating that America cease being America."

In *Listen, America!* Jerry Falwell quoted a similar statement from Milton Friedman's *Free to Choose:* "For all too many years, Americans have been educated to dependence rather than liberty. A whole generation of Americans has grown up brainwashed by TV and textbooks to believe that it is the responsibility of the government to take resources from some and bestow them upon others. This idea was alien to the Founding Fathers of our country." Citing the book of Proverbs, Falwell concluded that "Ownership of property is biblical. Competition in business is biblical. Ambitious and successful business management is clearly outlined as a part of God's plan for His people."

SUBSIDIZING SALVATION

Nor surprisingly, robber barons and business groups alike have invested heavily through the years in the crusades of the Super Savers. Moody, who advocated saving souls rather than saving society during a time when labor leaders and preachers of the Social Gospel were agitating for reform, was a particular favorite of tycoons J. P. Morgan and Cornelius Vanderbilt. Welcomed to Chicago by such paragons of success as Cyrus McCormick and George Armour, Moody warned his well-heeled hosts, "I say to the rich men of Chicago, their money will not be worth much if communism and infidelity sweep the land. . . . There can be no better investment for the capitalists of Chicago than to put the saving salt of the Gospel into these dark homes and desperate centers." Billy Sunday, too, had his wealthy champion in John D. Rockefeller, who had simplified the gospel of wealth, saying simply, "God gave me my money." Impressed by Sunday's businesslike approach to salvation, Rockefeller brought in Ivy Lee, a founder of modern advertising, to promote Sunday's 1917 New York City revival. As Sunday's biographer, William T. Ellis, observed, "Businessmen who found that a Sunday revival meant the paying up of bad bills of old customers were ready to approve a man whose work restored integrity in commercial relations."

In 1921, the *Christian Century,* which equated fundamentalism with premillennialism, defined the attraction of revivalism to the businessman: "When the capitalist discovers a brand of religion which has not the slightest interest in 'the social gospel,' but on the contrary intends to pass up all reforms to the Messiah who will return on the clouds of heaven, he has found just the thing he has been looking for."

Billy Sunday's blue-chip gospel, however, did not survive the stock market crash of 1929. It wasn't until the eve of the cold war that the wealthy and powerful found as charismatic a preacher of the character ethic. In 1949, after four moderately successful weeks, Billy Graham's tent crusade in Los Angeles was winding down. William Randolph Hearst got wind of Graham's impassioned attacks on communism, and the legendary order came down to the newsrooms of the Hearst empire: "Puff Graham." It was one of Hearst's last attempts at manipulating public opinion. Dutiful rewrite men breathed life into the myth, swelling Graham into larger-than-life size, a transfiguration through pulp and circumstance. Newspaper ads proclaimed, "Visit the Canvas Cathedral with the Steeple of Light! All-Star Supporting Party—Held Over by Popular Demand—Sixth Great Sin-Smashing Week." Moody and Sunday had both made good news copy, but Graham's headline-grabbing instincts soon surpassed them.

Graham captivated yet more captains of industry with such pronouncements as "Paradise is a place with no union dues, no labor leaders, no snakes, no disease." In 1952, maverick Wall Street broker Russell Maguire offered to subsidize Graham's revival crusades. Graham turned down the direct subsidy, but accepted $75,000 for his burgeoning cinematic industry. His first two films, already in the can, titled *Mr. Texas* and *Oiltown, U.S.A.,* were about two of Graham's converted magnates. *Oiltown, U.S.A.* was advertised as a parable of entrepreneurial righteousness: "the story of the free-enterprise system of America, the story of the development and use of God-given natural resources by men who have built a great new empire." Among Graham's Texas-millionaire claque was wildcatter Sid Richardson, whose funeral Graham conducted, eulogizing the reclusive Richardson as a man "willing to go to any end to see that our American way of life was maintained." As Marshall Frady observed, "Graham sturdily affirmed, for the nation's affluent and proprietorial, their own sense of the fitness of things."

ONE NATION UNDER GODLINESS

In the seventies and eighties, antihumanism inspired the same kinds of alliances between demagogues and tycoons as had the anti-Communist crusade of the fifties and early sixties. The Christian Freedom Foundation, originally founded in 1950 and funded by Sunoco tycoon J. Howard Pew to promote the cause of Americanism and free enterprise, was reconstituted in the midseventies by a group of preachers, politicians, and businessmen, including Bill Bright of the Campus Crusade for Christ, Congressman John Conlan, and Richard DeVos, president of Amway (the "American Way") Corporation. CFF found enthusiastic contributors in such moguls as John Talcott of Ocean Spray, brewer Joseph Coors, and silver-hoarder Nelson Bunker Hunt.

The entrepreneurial philosophy of the CFF was promoted in a series of publications issued by Third Century Publishers, a clearinghouse for right-wing propaganda. The first of these ideological broadsides, Rus Walton's *One Nation Under God,* argued that the constitution was designed to perpetuate a Christian order, and the second, *The Spirit of '76,* followed up that polemic with a practical guide for winning elections.

The key figure in drumming up the support of mission-minded millionaires for the CFF was the dark-haired, marshal-voiced Bill Bright, whose Campus Crusade for Christ was a gung-ho army of buttonholers trained to conduct a spiritual blitzkrieg of entire cities and countries as well as institutions. Bright, a former candy manufacturer whose California Confections was a model of West Coast enterprise, regarded the Great Commission that Jesus issued his disciples as a mandate for superior salesmanship. After a conversion experience in 1945, he looked around for prime territory in which to start his soul-winning franchise, and in 1951 he founded the Campus Crusade at UCLA, focusing his recruiting on athletes and student leaders—the opinion-makers.

Already a master at putting the Word into campus vernacular, Bright bolstered his campaign in 1958 by hiring a marketing consultant. The gospel was distilled into a seventy-seven–word crash course in Christianity known as the Four Spiritual Laws, to be distributed in booklet form. Soon Bright's Campus Crusade became a model multiministry campaign. Athletes from Athletes in Action ministered unto other athletes; soldiers from the Military Ministry ministered unto soldiers; businessmen from the Executive Ministry ministered unto other businessmen.

Bright remained undaunted during the sixties by the counterculture that was transforming campuses across the country. Initially, his conspicuously clean-cut troops worked as counterrevolutionaries, but Bright soon realized, as did the CIA, that infiltration and impersonation were more effective. Hippies should minister unto hippies. Appropriating the roiling spirit of the times and moving the battlefront to Berkeley, he portrayed Jesus as a revolutionary, using such slogans as "Solution—Spiritual Revolution" and "Revolution Now!" In 1972 he sponsored Explo '72, a mass rally in Dallas's Cotton Bowl stadium that drew some 85,000 young fans to cheer for Jesus and, incidentally, for our boys in Vietnam.

Bright's support from the business community for his Crusade had been substantial from the very beginning, but in 1976 he devised the most ambitious promotional campaign of his career. "Here's Life, America" was the code name of his billion-dollar plan to evangelize America—all 265 metropolitan areas and some

18,000 smaller communities—and then the world. Housewives held crusading coffee klatches for their neighbors, and specialized teams witnessed to singles groups and businessmen. In February 1976, Bright set up a Christian embassy in Washington for direct witnessing to the nation's political leaders. The cryptically triumphant declaration "I Found It" began to appear on bumper stickers and billboards across the nation.

Bruce Cook, the former advertising agent for Coca-Cola who directed the total-saturation "I Found It" campaign, explained the rationale for the slogan: "Back in Jerusalem when the church started, God performed a miracle there on the Day of Pentecost. They didn't have the benefit of buttons or media, so God had to do a little supernatural work there. But today, with our technology, we have available to us the opportunity to create the same kind of interest in a secular society." By 1981, Bright's blitz had secured $220,000,000 in contributions as well as the endorsements of ex-president Gerald R. Ford, Watergate prosecutor Leon Jaworski, Dallas Cowboys owner Clint Murchison, and football stars Roger Staubach and Terry Bradshaw.

Prominent among the contributors to Here's Life was Nelson Bunker Hunt, who also acted as chairman of the campaign's International Executive Committee, soliciting his financial peers to participate in the plan that would make the world safe for Christian entrepreneurs. (During a weekend retreat in Dallas during the spring of 1980, Hunt reportedly raised $20 million from his wealthy business colleagues.) Other members of that committee included Roy Rogers, W. Clement Stone, Wallace E. Johnson of Holiday Inns, and assorted businessmen from Switzerland, Canada, and South Africa. Hunt personally financed the filming of a miracle-laden life of Christ that he hoped would be screened by the Crusade for every infidel on earth before the century was out.

Another darling of devout millionaires, and of Bunker Hunt in particular, was James Robison, the Fort Worth evangelist famed for his denunciations of homosexuality and for his dramatic conversion of Cullen Davis, the eccentric heir miraculously acquitted of conspiring to murder the judge in his divorce case. (Robison and Davis subsequently earned a Bum Steer award from *Texas Monthly* by destroying a million dollars' worth of oriental statuary from Davis's private collection because they feared that the art works might be connected with idolatry.)

Although Robison's weekly Sunday morning broadcast reached only half a million viewers, located primarily in the South and Southwest, his reputation for slaying secular dragons was nearly as great as that of Jerry Falwell.

Born in a Houston hospital charity ward after surviving his destitute mother's attempt to abort him, God's Angry Man, as he came to be called, demonstrated his ability to wow the wealthy early in his career. At age twenty-three, he caught the eye of H. L. Hunt. Hunt had been so impressed with Robison's guest sermons at the First Baptist Church of Dallas that he offered to back the fiery young communicator in a political career. Robison wrestled with temptation, but turned down the podium in favor of the pulpit. Nevertheless, Robison's ties to the Hunt family remained firm, and H.L.'s son Nelson Bunker began to appear at Robison crusades.

Robison's brand of brimstone continued to impress leading lights of the business community, and in December 1979 he appeared on the cover of the magazine *Texas Business*. In the accompanying article, Robison cited among his backers H. E. "Eddie" Chiles, chairman of the Western Company of North America, and Mike Richards, chairman of the National Industrial Bank of Houston and the Northwest Bank and Trust of Houston. Robison proudly acknowledged his ties to the financial community, claiming, like Moody, Sunday, and Graham before him, that conversion was an asset for business: "When a man's attitude toward God is right, his quality of production will improve, and when he gives an honest day's work, he produces more. This improvement in productivity increases the gross national product and there is more for everybody. In this way, by steering employers and employees to Christian morality and influencing attitudes, preachers like myself can have an important impact on economic matters."

A powerful persuader, Robison was not out to cajole the lost into a little positive thinking but to pound fear into their hearts. He cast himself as a modern-day Jeremiah, called to cry out against wickedness. Like a parody of an old-time preacher, he sneered, he snarled, he sweated. In a speech at the 1982 National Religious Broadcasters convention, he even took on his own colleagues, warning of electronic preachers who watered down the gospel with entertainment.

Robison's own weekly broadcasts opened with a dramatic voice-over proclaiming, "James Robison, a man with a message, presents Jesus Christ as the only hope for a desperate and dying nation. James Robison is leading Bible-believing Christians to stand firm on the truth of God's word and reclaim America as one nation under God. James Robison speaks boldly concerning the spiritual cancers destroying the heart of families, churches, and our nation. James Robison, a man with a message." In February 1979, when his diagnosis of those cancers focused on homosexuality, citing the murder of San Francisco city supervisor Harvey Milk as evidence of God's judgment, pressure from the gay community forced the cancellation of "James Robison Presents" by Dallas/Ft. Worth station WFAA.

Robison's battle to reinstate his show on WFAA became a publicity campaign that boosted Robison to the top of the religious right, landing him the cochairmanship of Ed McAteer's Roundtable. His Freedom-to-Preach rally in Dallas drew thousands of supporters, who rallied to the Robison rhetoric. In a blast of poetic bombast, Robison outlined the skewed priorities of the American public, with its brief affairs with brand names, its fickle infatuations with big-name blonds: "It is a shame that America knows more about Mickey Mouse than about Moses . . . more about *Charlie's Angels* than about God's angels . . . more about Shell than hell . . . more about Phillips 66 than about the holy 66 books of the Word of God." Robison, unlike most Super Savers, did not approve of multifaceted ministries nor of mincing words. There were no fancy wrappers around the plain prophecies of the Bible for God's Angry Man. His loyalty was to men of plain speech, naked ambition, and hard money.

CHAPTER 6

Stations of the Cross: The Electronic Kingdom

An old man confined by infirmities and debt to his room in an old-folks home happened upon the Reverend Increase Matters's "Dialing-for-Donors" show one Sunday morning as he was switching channels on his TV set in search of "The Earnest Anguish Hour." Even as the Reverend Matters spoke, invalids from all over the country were calling the number on their screens to ask for prayers, to report unexpected healings. They testified to cancers cured in private parts, of boils vanished from public places, of assorted demons driven from broken homes and bodies. Full of hope, the old man called the magic number to ask for relief from his worsening emphysema and talked long and expensively with a DFD counselor. Soon the old man received in the mail a personalized condolence letter, a handkerchief imprinted in red by the Reverend Matters's fingertips, and a request to join the DFD Praise Partners for only $15 a month. The old man complied many times over, as he continued to cough into the colorful handkerchief. His gifts to DFD increased, but his breaths grew shorter, and his debts greater. One day he placed his hands on the TV set and cried out to the Reverend Matters, who kept smiling and smiling on the flickering screen. The old man died believing neither his faith nor his contributions had been enough.

Few televangelists in the Falwell era shared James Robison's dour attitude toward diversions behind the pulpit. Gone was the time when religious broadcasting meant merely stationing a TV camera in the choir loft or attaching a broadcast microphone to the preacher's tie. Dull sermons and droning voices were going the way of clapboard churches and Sacred Harp singing. Purists of old-time gospel preaching had to share the airwaves with enterprising evangelists who had learned the lessons of Christian capitalism about dressing up and diversifying their ministries. Preachers, after all, had to compete against each other as well as against secular programs for viewers.

Fulton Sheen, the original Electronic Christian, had claimed that radio was like the Old Testament because, when you listened to it, you heard the Word of God, and that television was like the New Testament because, when you watched it, you saw the Word of God incarnated right before your eyes. But Sheen, of the glowing dark eyes and snappy homilies, had been succeeded in the Electronic Kingdom by Super Savers who served up a new kind of gospel—a gospel of prime-time glitter as well as Sunday morning salvation.

One needed more than gumption and a Bible to mount the electronic pulpit these days; one needed a gimmick. If viewers wanted old-fashioned fire and brimstone (and new-fangled politics) they could stick to Jerry Falwell's "Old-Time Gospel Hour." For devotees of good-ol'-boy gospel, swaggering Jimmy Swaggart, a cousin of Jerry Lee Lewis and son of a moonshiner, who topped the religious-TV ratings in 1983, offered brow-mopping, piano-banging pentecostalism. And if they hankered for old-time wheelchair-stopping, crutches-dropping faith healing, there was always Ernest Angley, with his purple velvet jackets and deep-pile toupee, ready to slap the very deafness out of a child's ear or the devil out a man's innards with the flat of his hand.

Fans of Christian spectacle could flip to "The Rex Humbard Hour," formerly broadcast from the marble-and-glass expanse of the Cathedral of Tomorrow. Now transmitted from the verdant surroundings of Callaway Gardens, Georgia, the show featured guest celebrities and gala numbers from the singing Humbard clan. For viewers who preferred Schuller's California dreamin' to Falwell's down-home schemin', there was the "Hour of Power," as a wall of the Crystal Cathedral swung open to the bright, polluted sky of Orange County and the spray of an eternal fountain. For those who were looking for a Johnny Carson format but without the late-night innuendoes, there was Jim Bakker's "PTL Club," complete with an Ed McMahon-style sidekick in the person of Henry Harrison, otherwise known as Uncle Henry, who helped Bakker bring out a succession of born-again magicians, comedians, musicians, and miracle-workers.

For the Super Savers, all of this paratheological programing was part of the campaign to stop the metastasis of secular culture and implant a Christian culture in its stead. In the analogy frequently drawn by Raimundo Gimenez of the Hispanic Religious Broadcasters Association, evangelicals should use the media to "counteract the poison spewed forth by the secular media, just as the venom of the snake is used as an antidote." In other words, TV was a homeopathic cure for sin.

THE VIDEO VATICAN

Probably the most skillful converter of secular devices into sacred tools was Pat Robertson, founder of the Christian Broadcasting Network, who managed to build a defunct TV station into the Video Vatican of America. It was Robertson who was the most likely model for the character of the Reverend Freddie Stone in ABC's made-for-TV movie *Pray TV*. Actor Ned Beatty was so convincing in his portrayal of the smooth-talking Stone that when Stone, as part of the plot, asked troubled viewers to dial the 800 number on their screens, some 15,000 lost souls across America actually responded.

Robertson, like Jerry Falwell and Bill Bright, was a man with a mission. He had his own agenda, however, and his own methods. In 1959, Robertson, a former marine and Golden Gloves boxer who had graduated from Yale Law School but flunked the New York State bar exam, was dwelling with his family in a ramshackle pentecostal parsonage in a Brooklyn slum when he heard about a run-down hillbilly TV station for sale in Portsmouth, Virginia. He managed to buy it for a song even though, as he tells the story, he had been living on soybeans, and his assets at that time amounted to less than $70. He raised money by preaching in nearby Virginia churches, while technicians prayed over the equipment, and on October 1, 1961, the nation's first Christian TV station, WYAH, Channel 27, went on the air.

When finances remained shaky in 1963, Robertson sent out a call for 700 people to pledge $10 a month in order to keep the station alive, and the 700 Club was born. Christians paid their dues (which were shortly raised to $15), and in April 1977 CBN leased a transponder on RCA's Satcom 2 satellite, expanding its outreach through a maze of cable systems that served 14.5 million homes by 1982. By 1981 CBN's annual budget exceeded $68 million, and the 700 Club numbered close to 300,000 members.

Initially a talk/variety show hosted by Jim Bakker, who later left to found his own PTL network, "The 700 Club" resembled a cheap mock-up of the Johnny Carson show. There was the host's meet-the-press desk, with chairs set up alongside for cohost and guests, and there was the small, tinny-sounding band whose members tended to dress in primary-color leisure suits with rhinestone trim. When Robertson took over the show, he seemed to reign in secular splendor, as he joked with his guests, teased the bandleader, and goaded his sidekick Ben Kinchlow, a six-foot-four former Black Muslim who now found himself playing no-nonsense Sancho Panza to a Don Quixote who tilted at humanistic windmills. Whereas Carson would nervously steer his talkier guests away from tedious testimonials, Robertson would hang onto every detail, responding with an amen instead of a nervous twitch of his tie.

In the late seventies, "The 700 Club" began to tone down the banter and Good News and play up the bad news. Robertson's interviews with conservative political leaders and financial analysts took on the hushed, urgent tones of doctors conferring over the body of a patient in the operating room. The patient, of course, was America. What could be done to forestall the end, to prop up the invalid's faltering moral-support system? The Carson-nouveau desk had been replaced on the set by a pair of swivel chairs placed in front of a backdrop portraying the shattered dome of the U.S. Capitol, beneath which was printed the slogan "Christ or Chaos!"

Robertson had, in fact, branched out into politics even before Falwell emerged onto the national scene. Along with other evangelical leaders, he had helped to elect Jimmy Carter, with whom he subsequently became disillusioned. In Robertson's view, Carter had gotten slack with regard to the nation's defense, and he had surrounded himself with such backsliders as Hamilton Jordan and Andrew Young. Said Robertson of Carter, "There was this wonderful exterior charm to him. But underneath, terrible coldness." Ironically, a similar description had been applied to Robertson himself by his detractors.

In 1978 Robertson supported his friend, G. Conoly Phillips, a wealthy Virginia car dealer whom he had recently brought to Christ, for the U.S. Senate. Although Robertson did not donate cash directly, he tutored Phillips in fund-raising and media advertising. He advised Phillips on issues, masterminding the conservative platform on which Phillips ran as a Democrat, and he gave a nominating speech for his candidate at the state party convention. Although Phillips lost, Robertson continued his search for a political solution to America's spiritual ills. He became cochairman of the 1980 Washington for Jesus crusade because, he proclaimed, he wanted nothing less than to save America. He told *Sojourners* magazine in 1979 that "There's only one job in the United States and in the world, I suppose, that would give me any more opportunity to do good for my fellow man." That, he said, would be the presidency.

Robertson's disavowals during the Washington for Jesus rally of any overtly political aims seemed disingenuous, to say the least. Yet he claimed to have been instructed by God during his annual retreat earlier that year to withdraw from direct political involvement. Shortly after the National Affairs Briefing in August 1980, during which a suddenly God-fearing Ronald Reagan addressed a convocation of evangelical leaders on the campaign issues dearest to their hearts, Robertson resigned from the Roundtable, the religious lobbying group that had sponsored the event. In the September 15 issue of *Newsweek* he was quoted as saying, "God isn't a right-winger or a left-winger. The evangelists stand in danger of being used and manipulated."

Robertson decided to return to prayer and Christian programming as his means of building a Christian consensus. What America needed was a Christian culture that bombarded the senses with Christian messages. Secularism had called everything into question, and artists wandered about in the Unreal City of uncertainty instead of building the New Jerusalem. Robertson had told *Sojourners*, "We need to get into the arts and the media. I mean the church, after all, dominated the theater and music and art for centuries, and we've just totally given it up. We've given it up to nihilism. The art that comes out is nihilistic. Sartre, Camus, these people, they have no hope, nothing, and the art reflects that. . . . I'd like to see us get into all of this; that's the kingdom."

He made this point in more economic terms to the *Wall Street Journal*. Stating his disapproval of boycotts and dissociating himself from Donald E. Wildmon's Coalition for Better Television, as well as from Moral Majority, he explained, "I'm a great believer in free enterprise. Everybody does what he's called to do. I don't object to someone cursing the darkness, but I'd rather go out and light some candles."

Indeed, more than a few Roman candles had been lit at the October 6, 1979, dedication ceremony of CBN's new headquarters. The program concluded with a performance of Handel's hallelujah chorus, accompanied by an array of fireworks orchestrated by George "Boom Boom" Zambelli. As Robertson walked out on a platform and prayed over a milling crowd of 6,000, one was reminded of the Pope blessing the multitudes gathered before St. Peter's. Built in the shape of a huge cross with a circular prayer chapel at the center, the 160,000-square-foot structure, whose neocolonial brick facade would be right at home in Williamsburg, was designed to house four separate studios equipped with state-of-the-art technology. During the ceremony, Billy Graham commented that CBN represented the "most comprehensive use of technology in the service of the church."

Constructed at a cost of $21 million, CBN's new home put one in mind of patriotism and Patrick Henry and the glory of man as well as the glory of God. One of the most sophisticated communications centers in the world, at least in terms of equipment, CBN's studios were constructed to minimize the risk of human fallibility. Nearly everything worked by computer. CBN bought the first digital cameras on the market, for instance: RCA's TK–47s for studio use and TK–760s for both studio and remote work. The largest studio was stocked with "flying scenery," stored above the lights until needed in the show. Production was expedited by a Grass Valley switcher—the machine from which the director chooses camera shots and special effects—directly behind the director's console, which served as a learning device for students from CBN's graduate school of communications.

Despite its technical advantages, however, CBN faced some hefty competition from religious as well as secular broadcasters. In 1980, "The 700 Club" ranked only thirteenth among the Super Saver shows. But Robertson was determined to pump up the quantity as well as the quality of CBN shows. "The 700 Club" was modified into a TV-magazine format so that the show now resembled a cross between "60 Minutes," "Good Morning, America," and "That's Incredible." Bright-eyed correspondent Kathy Osbeck taped on-the-scene interviews with reformed child abusers, born-again entertainers, and former devil worshipers and occasionally contributed a session on home economics. Budget expert Malcolm McGregor, one of Robertson's "Scots buddies—they know how to save money," offered financial advice on a segment called "Money Matters." Kenneth Cooper, a Jim Fixx look-alike, contributed advice on health concerns—jogging, aerobic exercises, and diet.

As for politics, Robertson was doing more than praying on the subject. Interviewing politicians was a compulsion like snacking on potato chips—he couldn't meet just one. Despite his avowal the previous year, Robertson continued to entertain leaders of state he considered to be political heroes or allies, including Son Sann, president of Free Cambodia, the non-Communist faction at odds with the Heng Samrin regime. (In a film segment called "Cambodian Complicities," no mention was made of the havoc caused by the American bombing of Cambodia during the Vietnam War.) As Robertson discussed such issues as the sale of AWACs to Saudi Arabia, he called for instantaneous polls, in which viewers' opinions were registered by calls to a special phone number. (The vote on the AWACs sale: Yes—35 percent, No—65 percent.)

Shortly before Thanksgiving, 1981, CBN produced a ten-part series called "The American Covenant," a docudrama designed to set the record straight on the role of religion in the early history of America, from the Pilgrims to the delegates to the Continental Congress and the Constitutional Convention. Images of Pilgrims, Minute Men, the Liberty Bell, George Washington, and Christ were blurred in a montage of civil religion. The message: that our Founding Fathers never intended the complete separation of church and state; wary of a centralized government, what they feared was the establishment of a state religion. A position that Robertson apparently took to mean that ministers should interfere when it appeared that the judiciary was rendering too much unto Caesar.

Robertson found it impossible to stand idly on the sidelines as the Arkansas "Scopes" trial heated up in December 1981. He managed to upstage the trial proceedings by accusing Arkansas Attorney General Steve Clark of trying to lose the case—or "take a dive," in his erstwhile boxer's parlance. On his December 9 show, Robertson cited as evidence of possible collusion Clark's participation in a fund-raising auction sponsored by the American Civil Liberties Union—the very group that was representing the plaintiffs in the trial. During the broadcast Robertson had the name and telephone number of Arkansas Governor Frank White flashed onto the screen as he urged viewers to register their protests, and a number responded with angry phone calls and telegrams to Little Rock. Robertson's comments were deemed inflammatory even by advocates of the state's creation-science law.

In his continuing obsession with such controversial issues, Robertson clearly found it difficult to concentrate on the more mundane matters of, say, jogging and balancing a budget. In January 1982, after torrential rains and mudslides had ravaged the northern California coast, Robertson spoke almost gleefully about the possibility of an ensuing earthquake. Marin County, he observed, was famous for its hot-tub lifestyle, while San Francisco was known for its tolerance of homosexuals. "I think the time has come for God's judgment," he warned. "If I were you, I wouldn't get involved with Sodom and Gomorrah." And a week after Brigadier General Efraín Ríos Montt, a born-again Christian, staged a coup in Guatemala, Robertson was praying for the success of the bullets-and-beans strongman: "God, we pray for Ríos Montt . . . that you would . . . send the angels to watch over him."

Every subject on the show was tuned to an apocalyptic pitch. One should jog in order to keep fit for impending disaster, perhaps to outrun looters and incendiaries, and one should get one's finances in order before America fell into a depression that would make the thirties look like a picnic. A typical CBN commercial showed a man wobbling on a tightrope to suggest the plight of the average Christian in need of the safety net of financial planning—a convenience provided for viewers by CBN experts, of course.

Robertson's desire to travel simultaneously down Madison Avenue, Sunset Boulevard, and the King's Highway was particularly apparent during the 1982 National Religious Broadcasters convention, when his February 8 meeting of "The 700 Club" was broadcast live from the Sheraton-Washington (D.C.) ballroom. His guest celebrity for the evening was singer/dancer Carol Lawrence, who was dressed in a bright pink ruffled organza ball gown. Ms. Lawrence, who had recently joined the roster of born-again entertainers, pirouetted slowly as she sang an old Shaker hymn. At one point, when Ms. Lawrence sank impulsively to her knees during a testimonial, the show's floor director, unprepared for such unrehearsed fervor, gesticulated frantically at her to stand up.

Rex Humbard was also slated for a brief appearance, but he was welcomed by cohost Ben Kinchlow, while Robertson rested backstage. After Humbard spoke for a few moments, a series of cue cards began to appear, warning Humbard with increasing urgency that it was time for the guest choir from Atlanta, Georgia, to appear. The singing was to be followed by Jesse Helms and a head-on collision of religion and politics.

FROM SOAP TO NUTS

Robertson was trying to create a something-for-everyone network. The average Christian viewer who picked up CBN's shows by cable or on UHF (CBN owned four UHF stations outright) could watch wholesome TV almost around the clock, although a number of programs were repeated and secular sitcoms such as "Leave It to Beaver" were inserted to fill out the schedule.

From Chicago, for example, came a game show called "Bible Baffle," a kind of Christianized version of "Jeopardy," in which each contestant stood behind a pulpitlike blue podium equipped with a buzzer, behind which an arc of lights flashed like an electronic halo on the blink. Contestants were quizzed about obscure biblical references, and the winner of each round gained the chance to unscramble a Bible verse. The rather modest prizes ranged from selections of religious books to sets of TV trays made by Quaker Industries. From CBN's own school of communications came a children's show called "Bears and Blankets," which was aimed at children from one to four years old. Said Robertson of the new CBN kid-vid: "There might be some things on 'Sesame Street' that parents wouldn't want their kids to be exposed to."

The pride of CBN's programming, though, was the Christian soap opera "Another Life," produced by Continental Broadcasting Network, the wholly owned commercial subsidiary of CBN. Developed by Robert F. Aaron, a Boston-born Harvard graduate and former director of daytime programming for NBC, who had helped to develop three of NBC's most successful soaps—"Days of Our Lives," "The Doctors," and "Another World"—CBN's soap was designed to compete in the daytime secular market for advertising dollars as well as viewers. With such illustrious secular defectors behind its scenes as director/producer Peter Andrews, formerly the guiding light of "The Guiding Light," and executive producer David Hummel, former creative supervisor for Procter & Gamble, "Another Life" inspired such companies as General Mills, Oscar Mayer, and Richardson Vicks to sign on as advertisers.

The show's title, like that of many secular soaps, suggested both suds and salvation, and it brought to mind specifically the long-running "One Life to Live" and "Another World." Aaron's intent was to create a slick product that would deal with the same dilemmas as the secular soaps: alcoholism, drugs, child abuse, dallying doctors, unwed mothers, broken homes, scheming harridans, nosy neighbors. But floating above these scenarios of the beleaguered nuclear family, like a benevolent sponsor, would be the invisible, redemptive presence of God. Said Aaron, the difference between CBN's serial and others is its theme: that "faith in God can overcome the trials of life."

The devout, happily married core couple of the series, Scott and Terry Davidson, resided in the mythical town of Ravenscroft, a suburb of Richmond, Virginia, which had seen its share of Peyton Place perversities and intramural intrigues. Their daughter, Lori, a college student constantly fending off the advances of her boyfriend Russ Weaver, the school's football star, was wrongly accused in early episodes of seducing Paul Mason, a professor whose wife, Miriam, was the town's resident villainess. Miriam, the show's "female J.R.," was described by Aaron as "marvelously malevolent" and a "beautiful schemer."

In contrast to the picture-perfect Davidsons were their squabbling neighbors Jeff and Liz Cummings and their mistreated little daughter, whose patient suffering made Little Eva seem a bad seed. Other characters included Charles and Helen Carpenter, Miriam Mason's wealthy parents, who lived on Chicago's Gold Coast, scheming and drinking, and a divorced black friend of Scott Davidson's named Gene Redlon who lived with his son and mother.

When Aaron first took over the project in its early stages—the working title at the time was "The Inner Light"—he found the scripts to be too much like biblical parables, "didactic" and "smug." He wanted to create a soap with hope and happy endings, but felt that an overtly religious message would turn off much of the college-age audience he wanted to build up for the show. The responsibility for writing the show was handed to Dallas and Jo-Anne Barnes, a born-again husband-and-wife team who also happened to have over eighty hours of secular prime-time credit. Aaron felt that the moral message should emerge from the situations of the plot—not from Bible-quoting preachers. For example, Lori would counter the panting Russ's passes with such lines as "Some day, you'll share my faith and then there won't be any more fighting."

Yet one episode in the fall of 1981 featured an outright miracle —perhaps as a concession to Pat Robertson's belief in faith healing. As the alcoholic profligate Jeff Cummings lay near death in a hospital room, the doctor at his bedside remarked gravely, "If you're going to speed through life, you've got to realize you're gonna crash." As Jeff's wife and child prayed fervently for his recovery, a bright orange glow surrounded the miscreant, and he awoke from his coma, removing his oxygen mask in bewilderment—a miraculous cure that would never have occurred even on "General Hospital." Jeff, of course, mended his ways, and even opened a Christian bookstore. Scott Davidson, played by John Corsaut, unfortunately passed on to greener pastures when Corsaut decided to leave the show.

Robertson himself would seem to have cause to believe in miracles. Not only was there the evidence of the many-splendored CBN complex that sprang forth like a mighty tree from a mustard seed of faith planted on the sands of Virginia Beach. There was the time when Robertson turned back a mighty hurricane—just commanded it in the name of Jesus to do an about-face and head back out to sea. And then there were the healings. On a typical show in November 1981, Robertson declared, "At Lourdes there have been only eleven cases of miraculous healing. But we have seen documented tens of thousands. You don't have to go to some shrine somewhere."

One of the benefits of membership in the 700 Club, then, was divine Medicaid. A consistent feature of the show was the pray-for-a-miracle segment. Shifting roles easily from chatty talk-show host or earnest economics lecturer to pentecostal preacher, Robertson would fall to his knees beside Ben Kinchlow and his guest *du jour* and begin to pray, his eyes shut tight as sweat and tears threatened to flow. *"Heal a broken home now . . . bring a husband and wife back together . . . heal a sick mind . . . Thank you, Jesus! . . . mend broken bones . . . Right now, Lord! . . . heal a cancer."* Asking viewers to place their hands on their TV sets, Ben Kinchlow would murmur reassuringly, "There's no gimmick involved."

The phones would start to ring as people dialed the 700 Club to ask for help or to report their miraculous recoveries. But Robertson knew already; he had received "words of knowledge"—visions from the Lord—of healings all across the country. *"There's a deeply inflamed eye, a bloodshot eye that's being healed right now . . . tennis elbow is being healed . . . somebody named Charles is praying about a job . . . there's a man who's in need of financial help, somewhere in Washington, and help is on the way . . . Thank you, Jesus! Amen! Amen!"*

Robertson knew the loneliness, the despair, the anguish of the wounded or lost sinners of America—the people who needed a miracle just to get by until the next day. As a tongue-speaker who had come of age in a small pentecostal church, he understood the hunger for immediacy, the need to believe that God's grace could suddenly become manifest. His show offered the electronic version of group prayer, the instant display of the miraculous charisma sought by pentecostal Christians. Unfortunately, however, he could offer only an illusion of the spontaneity and sense of community that tongue-speakers created in their churches. For the televangelist, communications from God had to come on cue.

Robertson followed up his scattered barrages of faith healing
with well-aimed rounds of fund-raising. Since so many of his viewers were elderly, invalid, or jobless, confined to their living rooms
or sickbeds, the odds were favorable that both appeals would hit
home. Concluding that the Bible taught that the more one gave the
more one would receive, Robertson formulated his very own Kingdom Principles, a code for Christian charity. According to the
Kingdom Principles, the Lord was the benign Exchequer who re-
paid one's deposits with interest. If viewers sent their rent money,
their medicine money, their pin money, or their mad money to
Jesus, c/o CBN, Virginia Beach, Virginia, they could expect a
quick return on their investment. The Texas oilman, for example,
who donated a 4 percent override on his gusher could expect the
law of reciprocity to bring him an outpouring of divine grace. Not
even the Pope would promise such a return back in the Middle
Ages when transgressors could buy indulgences in a sort of sin-
abatement plan.

The Kingdom Principles operated as a religious IRS—an Eternal
Revenue Service—to keep CBN's coffers filled and those "Bible
Baffle" lights blinking. Since video evangelists couldn't exactly pass
the offering plates during a service, they had to devise other means
of extracting tribute. In fact, the Super Savers had become so ingenious at raising funds to cover their enormous operating costs (annual budgets for the top shows consistently exceeded $50 million)
that they had to buy money-sorting machines and such devices for
mass correspondence as the ESP (Electronic Signature Production)
computer that could replicate signatures at the rate of 400–700 an
hour. Jerry Sholes, formerly of the Oral Roberts Evangelistic Association, reported that Roberts, whose ratings consistently topped
those of all other religious broadcasts during the late seventies,
received so many prayer requests (some 6 million a year) that the
evangelist simply blessed the computer printouts of supplicants'
names, categorized according to affliction.

CASHING IN ON JESUS

Super Savers used essentially six different fund-raising techniques. The first was selling sacred space: convincing viewers to buy a piece of the Rock of Ages. Generous donors could have their names inscribed on Oral Roberts's Tulsa prayer tower, on individual cushioned chairs in Robert Schuller's Crystal Cathedral, on chalets in Jim Bakker's Heritage U.S.A., or on "living memorial" bricks in Jerry Falwell's new Liberty Mountain prayer chapel. In 1982, those who contributed to Falwell's pro-life Save-a-Baby campaign also paid for the construction of the Tomb of the Unborn Baby, dedicated to the "memory of the millions of aborted babies that have died in America" since the day of infamy—January 22, 1973— when the Supreme Court legalized abortion.

The second tactic was selling prayer time, which could be almost as expensive as broadcast time. Oral Roberts, who chummily asked viewers to drop him a line about their problems, promising to say a personal prayer for each supplicant, was the master of this appeal.

Tactic number three was a more formalized version of the second. This was the join-the-club approach. In order to ensure that one's prayers would be answered, one could join Roberts's Faith Partners, Rex Humbard's Prayer Key Family, or Robertson's 700 Club. But there was also a club-within-a-club at CBN. If one donated $100 along with "Seven Lifetime Prayer Requests," one's name and problems could become part of posterity—they were recorded on microfilm and entombed in the CBN prayer pillar located in the very center of CBN's circular prayer chapel.

The virtue of belonging to these religious clubs—and indeed to video congregations—was that you never had to leave the sanctuary of your own home; you never had to shake hands with or smile at the undesirables and troublemakers who inevitably disturbed one's peace of mind at any religious gathering. To consider a scattered group of contributors like the 700 Club as a "cult," as some critics did, was absurd; to consider it an expensive club from which one could never be blackballed and for which one never had to get out and sell cakes and cookies was more accurate.

Joining a religious club also entitled one to become a souvenir collector. Accordingly, the fourth fund-raising strategy involved hawking holy molies. Instead of buying a splinter of the true cross or the mummified thumb of St. Expedite to clutch when times got tough, the TV viewer could buy a Pocket Sermon Coin resembling an Olympic gold medal from Robert Schuller Ministries or a cloth with the imprint of Oral Roberts's healing hand. It was a practice that seemed to come perilously close to promoting the trappings of ancient Roman Catholicism—the relics, icons, statues, and superstitions—that the remodelers of the Reformation tried to remove from their churches.

When believers joined the 700 Club, they received a lapel pin, bumper sticker, auto decal, and certificate of membership—not to mention a monthly newsletter called *Perspective* and cassette tapes of Robertson's most recent revelations. If you joined Jerry Falwell's Faith Partners, you received a gold-plated Jesus First pin, a special pocket secretary, and a Faith Partner Giant Print Bible. For antiabortionists, Falwell offered the Precious Feet lapel pin, not representing the hallowed soles of Jesus but the tiny feet of unborn fetuses. Jim Bakker offered the PTL Masters' Art Collection, featuring a portrait of the baby Jesus guaranteed to get even an atheist all choked up. (Perhaps this is the kind of Christian art Pat Robertson felt should replace the nihilism that passed for art in the secular marketplace.) And Jimmy Swaggart would even let you travel with him on a pilgrimage either to the Holy Land or to Hawaii, depending on the season.

If these techniques did not soften up the stingy viewer, there was always the hard-sell strategy: the personal appeal. Most shows fostered the illusion of intimacy, as the preacher zeroed in on that dear phantom lady with cataracts in Chattanooga, that hypothetical young girl in Akron who had been tempted by demons, drugs, and alcohol. Then, as viewers called in for prayer or counseling, their life stories were recorded on data sheets that ultimately entered the show's computerized memory banks. Soon they were receiving letters that referred specifically, uncannily, to their hometown, occupation, age, or even disease. It was even alleged that one Super Saver had a special task force to relieve elderly viewers of their jewels. Perhaps he referred potential donors to that beautiful passage in the sixth chapter of Matthew: "Lay not up for yourselves treasures upon earth, where moth and rust doth corrupt, and where thieves break through and steal." The vaults of the Super Saver would presumably be more secure.

For those stubborn viewers who were still holding back their earthly treasures, the TV preachers employed the last-resort technique used by secular merchants: the going-out-of-business sale. Just when things appeared to be going so well for the TV ministers, their empires were actually crumbling at the edges, their cash flow drying up like the Dead Sea. In 1979, Rex Humbard, whose Midwestern ministry had been languishing, bombarded his viewers with pleas for support, claiming debts of $3.2 million. Soon thereafter Humbard sought refuge within the generous girth of the Sun Belt, buying a Florida condominium worth $650,000 and setting up an alfresco pulpit in Georgia's Callaway Gardens.

In the spring of 1981, viewers on Jerry Falwell's mailing list received a communication stamped "Urgent." The letter began, "It now appears that after 25 years of broadcasting and televising the Gospel, the Old-Time Gospel Hour may go off the air." Viewers were urged to send "an emergency gift of $25 right now. . . . Remember, within the next few days, we must have a miracle. We cannot go into the month of June without a supernatural intervention."

Similarly, regular viewers of the "Hour of Power" were distressed during late summer, 1980, to receive a message from Robert Schuller, datelined Norway, saying that "The cash flow the last two months that sustains Hour of Power on the air has dropped to the point where we must drop, that means cancel—translated *go off the air in September*—in more cities than I can accept." All this only shortly before the grand opening of the multimillion-dollar Crystal Cathedral, to which celebrities would flock from all over the country. Lamented Schuller, "God knows how empty my soul would be if *any city* in America missed *the first telecast* in September from the Crystal Cathedral!"

Schuller's rhetoric was the essence of constraint compared to that of fellow Californian Dr. W. Eugene Scott, of the "Festival of Faith" show, who was zapped off the air in midbroadcast by the FCC in 1983. Scott, who contended with James Robison for the title of "God's Angry Man," was famous for his insulting Don Rickles approach to fund-raising. For Scott, every minute could be the last, and any viewer who dallied was a fool. When the pledges weren't coming in fast enough, he would glare at the camera, taunting the viewers, "You just sit there glued to your chairs. This is war!"

As his battle with the FCC intensified (he refused to turn over the donation records of his contributors), the blue-eyed, white-haired Scott bought a collection of wind-up monkeys that he used as totems of the Washington bureaucrats who were plaguing him. In one segment of a documentary by German director Werner Herzog, Scott was caught in all his angry glory. Bashing the simians over the head with a paddle as they chattered and clashed their cymbals, he cackled, "Hit a bureaucrat on the head—that's all he knows how to do." (As recorded by Herzog off-screen, Scott appeared considerably calmer and more thoughtful about his dilemma; he told Herzog that he would like nothing more than to get away from all the hullabaloo, perhaps moving to Australia to teach Plato in college.)

The most famous last-hour appeal, however, was made by Jim Bakker, shortly after he was hired by Pat Robertson. Robertson recorded the event in his autobiographical book, *Shout It from the Housetops*. It seems that one night during station WYAH's regular sign-off, Bakker appeared on camera and announced, "We're on the verge of bankruptcy and just don't have the money to pay our bills," and proceeded to break down and cry. As the tears splattered on the station floor, the camera remained fixed on Bakker's face, and phones began to ring. Bakker managed to raise over $100,000 in less than four hours and earned himself the title Jack Paar of the Preachers. Clearly this was a man destined for his own Total Image Center.

The tears continued to flow sporadically and effectively over the years when Bakker joined the PTL Club and occasionally fell into difficulties with the FCC or with his creditors. Christian culture, it seemed, was well watered by its cultivators.

CHAPTER 7

Selling the Word:
The Christian Publishing
Industry

*The Salesman from Nazareth knew His business.
Which, in no small measure, accounts for His success.
He simply had to know His stuff. His prospects
challenged Him at every step He took. So did His
competitors. When He said, "Verily I say unto you
. . ." He knew what He was talking about.*

Josef Daikeler,
The Salesman from Nazareth

The new evangelical revival, like the Protestant Reformation itself, resulted in part from a revolution in communications. In sixteenth-century Germany, the printing press and crusading translators made the gospel accessible to the laity. And in the latter part of the twentieth century, television and popular evangelists put Jesus into the vernacular for millions. However, the printing press was still crucial to the creation of an evangelical culture. Just as important to the promotion of Christian values as the Christian TV station was the Christian bookstore, which operated as a kind of all-purpose Christian shopping and counseling center.

Despite all the banning and bowdlerizing incidents across the country that involved conservative evangelicals, books—particularly the Good Book—were very popular among born-again consumers. By 1981, there were more than 6,300 Christian bookstores in operation aross the country, most of which belonged to the Christian Booksellers Association, the evangelical analogue to the American Booksellers Association. An average of one new CBA store was being opened every day.

The religious publishing industry was approaching the billion-dollars-a-year mark, with some 4,500 new titles being offered every year and a total of nearly 30,000 titles in print. *Publishers Weekly,* quickly recognizing the potential of the religious market, began to cover CBA conventions and devote special issues to religious books. It seemed that the Christian marketplace remained bullish even when secular markets faltered.

There were several causes for the "explosion" in Christian bookselling, according to CBA vice president John Bass. While denominational houses accounted for most Christian book sales even after the CBA was established in 1949, today's Christian books were "appealing more to the general public." They were "addressing such important issues as personal health concerns, rearing of families, divorce, homosexuality, and depression." The "uncertain world climate of the 1980s contributed to the interest in Christian literature." Moreover, publishers, growing more competitive and aggressive, had "upgraded the quality of their marketing concepts and their products' appearances and graphics."

Annual CBA conventions were festive affairs that displayed Christian capitalism at its most colorful. The first one I attended was held at the Anaheim Convention Center, a UFO-shaped hall located in the heart of Orange County, California, equidistant from

Robert Schuller's Crystal Cathedral and Disneyland's miniature Matterhorn. As one bookseller described the convention, it was as much a circus as a business gathering. Authors autographed books in booths built to resemble high-tech modules or Spanish missions, and blenders, luggage, and other prizes were raffled off to lucky buyers. A hot-air balloon was tethered at the entrance during the first night of the convention, and inside was a huge balloon in the shape of a little boy perched on his bed, reading a book. A man dressed as a giant hymnal walked around greeting the booksellers, and a puppeteer in one booth occasionally reached out a furry paw to grab a customer. Guards at the convention center remarked that it was the most spectacular trade show they had ever seen in Anaheim.

Obviously the image of the Christian bookseller had changed since Flannery O'Connor wrote about the traveling Bible salesman who seduced a customer in order to steal her wooden leg. So positive-minded, professional, and prosperous were the religious publishers I met that I was inspired by Norman Vincent Peale to devise the Eleven P's—or Principles—of Christian Publishing in order to describe the evangelical approach to bookselling.

Perennials. Once religious titles arrived on the Christian bestseller lists, they could linger for years. In 1982, Hal Lindsey's apocalyptic *The Late Great Planet Earth,* the best-selling trade paperback of the seventies, was still on the Top 10 paperback list of the *Bookstore Journal,* the CBA's official publication. Returns on religious titles averaged only about 5 percent (often as low as 2 percent), so that the publishers' backlists were often much bulkier than their new catalogs.

Bibles, of course, were the perpetual blockbusters. Although the King James Version was still the best-selling Bible, and the best-selling Christian book, there was increasing demand for "readable" Bibles. Nashville-based Thomas Nelson Publishers, the world's leading producer of Bibles, "updated" the King James Version at a cost of $4.5 million and spent a million dollars promoting it. Nelson hoped to steal some of the thunder from their chief rival, Zondervan Corporation of Grand Rapids, Michigan, whose New International Version had sold more than 6 million copies since it was first introduced in 1978.

Even these versions were not readable enough, however, for some Christians. The best-selling "easy-reading" Bible was *The Living Bible,* which was not actually a new translation but simply a new paraphrase, written in ultrasimplified language by a concerned father for his family. *The Living Bible* was born when Kenneth Taylor, a father of eight who commuted to his job in Chicago from the pastoral suburb of Wheaton, was pondering the difficulties he had encountered in conducting daily devotional Bible readings around the dinner table. It occurred to Taylor that what was needed in communicating the meaning of the Scriptures was not a better word-for-word translation but a simple thought-for-thought paraphrase of the Good Book. After testing his initial efforts on his children, Taylor tried unsuccessfully to find a publisher for his *Living Letters.* Finally, he published the manuscript himself, selling 800 copies at the 1962 CBA convention. When a copy of *Living Letters* reached Billy Graham, then recuperating from an illness in a Hawaii hospital, the rest was publishing history. Graham ordered 50,000 paperback copies to give away during his crusades, and eventually distributed 650,000 copies. *The Living Bible* was the best-selling book of both 1971 and 1972 and sold more than 25 million copies by 1982.

A recent edition of *The Living Bible* by Chariot Books, a division of David C. Cook, combined the *Living Bible* text and comic-book-style illustrations with dialogue balloons. But this edition was not the only comic-book Bible on the market. In 1980, Scarf Press in New York released a 144-page book called *Picture Stories from the Bible: The New Testament in Full-Color Comic-Strip Form,* which combined in hardcover form a series of three comic books that had been published in the 1940s. The original *Picture Stories* series was created by Maxwell C. Gaines, the "father of the comic book," who first published the exploits of such superheroes as Superman and Wonder Woman in comic-book form. Zondervan, too, had its own visual-aid Bible called *The New Pictorial Bible,* which had been designed, according to Zondervan marketing director Phil Wolfe, for "the generations who have grown up with television."

The proliferation of new, consumer-friendly Bibles inspired cartoonist Doug Marlette to poke fun at the more "accessible" translations. Preacher Will B. Dunne, in one *Kudzu* installment, reads from a hip version of the Beatitudes: "Blessed are the bummed out: for they shall be mellowed. . . ."

With so many varieties of the Good Book to choose from, not even biblical literalists could agree on which version to interpret literally. There was a Bible for every budget and taste, including a trendy paperback edition of the *Good News Bible* with a mock denim cover. Even stately Oxford University Press was holding its own in the highly competitive Bible market. Oxford's *Scofield Reference Bible,* which incorporated the prophetic end-time commentaries of premillennialist John Nelson Darby into the text, had been selling steadily since it was first published in 1909. In 1981, Oxford won the CBA's runner-up advertising award for its campaign to sell a buffalo-calfskin-bound edition of the Scofield Bible as a graduation gift.

Pastiche. As Bibles became progressively more idiomatic, other Christian literature began to range wider and wider from traditional models, interpolating ancient and contemporary elements in order to make Jesus "relevant." The practice actually began in the late nineteenth century with a series of books that attempted to place Christ in a modern context. Charles Sheldon's best-selling *In His Steps* asked readers to imagine what Christ would do if he were in their situation: Would he ignore that young child's plea for help? Would he take that tempting drink of whiskey? Would he bet the rent money on the next turn of the roulette wheel? Southern writer Shirley Abbott recalled her own interpretation as a young girl of Sheldon's work: "Would Jesus have drunk the glass of ginger ale my mother had just given me? Was there a Baptist position on soda pop?"

In 1894, Edward Everett Hale wrote a book asking what would happen if Jesus came to Boston, and William Thomas Stead asked, similarly, what would occur if Christ came to Chicago. A reviewer for the New York *World* was particularly impressed by the cover of Stead's book: "The striking cover of this dynamite-laden book, soon to be exploded in the hardened heart of Chicago, bears the figure of Christ, with one hand raised in rebuke against a half-score of typical Chicagoans who have just risen from the gambling table, their arms laden with gold."

The intent of these sermonizing writers was to satirize or criticize the sins and shortcomings of their own historical context—a technique used by comedian Lenny Bruce in his famous routine involving a vist by Christ and Moses to St. Patrick's Cathedral in New York. Other writers, however, used similar fictional techniques to glorify their own enterprises. The pioneer of this technique was Bruce Barton. In *The Man Nobody Knows* Barton had used Jesus not only to glorify business but to elevate the masculine ideal of strength and vigor. For Barton, Jesus was no sissy, no meek, sad killjoy: "A physical weakling! Where did they get that idea? Jesus pushed a plane and swung an adze; he was a successful carpenter. . . . A kill-joy! He was the most popular dinner guest in Jerusalem! . . . A failure! He picked up twelve men from the bottom ranks of business and forged them into an organization that conquered the world."

It was this notion of an encultured Christ that eventually inspired contemporary evangelicals to place Christ in the most unlikely settings—the football field, the kitchen, the executive boardroom, the battlefield. In their search for a relevant Jesus, Christians had gone from *Are You Running With Me, Jesus?* to *Twelfth Man in the Huddle.*

The Christianizing of culture in the publishing industry also extended to fiction. A number of Christian novelists, using the example of Lew Wallace's *Ben Hur,* took stories from the Bible as the bases for plots and relied on their own imaginations to fill in the details. Unlike Kazantzakis or Anthony Burgess, however, they did not stray very far from the Scriptures. Evangelical writer Harold Pickett described this technique of "interlinear manuscript illumination" with a certain skepticism: "Since they are excluded by their own theological position from recreating the heart of their narrative, they can only embellish their stories, fitting them out with clichéd similes and melodramatic emotions."

Best-selling evangelical author Joyce Landorf, undaunted by Thomas Mann's treatment of a similar theme, turned the story of Joseph and Potiphar's wife into a "frustrated housewife myth." Elsewhere, she revised Swinburne's image of Jesus as the pale Galilean; he was probably sunburned, she concluded, because he was outdoors so much.

Venturing a bit further from the Scriptures, some Christian novelists, like Christian TV producers, borrowed a few tricks from the secular competition. They attempted Christian whodunits, thrillers, and fantasies. But it was the writers of children's books who took the most whimsical liberties with traditional genres. Crossway Books offered a children's version of the story of Jonah in which the hapless prophet who took a ride in the belly of a whale was a mouse called on by God to chastise the wicked city of Nineveh—inhabited, of course, by cats. The list of children's comic books included an inspirational Archie series ("Archie's Clean Slate"), a tribute to Dallas Cowboys coach Tom Landry, and a version of Charles Colson's *Born Again*.

At one point, there was not one but two Christian Mother Gooses in Christian book catalogs. Marjorie Decker, a British grandmother whose *Christian Mother Goose Book* lingered on the *Bookstore Journal* bestseller list for three years, took the terror out of nursery rhymes by turning "Three Blind Mice" into "Three Kind Mice" and straightening out the crooked man. Explained Decker, a tiny woman with a beatific smile, whose funny hat and toy stuffed goose were familiar sights at CBA conventions, "Mother Goose is cannibalistic and murderous, but we couldn't see it because it's traditional and has an aura of respectability. Our Mother Goose is more typical of humanity; she has good points and bad points. The character of Grandpa Mole emerged as the hero because we need to honor old people."

Positive Thinking. The upbeat genre popularized by Dr. Peale himself continued to thrive. Like secular how-to-succeed books, which were in fact influenced by evangelical prototypes, Christian get-ahead and feel-good books used pep talks and pop psychology to work on the reader's feelings of insecurity, guilt, ambition, or greed. Success, accompanied by prayer and/or Bible-reading, seemed a surefire cure for spiritual as well as social problems. Dr. Peale continued to produce spin-offs of his original formula, while other cockeyed optimists invented their own versions of self-fulfilling prophecy. The most prolific of these was Robert "Turn Your Scars into Stars" Schuller, who seemed to have a new title every six months, from which he quoted generously on the "Hour of Power."

As Zondervan's Phil Wolfe told me, "In the Christian community, there are two sides. There are people who have grown up with a positive emphasis, and there are those who grew up with guilt feelings, the mentality that says you can't have a good time if you're a Christian. So many people who come out of a negative religious background need the positive; they have to be taught how to enjoy the good life."

Some well-published evangelists based entire ministries on their own rags-to-riches stories, in which material and spiritual success seemed to coincide. Bill Basansky's popular *Total Success: How You Can Have It* revealed, according to its catalog entry, "the principles of God which have been working in his life, bringing him from a life of total physical and spiritual poverty and bondage in Russia to a life of prosperity and liberty and total success."

Secular publishers also entered the optimism business. Bantam Books, whose religious division turned out one or two titles a month, offered Og Mandino's *The Greatest Success in the World.* (Modest titles were scarce in the Christian marketplace; Mandino's previous blockbuster was called *The Greatest Salesman in the World.*) Putnam's featured Pat Boone's *Pray to Win: God Wants You to Succeed,* which had been packaged by agent Bill Adler, a celebrity specialist. Boone, like Peale, Mandino, and Bruce Barton, used frequent references to business in his outline for successful prayer: "God is like the Chairman of the Board who founded the company and who wants to bring His sons up through the structure he created, learning the business from the ground up, eventually reaching the place where they can take over, completely!"

One would think Christianity was all rainbows, smile buttons, and success stories. A Christian-bookstore worker from Anaheim told me that rainbows had been the theme of her daughter's prewedding shower, and the presents had included rainbow towels, rainbow soap, even a rainbow shower curtain. A Christian card and gift manufacturer from Arizona who had renamed his business Rainbow Productions said that he had been lucky in his choice of names; he hadn't even realized at the time that rainbows were "in" for Christians.

Christian publishing was itself a success story, as were the careers of many individual publishers and writers. Millionaire Jarrell Mc-Cracken, whose company, Word, Inc., was bought as an independent subsidiary by ABC in 1973, began his business in Waco, Texas, with a single tape called "The Game of Life," a sports allegory in which Jesus Christ was the coach and the Bible the rulebook. Eventually McCracken offered the most varied catalog in Christian publishing, with books ranging from *Casseroles I Have Known* to *All We're Meant to Be: A Biblical Approach to Women's Liberation* and records ranging from *The Singing Governor* by Jimmie Davis to *Horrendous Disc* by Daniel Amos.

When I asked McCracken about the secret of his success, he responded that Word had gotten more "sophisticated in its approach" over the years. The elegantly dressed and urbane McCracken, who is hardly the man one would picture as the creator of "The Game of Life," nor the kind of man one would picture as the genius behind a "notoriously sanitized Christian publishing house" (as Word had been called in a Dallas *Morning News* article), said that "as a Christian in business, there are certain principles I have that are the same as those of secular businessmen—marketing and advertising strategies. The major difference would be in aspects of the human equation. Our relationship with artists and authors is on a more meaningful basis; we're seeking goals that transcend selfish interests. But when somebody else gets tough, you're not going to turn the other cheek and run."

McCracken, a paragon of Christian capitalism, admitted, "I'm a very competitive person. It's not a position of weakness to be a Christian; Christianity places a high premium on self-realization, not strictly for one's ego satisfaction, but for the higher good. It's a form of higher selfishness. You have to be competitive, not in causing someone else to lose, but to show yourself that you can develop your gifts to a higher degree. In this business, we're dealing with competitors who have been around for a hundred years, and we've become one of the strongest forces in the industry. And in another interest of mine, Arabian horses, it was the same thing. I got scared enough by the first price I was cited on an Arabian that I studied pedigrees for three hours a day for a year. I discovered that most people breeding Arabians didn't know what they were doing. That's why I've ended up in a dominating position in that industry."

Products and Promotion. In addition to higher selfishness, the secret of growth for Word and for most other successful companies was diversification and marketing. In 1981, Word led the industry in

Christian records and tapes, and in 1982, the company put out its first catalog of videotapes. Also in 1982, Word entered the physical-fitness market, introducing two Christian competitors to Jane Fonda's workout records: *Firm Believer* and *Believer-cise*. Women who wanted to simultaneously tone up and tune in to God could work out to gospel music rather than jazz or rock and roll: "Waist, toes, heavens! Waist, toes, heavens! Reach for the heavens! Praise the Lord!"

McCracken was willing to take risks to increase his market, even though he had occasionally been burned. For example, Word lost $150,000 on Eldridge Cleaver's born-again confession, *Soul on Fire*. Said McCracken, "I had never dealt with someone from such a different culture, and I saw him as a sequel to Martin Luther King; we stuck our necks out." At the 1978 National Religious Broadcasters convention, McCracken, who had planned to promote *Soul on Fire* with a special film and a personal appearance by Cleaver, had to convince Cleaver to stay away from the press when news stories appeared that discussed a new line of trousers he had designed called "Cleavers," which reintroduced the concept of codpieces into men's clothing. However, McCracken had better luck with another redeemed black miscreant—Al Green. Green's first album for the gospel division of Word, which quickly hit the top of the charts, was the first gospel album to go gold in several years.

Many publishing companies offered marketing expertise and merchandising aids along with their products. During the 1981 CBA convention, Zondervan, which also owned a chain of bookstores, sponsored daily demonstrations of book displays "cooked up" by clerks in chef hats. Using such snappy display techniques, Zondervan outlets were able to attract enough browsers to warrant locations in shopping malls. Zondervan's Phil Wolfe, who transferred into Christian publishing from the Hewlitt Packard Company because he wanted to "pull my career closer to where I was spiritually," said that Zondervan could offer booksellers a profile, based on test marketing, of potential readers for both Bibles and other titles.

Other companies diversified in different directions. The Swanson Company of Murfreesboro, Tennessee, for example, offered over 100,000 different items, including jewelry, art supplies, and Bible covers. Although the company got its start by making cross-corner wooden frames for religious texts, it had become the largest manufacturer of plastic molds in the world. According to owner Joseph Swanson, who bought the business from his parents, "The key to our success is management. At first we were sentimentally attached to wood, but we had to change." The company, said Swanson, which was also involved in a car dealership, powdered-metal production, a construction company, and warehouse rentals, grossed $20 to $25 million for all of its operations.

Warner Press, of Anderson, Indiana, which had recently celebrated its hundredth anniversary, also branched out in the marketplace. Formerly known as the Gospel Trumpet Company, Warner's was doing so well, according to wholesale manager Bill Baxter, that "If we were doing any better, we couldn't stand it." Warner's produced the world's largest selection of "Christian Witness" jewelry and games such as "Bible Tic Tac Toe." Said Bill Baxter, the stores were buying "modern versions of the same old stuff," but they were getting more adventurous in their merchandise. "Ten years ago we wouldn't have dared to put out something like this," he said, pointing to the company's new collection of ceramics called "Luv-ums," which consisted of tiny tots in various poses guaranteed to elicit a tear or a smile.

The Christian bookstore had become a complete religious center, although much of the merchandise in the typical store seemed more appropriate for Woolworth's than for outlets of the gospel. In addition to categorized book racks, and a room at the back of the store for informal counseling when literature was not enough, the model store featured stacks of such items as rubber welcome mats decorated with rainbow motifs; poster display racks; counters spilling over with inspirational T-shirts; portable trees sprouting bumper stickers with mottoes like "In Case of Rapture This Vehicle Will Self-Destruct"; walls lined with greeting cards and records; and nooks dedicated to plaques, statuary, and jewelry.

The proliferation of this Christian version of disposable pop culture prompted evangelical writer Virginia Stem Owens to charge that "Where the spirit needs nourishing by dreams and visions, we are substituting the junk food of media hype. . . ."

Personalities. Like secular culture, evangelical culture was cued to certain media superstars (like Billy Graham) whose books seldom failed to become bestsellers. Even being related to an evangelical celebrity was often enough to sell books. In 1983, Word published a best-selling confession called *From Ashes to Gold,* written by Patti Roberts, ex-wife of Oral Roberts's son Richard. Patti revealed that the younger Roberts had insulted her on their wedding night by exclaiming, "You know, you look fatter with your clothing off." Her revelations about the elder Roberts were so unflattering that the book could have been titled *Oral Dearest.*

Publishers frequently had to compete for the "name" writers, who seemed to evince little company loyalty. Writers often had titles or "products" out with as many as half a dozen different publishers. Joyce Landorf, for example, appeared at several booths during a CBA convention I attended, promoting a novel for Revell, greeting cards for Dayspring, and a film for Word. Word was also able to attract best-selling writer Joni Aerickson, a quadraplegic since her late teens, not to do a book but to do a record. Aerickson, who painted landscapes and designed greeting cards in addition to writing books, said during a CBA convention banquet that "the people at Zondervan and World Wide are great, but the people at Word are really super. They made it easy for me to make an album."

Now that religious publishing had become such a lucrative business, Christian-celebrity books, like country music, were experiencing the "crossover" phenomenon—the temptation to go mainstream. Hal Lindsey, for example, abandoned Zondervan, which originally published *The Late Great Planet Earth,* for Bantam, which had copublished the paperback version. But the crossover worked both ways. Many secular celebrities published their Augustinian confessions with religious houses and temporarily joined the celebrity revival circuit. The preponderance of these were athletes. Terry Bradshaw's *Man of Steel* and Roger Staubach's *Time Enough to Win* proved brisk sellers, as did *The Making of a Super Pro,* the collection of interviews with born-again players by Bob Hill, founder of *The Christian Review.*

My erstwhile idol, Bill Glass, published several titles with Word, in addition to *Born to Win,* which applied positive-thinking principles to sports. His best-known book, *Don't Blame the Game,* was an apologia for pro football, written in response to hedonistic books like Joe Namath's *I Can't Wait Until Tomorrow* and bitter exposés like Dave Meggyesy's *Out of Their League*. For his first book, Glass had broached the idea of a day-to-day sports diary to World Publishing Company in Cleveland, but he ended up writing the book for Word instead, whose editors modified his manuscript to a more conventional series of chapters. In the meantime, as Glass liked to point out, World used the diary format, minus the Christian message, with great success in Jerry Kramer's guts-and-sweat memoirs.

The world of politics also produced a number of latter-day confessors. Senator Mark Hatfield, former representative and presidential candidate John Anderson, and former senator Harold Hughes published books with religious messages, and both Charles Colson's *Born Again* and Jimmy Carter's *Why Not the Best* became all-time bestsellers. (Colson's book was still going strong in 1983, as was his sequel, *Life Sentence*, but according to Broadman Press, Carter's book did not sell as well after his second year in office.)

Another Christian memoir to emerge from the Watergate era was Leon Jaworski's *Crossroads*, an account of the Watergate prosecutor's calls for divine guidance at times of crisis. At a CBA press conference to promote the book, Campus Crusader Bill Bright announced that 4,000 copies of the book had been sent to government leaders. It was at Bright's urging, in fact, that Jaworski wrote the book. Said Jaworski, himself the son of a preacher, "I'd rather have his [Bright's] endorsement than anyone else's because his record speaks for itself." Of his decision to come forward with his faith, Jaworski said, "I had always treated my religion and my relationship with God in heaven as so private and confidential I didn't feel the need to share it with others. But I had been the recipient of public accolades and I had spent some time thinking how I was accepting these. I knew in my heart that credit was given where it wasn't due. I knew how many times when matters got complex and difficult, I turned to Him."

When I asked Jaworski whether he was apprehensive about the increasing traffic between church and state, he responded, "I know of no reason why there should be a big problem with the use of religion in government centers. The doctrine of separation of church and state is misunderstood. It was put there so no one would ever be forced into religious belief, to keep the government from ever saying to an individual he has to believe a certain thing. I think it can be carried too far. There are instances in which a church should take a position. Corruption, for instance."

As for the failure of Jimmy Carter, who apparently had sought God's guidance frequently, Jaworski said, "We're told that we're not supposed to ask for a certain result in prayer. He has been described to me as a very obstinate man who would not take advice. Maybe he wouldn't take God's advice." And as for Charles Colson's conversion experience, Jaworski said, "I was skeptical about it. No sooner was he sentenced than he began telling stories about his dealings with us that weren't factual. And I can't get over those conversations he had with Nixon at night. But maybe I have done him an injustice. Who am I to say that Chuck Colson isn't as good a Christian as anyone today?"

Crossroads itself was a calm recollection of personal sorrows and national tragedies—of deaths in the family, the Ku Klux Klan in Texas, Nazi war-crimes trials, and the Watergate cover-up. Despite a restrained outburst of indignation near the end of the book about the erosion of morality in America, Jaworski concluded with resigned affirmation: "To all that shall be, yes." Evangelical readers found such a mild-mannered style of witnessing to be lukewarm. Apparently the confession of the penitent felon was more riveting than the story of the virtuous prosecutor. Said a bookstore saleswoman from Anaheim of the book's sales in California, "It hasn't generated much interest out here; it takes a Chuck Colson for that."

Prophecy and Pragmatism. Celebrity status was important, but it no longer guaranteed instant success for a Christian book. Perhaps it was because, as one bookseller remarked wistfully, "We're running out of celebrities." Sales of Billy Graham's *How to Be Born Again* fell far short of Word's optimistic first printing of 800,000, and Jerry Falwell's *Listen, America!* sold fewer than 25,000 copies in hardcover for Doubleday. Christians appeared to be looking primarily for two seemingly disparate qualities in their inspirational literature: prophecy and pragmatism. Graham's subsequent book for Word, *Till Armageddon,* proved a blockbuster, as did Hal Lindsey's *Countdown to Armageddon* and other sequels to *The Late Great Planet Earth.*

These books of prophecy, like the Sibylline oracles of the Middle

Ages, drew upon the social and political conflicts of the day. Constantly updated to address the anxieties and preoccupations of the moment, they offered the reader a clear if terrifying vision of the future.

Most patrons of CBA bookstores seemed to be premillennialists, longing for the Rapture that would spirit them away from the earth before the great Tribulation. They would agree with former Secretary of the Interior James Watt's statement to the House Interior Committee, "I don't know how many future generations we can count on before the Lord returns." But despite an eschatological urge to float away from the mundane business of living, those same readers were looking for concrete answers to the questions of how to raise a family, how to lose weight, how to keep a spouse from straying, how to invest for the future. Consequently, "cope" books, particularly those concerning family problems, were now the biggest-selling category of Christian books other than Bibles, and women from the ages of twenty-eight to forty-five continued to be the largest category of readers. Family counselor James Dobson sometimes had as many as five books on the bestseller list. Bantam's Brad Miner, who moved into editing from the marketing end of the business, observed, "We've gone beyond that born-again phase when people were into that exhilarating experience of finding Christ to a recognition that a lifelong commitment involves a thinking through of every aspect of one's life."

Politics and Paratheology. The changing evangelical attitude toward politics resulted in a new category of books that assailed humanism and advocated various forms of Christian activism. One of the most influential of these among leaders of the religiopolitical right was John W. Whitehead's *The Second American Revolution,* which detailed the causes of humanist dominance in the Western world and discussed the rise of a "judicial and governmental authoritarian elite" in the United States. Even more popular was a book by Dr. Francis Schaeffer called *A Christian Manifesto.* The founder of L'Abri Fellowship, a Christian community and study center in Switzerland, Schaeffer had come to be regarded as the guru of fundamentalism. *A Christian Manifesto* argued that Christians who had become disturbed over individual issues—permissiveness, pornography, the breakdown of the family—failed to see that all these problems were due to one larger problem: the shift in worldview away from the teleological Judeo-Christian tradition to "the idea that the final reality is impersonal matter or energy shaped into its present form by impersonal chance." Schaeffer advocated civil disobedience in order to combat the materialist/humanist worldview, citing the American Revolution as a precedent.

Paradox. Despite the obvious success of Christian writers and publishers within the world of evangelicalism, they never seemed to get much recognition from the secular world. Christian books might sell hundreds of thousands of copies and dominate the *Bookstore Journal* bestseller list for months, but they never seemed to crack the major secular bestseller lists, mainly because Christian bookstores were not among those stores used to compile the lists. Secular stores seldom stocked many evangelical titles, other than the latest positive-thinking bestsellers.

In previous years, such benign neglect would not have disturbed evangelical leaders. But now, evangelical entrepreneurs were not content with a separate-but-equal status; they wanted the kind of legitimacy and respect that only secular recognition could bestow. Evangelicals who were involved in a drive for moral, political, and social recognition interpreted the bestseller blackout as yet another sign of anti-Christian sentiment—of de facto censorship. Just as Donald Wildmon had deplored the lack of Christian representation on prime-time TV shows, other evangelical spokesmen asserted that Christian writers and publishers were being treated as second-class citizens by the secular media.

Moral Majority spokesman Cal Thomas was incensed that although *A Christian Manifesto* outsold *Jane Fonda's Workout Book* by two to one in May 1982, Fonda was number one on the New York *Times*'s bestseller list and Dr. Schaeffer "was relegated to ignominious oblivion." In his own 1983 manifesto, *Book Burning,* Thomas complained that Christian publishing was the "Negro league" of publishing: "Before the 1940s, the 'Negro league' baseball players played the same game as did the all-white majors (and in many cases played it a lot better), but the majors didn't want them because of their (and the fans') prejudice against blacks. . . . Religious publishing and books by Christians, whether overtly religious or not, have for too long received the same kind of treatment."

Thomas, who had worked for a time in the secular world as a television reporter and newscaster, was more aware than most conservative evangelicals of the credibility gap that existed between the media and the world of evangelicalism. It was Thomas who lectured other conservative evangelicals in Moral Majority training sessions on how to establish credibility with a hostile or condescending reporter. Perry Deane Young described one such session in which Thomas told aspiring Moral Majority activists, "If you don't look the way they think you ought to look, then you're dumb. . . . I don't care how much you may love those polyester pantsuits, don't wear them. That's not an option. Don't do it. No white shoes and socks—especially in winter. No matter how much you like them. I'm serious. Take stock of your wardrobe. Some of you guys look like you got dressed in a closet with the lights off. . . . The way you look can speak volumes. . . . And go to a hairstylist—those of you who still have something to style. Sorry, fellas—no burrs and no flattops." Thomas understood that differences of class and taste were often inseparable from those of creed.

Other evangelicals were more interested in bridging the gap between evangelicalism and mainstream thought than in impressing the press or making the New York *Times* bestseller list. In September 1983, a group of noted evangelicals announced the beginning of a publishing venture called *Studies in a Christian World View,* designed to redress the neglect of Christianity by intellectuals in America. Ten volumes relating Christianity to other fields of study, including psychology, science, literature, and the arts, were planned in the series. The director of the project was Dr. Carl F. H. Henry, author of his own weighty series of studies in evangelical theology, called *God, Revelation, and Authority,* and director of his own one-man think-tank, the Institute for Advanced Christian Studies. It was Henry who, along with Billy Graham and Graham's father-in-law Nelson Bell, had founded the highly successful magazine *Christianity Today* in 1956 in order to relate evangelicalism to the serious issues of the day.

In 1970, an article in *Christianity Today* had chastised evangelicals for failing to do just that—for failing "to articulate, except in broad generalities, to the positive requirements of a Christian civilization. Here, perhaps, lies our greatest failure. So often we have concen-

CHAPTER 8

Making a Joyful Noise:
The New Christian Music

God intended for Christians to be the "salt of the world," to have a preserving influence on our nation, holding it back from moral spoilage and decay.

Jerry Falwell,
*Christians in Government:
What the Bible Says* (a pamphlet)

*I ain't knockin' the hymns
Just give me a song that has a beat
Just gimme a song that moves my feet.*

Larry Norman

trated one-sidedly on purely spiritual activities and have left social problems, politics and education and other important areas to their own fate. . . . Often we think only in terms of personal witness, of winning individual persons to Christ, and neglect the many burning social problems of our time and the broad and difficult questions of culture in general."

Even with a booming Christian publishing industry, a burgeoning Christian culture, a myriad of Christian schools, and a plethora of issue-oriented preachers, and perhaps even with such serious intellectual efforts as *Studies in a Christian World View,* evangelicals still had a long way to go to overcome that failure. Most important, they had yet to understand or recognize the rights and needs of other groups who had also come to claim America as their own.

The profusion of new books and albums that began replacing the old King James Bibles and traditional hymns of evangelical worship in the 1970s broke up the monotony of old-time religion and established a new consumer culture for evangelicals. But it was not merely the movers and shakers of Moral Majority who were responsible for this cultural renaissance. The Tupperware conservatives of Moral Majority were not as concerned with creating fresh cultural alternatives as they were with preserving for eternity what was left of their disappearing world.

The explosion of Christian pop culture actually began with the Jesus movement of the late sixties and early seventies, with its Bible rap sessions, Jesus newspapers, Christian Woodstocks, and redemptive rock musicals. The Jesus People, who had become disillusioned with drugs and other secular diversions as well as with the smugness of established religion, found their own way to God. Their intention was to rescue Jesus from the preachers and give him back to the people.

Already colonized by the tripping visionaries of psychedelia, the West Coast also became the center of a Jesus revolution. The Christian flower children resembled their secular counterparts, except that they got high on salvation rather than LSD. Shaggy and unshorn, but resplendent in bandannas, boleros, and Jesus buttons, they looked to John the Baptist as the original Jesus freak. An editorial in a Jesus weekly called *The Truth* explained, "We know he lived in the wilderness, ate grasshoppers and honey, had long hair, and he stank!"

At the height of the Jesus movement, born-again surfers were hanging ten for the Lord, and repentant hippies and burned-out bikers were being baptized by the blood of the Lamb in the Pacific, in the reflecting pool near Lincoln Memorial in Washington, D.C., even in Pat Boone's swimming pool. Drug-culture dropouts were singing and testifying in Christian coffee houses across the land. When February 13, 1971, was declared "Spiritual Revolution Day" by the California state senate, some 8,000 young pilgrims converged from around the Pacific Coast, including one penitent who carried a 150-pound cross for the last fifty miles.

In June 1971, Jesus graced the cover of *Time* magazine, and the accompanying story concluded that "Jesus is alive and well in the radical spiritual fervor of a growing number of young Americans who have proclaimed an extraordinary religious revolution in his name." This was the era of Day-Glo disciples and dunning for Christ. While secular street people panhandled for a precarious living, Jesus freaks were busy buttonholing pedestrians. During a typical day on Hollywood Boulevard, for example, one might have witnessed some strange sights: long-haired evangelist Arthur Blessitt chained in protest to a pole in front of His Place, the endangered Christian nightclub; assorted street chaplains wearing mime makeup and Jesus watches, quoting end-time scriptures, and passing out tracts; the Heaven Bus from Tony and Susan Alamo's Christian Foundation loading up with the unsaved for a trip to the ranch of the recently redeemed.

Despite their flamboyant appearance and pentecostal spontaneity, most Jesus freaks were fundamentalists and grim premillennialists. Sometimes they invaded "straight" evangelical churches as an admonishing tribe, with a flourish of tambourines, in order to announce that the hour of judgment was near. Some evangelicals welcomed them as a fulfillment of the vision set forth in Acts 2:17, echoing the ancient prophecy of Joel: "And it shall come to pass in the last days, saith God, I will pour out of my Spirit upon all flesh: and your sons and your daughters shall prophesy, and your young men shall see visions. . . ." A number of churches tried to keep up with the times and modernize their youth ministries. The First Baptist Church of West Palm Beach, Florida, led the way to reconciliation by appointing a "Minister of the Generation Gap." Generally, however, the Jesus people attended their own "hip" churches, such as the Bethel Chapel of Redondo Beach and the Calvary Chapel in Santa Ana, which held baptisms at Corona Del Mar beach.

The Jesus revolutionaries demanded their own culture—their own rituals, rallies, and music. Music was the heart of their ministry, as it had once been for the fast-growing evangelical churches of the frontier, whose congregational singing brought popular religion to the outback. The Christian Woodstock nation gathered together all across the country in mass festivals of love, song, and praise. The first of these convocations, the Faith Festival, held in Evansville, Indiana, which drew some 6,000 celebrants to hear Pat Boone and other stars, was the prototype of the New Age camp meeting.

Through the early seventies, Jesus people adulated their own rock stars at such festivals as the Sweet Jesus Prince of Peace Rock

Festival at Willamette University in Salem, Oregon, and the Jesus Festival of Love at Kent State in Ohio. Students who had tired of simple Sunday school anthems like "Do Lord" and "I've Got the Joy, Joy, Joy, Joy Down in My Heart" could thrill to "The Eve of Destruction" and "Day by Day." Christian yell-leaders introduced the crowds to Jesus cheers: "Give me a J, give me a C. . . ." The most famous of these early Jesus festivals was Expo '72, Bill Bright's week-long extravaganza chaired by Billy Graham and headlined by Kris Kristofferson and Johnny Cash. Expo launched the careers of a number of Christian entertainers and served as a kind of giant pep rally for faith in America, a showing forth of young fundamentalists for freedom.

Disc jockey Paul Baker, who had begun to collect examples of the new Jesus music, aired the first "all-Jesus rock radio show" on station WLCY in St. Petersburg, Florida. Said Baker, "In the true spirit of a rock and roll disc jockey, I wanted to shock everyone. Not in a negative way, but in a way which would open everyone's eyes to the reality that there *could* be dynamic rock music about the Maker."

Larry Norman, the pop music dropout who became the poet laureate of the Jesus revolution, expressed the exuberant spirit of the movement: "Wowie, zowie, He saved my soul!"

Jesus had become an underground hero, a cult figure whose message of love, peace, and brotherhood had become the anthem of the age. The Byrds, whose "Turn, Turn, Turn," a revery based on the book of Ecclesiastes, chapter 3, had been a secular smash, bridging the fading folk revival and the British rock invasion, were now singing "Jesus Is All Right with Me." *Jesus Christ Superstar,* which brought the Jesus revolution to Broadway, equated Jesus with the rebellious rock stars of the counterculture. Was Mary Magdalene a devoted follower or a groupie? To lyricist Tim Rice, Jesus as long-haired revolutionary was more relevant than divine, and Judas was Everyman. In *Godspell,* which adhered more closely to the gospel, Jesus was portrayed as a street clown, a merry urban prankster persecuted by the cops.

Both musical lives of Christ were compared in the secular press to medieval mystery plays and to Bach's *St. Matthew Passion,* but for many Jesus people, *Jesus Christ Superstar* represented the crass commercialism that was co-opting their culture. Folksinger Tom Paxton satirized the Jesus-in-footlights phenomenon in "Jesus Christ, S.R.O. (Standing Room Only)": "Jesus loves me, this I know/ Gave me house seats to his show." However, despite predictions made by both *Variety* and *Billboard* in 1971 that religion would replace sex and psychedelia in pop music, most of the new Jesus music was too "Up with People"—too tame, too well scrubbed, too preachy—to cross over from the sacred to the pop market. Much of it was produced by enthusiastic amateurs, who favored such lyrics as "I don't worry, I don't fret, God ain't failed me yet," and even professional pop groups who converted to Christianity—the Wilson McKinley and Chuck Girard's Love Song—tended to tone down their sound from electric acid to acoustic croon.

A Christian folk musical called *Tell It Like It Is,* written by Ralph Carmichael and Kurt Kaisin, was televised by NBC in 1969, but its popularity failed to spread much beyond youth fellowship halls. Nevertheless, Carmichael, a composer who had scored soundtracks for Billy Graham films and who had once worked as orchestral arranger for Ella Fitzgerald, had become a significant force in contemporary gospel music. In 1964, he had founded Lexicon Music, with Jarrell McCracken and Word, Inc., as co-owners.

A few years later, since Word was turning out mainly traditional white gospel music—with such stars as Jimmie Davis, the singing ex-governor of Louisiana—Carmichael started Light Records to record the contemporary music he had published. He discovered Andrae Crouch, a young black singer and songwriter involved with a Christian drug rehabilitation program who had been touring with a group called the Addicts Choir. With Crouch, Carmichael was able to add accessible black gospel to Light's roster of lush orchestral extravaganzas and folky youth-outreach rock. Roll over, Wesley and Watts.

Contemporary gospel outlasted the nonconformity of the Jesus movement. Mass rallies of Christian youth continued through the late seventies, but the participants had cleaned up their act. Hair tended to be short for men, nicely flipped for women, and clothing ranged from standard-issue Bob Jones University for men to Charlie's-Angels-cute for women. Festivals were orchestrated by Christian entrepreneurs and grew into perennial events. Jesus '77, for example, sponsored by Jesus Ministries, a nonprofit consortium of

Christian businessmen, led to the establishment of a year-round retreat center called Agape Camp Farm. Services offered by Jesus Ministries during festivals included alfresco baptism. Even ostensibly secular amusement parks diversified into the business of Jesus bashes. Beginning in 1974, Knott's Berry Farm offered a series of contemporary gospel Maranatha Nights.

The new evangelicals were ready to stand up for Jesus, to cherish the old rugged cross, and praise Him from whom all blessings flow, but evangelical music would never be the same. Church choir directors were expected to reach beyond volunteer solos of "How Great Thou Art" and provide real entertainment. Many music directors added percussion attachments to their organs and bolstered their piano accompaniment with multitrack tapes. Soon it was not merely small pentecostal churches but large suburban institutions that encouraged a spirit of holy shake, rattle, and roll. Some ministers even became concert promoters. The Reverends Chris Greeslin and Ron Davis of the Frederick Worship Center in Frederick, Maryland, initiated a series of King Jesus Concerts, headlined by some of the top names in Christian rock.

The ministry of music had come a long way from the austere harmonies of Sacred Harp and shaped-note singing. In this new age of evangelical culture, fans of Christian music could choose their albums from some 750 titles a year. For live music and mass fellowship they could attend Jesus nights at the Roxy in Los Angeles or jubilation rallies at Knott's Berry Farm. For longer and more concentrated doses of musical ministry and sunshine, they could bask in the glory of the Lord on a Christian voyage. Sonshine Concerts of Tulsa, Oklahoma, chartered the luxury liner *Flavia* for a four-day cruise from Florida to the Bahamas, to be highlighted by a "live island concert" featuring the Imperials, a lively Christian combo for the whole family.

By 1981, contemporary gospel music had become a $100-million-a-year business. As Mark Humphrey of the Los Angeles *Reader* commented, such a modest annual gross was a "slow month's budget for nose candy in the record industry at large," but gospel had become the fifth-largest-selling category of music—bigger than classical or jazz. In 1983, gospel accounted for 5 percent of the total market in records and tapes, as compared to 4 percent for classical and 2 percent for jazz. Christian radio stations had boomed along with Christian product; more than 300 stations were spinning Christian discs exclusively, and most of the one-in-eight stations in the country classified as religious broadcasters were airing gospel on a regular basis.

Although gospel charts were now being tracked in secular trade magazines, the Christian music business had its own version of *Cashbox, Billboard,* and *Record World. Contemporary Christian Music,* founded in 1978 by former disc jockey John Styll, grew from a small Christian-bookstore giveaway into a slick monthly that embellished the traditional trade format with fan-magazine interviews, profiles, and gossip. *CCM* kept track of such innovations in the industry as "Christian Night at the Roller-Rink," a "blend of ccm, people, skates and fun" and related the trials and temptations of such Christian rockers as Mylon LeFevre, the songwriter and session man who was once kicked out of Bob Jones University for singing Jesus jazz. LeFevre, who performed briefly with the dope-indulging Holy Smoke Doo Dah Band, as well as with such notables as George Harrison, Willie Nelson, and the Who, kicked a drug habit and became a full-fledged gospel singer who counted his success in converts rather than in cash.

Moguls of the secular music industry began to notice the success of their devout colleagues. The "Barbara Mandrell and the Mandrell Sisters Show," with its crude cornball humor and smooth country gospel, was a surprise hit on NBC. Andrae Crouch kept popping up on TV—on the "Today" show, on the "Mike Douglas Show," even on "Saturday Night Live." Crouch, who was on his way to becoming the Sammy Davis, Jr., of gospel, was a featured performer during the 1981 Grammy awards show, when Reba Rambo and Doug McGuire's disco version of the Lord's Prayer, presented live by a large cast of Light Records stars, won the Contemporary Gospel award.

Not only did contemporary gospel command a sizable loyal following; it appeared that gospel had begun to cross over into pop territory, just as country music had done. With the rise of evangelicalism and conservative values in America, both the secular and sacred products of rural and small-town Protestant culture were becoming popular. Moreover, as country and gospel music were fed into the star-making machinery of mass popular culture, the rough edges were smoothed out and polished.

Late in 1981, Columbia Records announced that it was starting its own gospel label, Priority. MCA, which already boasted its own gospel label, Songbird, signed a distribution deal with Sparrow, a major Christian label. Polygram Records established a new division called Lection to promote "neogospel." But the biggest crossover surprise came when Ralph Carmichael, who had bought out his shares from Word, signed a deal with Warner/Elektra/Asylum. E/A agreed to distribute albums to all its regular accounts except Christian bookstores, which remained the responsibility of Lexicon/Light. Said Carmichael at the time, "I feel they look on gospel music as not only an extremely viable product for the secular marketplace but something the world needs now."

However, secular record company executives weren't born-again yesterday. During a gospel music forum sponsored by *Billboard,* at which secular representatives easily outnumbered the Christian advocates, CBS Records president Dick Asher explained why CBS had entered the gospel field: "I'll not pretend that we're here because of some new burst of religious faith. We're here because of the potential to sell records in the gospel market. We want to put gospel records in stores that don't currently carry them. We want to transform gospel from a specialty market to a mass-appeal market." Like Tammy Wynette, they wanted to see Jesus on "The Midnight Special."

It was tempting to imagine how the sales pitches of more zealous secular record promoters, notorious for their embroidered satin jackets and illicit goodwill gifts, might be applied to the Christian market. Perhaps deals would be consummated by prayers rather than puffs, and incentives would be measured in blessings rather than grams. And surely big record company executives would insist on make-overs for the less comely Christian stars. The come-hither perkiness of the Mandrell Sisters was fine for consumers of "Hee Haw" and Lawrence Welk, but other singers might not be so marketable. Despite the popularity of Donny and Marie Osmond, which indicated an insatiable need in the American public for perpetual innocence and perfect teeth, sanctimoniousness was tricky to sell. Pentecostal balladeers could never stir rock audiences for whom the trinity meant sex, drugs, and rock and roll. Nor could a chubby gospel trio in A-line princess dresses ever make it on the Carson show. One could envision losses of innocence and pounds as contemporary white gospel music made it to the big time.

> *Brother Banlon Grimm reminded the children of suburbia of the Lord's angry words to Moses on the mountain when the Israelites below were bowing down to the golden calf: "Now therefore let me alone, that my wrath may wax hot against them." And Brother Grimm brought to the parking lot of the First Baptist Church of the Perpetual Mall a number of discs engraved on both sides, which he cast out of his hands and brake atop a sacrificial pyre. The children of suburbia also cast many discs into the flame, making burnt offerings of their heavy metal idols, and they watched the wrath of Brother Grimm consume the hot wax of their sins.*

Not all evangelicals were cheered by the success story of ccm. The rock of ages they clung to did not roll with the times. Not surprisingly, Ralph Carmichael's first concert at the National Religious Broadcasters convention stirred few amens. The growth of contemporary Christian music and the opening of gates between sacred and secular genres stirred up a long-simmering controversy over the devil's role in rock and roll.

Larry Norman had written an influential song called "Why Should the Devil Have All the Good Music," implying that rock and roll could be Christianized. (The title echoes Martin Luther's famous query.) But many evangelicals disagreed, feeling certain that rock music and redemption didn't mix any better than snake oil and baptismal water. In the summer of 1979, a reborn Richard Penniman, the Little Richard of "Tutti Frutti" and "Good Golly, Miss Molly" fame, announced that "rock-and-roll singers are the Devil's evangelists." In order to avoid temptation, the forty-three-year-old singer vowed to sing nothing but gospel.

Ironically, Penniman seemed to forget that gospel music itself, the jubilant music of golden-toned quartets and swooping, spine-tingling solos that we associate so closely with black Christianity, was not always greeted at the altar with open arms. Thomas A. Dorsey, the father of modern gospel music, who first began to jazz up the good news of salvation with the bad-news rhythms of the blues in the 1930s, has admitted, with a hint of pride, to being "thrown out of some of the best churches."

Evangelist Jimmy Swaggart, whose own old-time white gospel albums sold briskly among the moldy figs of Christian music, was convinced that rock and roll was forged in the devil's sweatshop, and that Christian rock music was "spiritual fornication." For Swaggart there could be no trifling with satanic riffs. In October 1981, *Contemporary Music* reported that Swaggart had dismissed employees working on his syndicated radio program who had dared to air Christian rock music.

Swaggart, it seemed, knew about the devil's music firsthand. He had pounded the same rickety old Assembly of God piano as his cousin Jerry Lee Lewis when the boys were growing up in Ferriday, Louisiana. He had been gifted with the same wavy blond pompadour, tormented by the same twinkling temptations as the hell-bent Jerry Lee. But one night, during a bout with pneumonia, Swaggart had been swept by a fever of resignation, and he had let it all go: "Jerry Lee can have 'Great Balls of Fire,' but I'll take the fire of the Holy Ghost! Hallelujah!"

The devil's pursuit of Jerry Lee became a common theme in Swaggart's sermons, illustrating in lurid detail the consequences of dabbling in demonic music. Periodically, Swaggart would manage to get his carousing cousin down on his knees in repentance, particularly during Lewis's hospitalized respites from dissolution, but it seemed that the devil had a lien on the soul of the wild man of rockabilly. As Jerry Lee had told Sun Records producer Sam Phillips in a long theological debate before recording "Great Balls of Fire," "Man, I got the Devil in me! If I didn't have, I'd be a Christian!"

Few preachers in the 1950s would have disagreed with Jerry Lee about the devilish nature of all the shaking going on in rock and roll music. According to Lewis's biographer Nick Tosches, the same year Elvis Presley made his first record, the Reverend Robert Gray of Trinity Baptist Church in Jacksonville, Florida, preached that the singer had "achieved a new low in spiritual degeneracy." Tosches also noted that in the summer of 1977, five days after Presley's death, the plastic display letters of a trailer sign outside a Baptist church in Orangeburg, South Carolina, informed the world that ALL THAT HIP SWIVELING KILLED ELVIS.

By the time of the Falwell era, with-it preachers had realized that rock and roll was here to stay. Nevertheless, a number of stubborn evangelists chose to specialize in the sin of rock and roll. For these rock and roll teetotalers, rock music came after the Fall and before the Flood—it was about temptation and rebellion, not self-denial and salvation.

A leading expert in uncovering the decadent and demonic implications of rock music was evangelist Bob Larson, the author of such studies as *The Devil's Diversion, The Day Music Died,* and *Babylon Reborn.* Larson studied the lives and lyrics of rock bands closely, discovering that not only did the popular California group, the Eagles, base their name and their music on the peyote-crazed principles of Carlos Castaneda but that singer Joni Mitchell credited "her creative impulses to a 'male muse' named Art" with whom she often "roamed naked" on her forty-acre retreat. Moreover, according to Larson, the elephantine lead singer of the group Meat Loaf, whose album *Bat Out of Hell* "featured pictures of demons and tells of a mutant biker who rides out of the pit of Hell," admitted to getting "possessed" when on stage.

Other evangelists were even more aggressive than Larson in their antirock crusades. Jim and Steve Peters of the Zion Christian Center in north Minneapolis became known as the Barbecue Brothers for the numerous pyres of pernicious LPs they had lit. Things heated up even more when James "Gibby" Gilbert, minister of youth at the Church of Christ in Kaufman, Texas, a small town southeast of Dallas, discovered "backward masking"—the insertion of subliminal messages into rock music. According to Gilbert, these subversive messages sound garbled when a record is played in the usual way, but when the record is played backward the words become clear. Examples given by Gilbert included Led Zeppelin's "Stairway to Heaven," in which one could discern the lines "I will sing because I live with Satan" and "There's no escaping it my sweet Satan," and a song by Black Oak Arkansas called "The Day Electricity Came to Arkansas" which allegedly contained the words "Satan, Satan, Satan. He is God."

In 1982 a legislative committee in California heard testimony from Trinity Broadcasting Network's Paul Crouch, Jr., on the satanic anthems being slipped into rock records, and in late April of that year, California Assemblyman Philip D. Ryman introduced a bill (AB 3741) that would require backward-masked records to carry a label informing consumers of the subliminal message contained on the album.

These watchdogs of musical purity feared that the damage caused by rock music would go undetected by gullible fans. According to fundamentalist writer Lowell Hart, the dangers went even deeper than suggestive lyrics or licentious singers. The very beat of the music could cause mental and physical illness. The rock beat, said Hart, was "demonic," "pagan," and inspired by "voodoo." "Dissonance," he theorized, "accounts for increases in nervous and psycho-neurotic ailments." Given all these disturbing attributes of rock music, the very idea of such a thing as Christian rock seemed outlandish, blasphemous; Christian rock was a contradiction in terms. Listening to "contemporary Christian music," wrote Hart, "is like trying to get my meals from the garbage can—not very appetizing."

Gradually, however, a number of evangelists who had been completely opposed to rock music, both pagan and Christian, began to change their tune. If righteous rock and rollers pitched their revival tents on the devil's campground, at least they wouldn't be preaching only to the converted. In the fall of 1981, *Contemporary Christian Music* published a three-part series on the religious rock controversy, carefully presenting both sides, including the dangers of idolatry and superficiality as well as the virtues of youth ministry and making a joyful noise.

Even Bob Larson conceded that Christian rock was an acceptable substitute for secular rock. Admitted Larson, somewhat grudgingly, "even the worst attempts at expressing the Christian faith in modern vogue are bound to be better than the sex-drenched paeans to hedonism found in the secular marketplace." Relaxing his guard even further, in August 1982 Larson introduced the first in a series of columns for *CCM* with a meditation on religious gullibility—the "inclination some evangelicals have for believing rumors of conspiracy that cater to a fearful and suspicious mentality." Larson, who had once warned Christians about the invasion of demonic symbols into modern culture in the guise of exotic jewelry, figurines, and folk art, was now chiding evangelicals for their rumormongering about the Procter & Gamble man-in-the-moon logo and the subliminal messages of rock and roll.

Larson pointed out that in all probability there was little danger of satanic collusion in brushing with Crest toothpaste, swaddling a baby in Pampers, or even listening to rock music played backward. To expose the folly of the backward-masking rumors, Larson conducted an experiment with one of his own songs. When played backward, the innocuous lyrics of praise revealed a semblance of the words: "Satan is here in this building." As Larson proved, what the backward unmaskers like Gibby Gilbert had uncovered was a Manichaean universe in which evil was always on the flip side of good. Those in search of Satan could always find him. He was lurking behind every doorway, within every voice, inside every symbol.

THE BLAND LEADING THE BLAND

The irony of all this ruckus being raised about Christian rock was that most of it was so dull it would have lulled any lurking demons. A driver who listened to Christian radio on the road was in danger of falling asleep at the wheel. One Christian writer complained of the uninspirational blandness of the music he heard at a contemporary Christian rock concert: "The words were Christian—even truthful—but the poetry was on the level of a cheap greeting card. The music was bright and lively, but forgettable; the compositions were mostly new, and the few familiar hymns were treated to the same tepid style of cocktail lounge music featured in a thousand motels every night." In their efforts to weed out the devil's influence from pop music, Christian musicians tended to create a curiously rootless sort of music.

In place of hymns that had been sung for generations, contemporary Christian music supplied instant hits. The bright new music was supplanting the dour old standards, just as Ira D. Sankey and P. P. Bliss's *Gospel Hymns and Sacred Songs* had replaced Isaac Watt's *Psalms and Hymns* when the evangelistic revivals of the nineteenth century called for a more popular hymnody. An introduction to a new hymnal, *Hymns for the Family and God,* published by Paragon Associates of Nashville, proclaimed, "Whereas it used to take decades or centuries for a hymn or song-style to become an established part of the Christian's repertoire, today this can happen in a few months time."

Similarly, Grady C. Cothen, president of the Sunday school board of the Southern Baptist Convention, had prefaced the new 1975 Baptist hymnal with a testament to nontraditional Christian music: "During the dynamic days of the sixties and seventies the stream of Christian music has been joined by many new rivulets. The sounds of haunting folk melodies with biblically based texts join the stately grandeur of traditional hymns. The surge of new rhythmic sounds contrasts with more familiar gospel songs, bringing new dimensions to proclamation." That hymnal included a number of black spirituals as well as new, space-age hymns. Thad Roberts's "God of Earth and Outer Space" called for a special blessing on America's astronauts, while "Here Is My Life," by Ed Seabough and Gene Bartlett, acknowledged the sights, sounds, and stresses of modern life: "Lord, you placed me in this world/of time and space and missiles hurled,/With eyes I've seen the ghetto gloom/With ears I've heard the sonic boom/And man cry out for breathing room."

Contemporary Christian Music divided Christian product into six categories—contemporary/rock, adult contemporary, black contemporary, children, worship and praise, and inspirational—but much of it simply made mellow Muzak unto the Lord by sanitizing various secular styles. There were rock songs without the romance and the rebellion, and there were torch songs without the flame. "Adult contemporary" or "inspirational" songs tended to end with a trumped-up crescendo of voices and strings, so that the effect was like a segue from "Day by Day" to Handel's hallelujah chorus.

A popular standard of Christian entertainment was a medley of secular styles delivered by smiling young people who extracted upbeat highlights from the history of rock, condensing the sixties into a safe and smarmy decade. The epitome of this cheerful collagism was the "Up with People" extravaganza during the halftime of Super Bowl '81, in which over 400 young participants wearing tight chartreuse-and-fuchsia costumes sang "Monster Mash" and a collection of songs by the Beach Boys, Simon and Garfunkel, and the Beatles. The finale was a rousing version of "All You Need Is Love," chanted in the dark as hundreds of pen lights flickered on

the field. Secular rock and roll devotees who witnessed this spectacle found murder, not love, in their hearts.

Christian musicians who didn't sanitize the secular styles they had
adopted faced a different problem. Often there was no organic connection between the message and the style. Lowell Hart and other
antirock crusaders were at least partially correct about Christian
rock being a contradiction in terms. When no attempt was made to
fuse form and content, the result was the creation of strange hybrid
beasts that headed off in two directions at once: Christian punk,
Christian new wave, Christian heavy metal. The skewed hipness of
these new Christian minstrels resulted in such songs as "Don't Let
Evolution Make a Monkey Out of You" by the Bethlehem White
Sox.

Religious rock and rollers who performed outside Christian arenas felt less constrained to yoke the eternal with the topical. Robin
Lane and the Chartbusters and the Alpha Band, for example, created folky new-wave music with a fragile icing of euphoria that
transformed the alienation of the blank generation into subtly
Christian affirmation. And Canadian folk-rock singer Bruce
Cockburn, referred to by *Contemporary Christian Music* as the
"thinking man's artist," regarded himself as a songwriter who only
coincidentally happened to be Christian. Like Bruce Springsteen in
another context, Cockburn found it hard to be a saint in the city.
He drew on a motley collection of musical styles to stretch the
emotional range of his songs—from the calm folk poetry of meditation to the jazzy despair of the beat generation to the joyous shout
of a Caribbean psalmist.

Unfortunately, few Christian rock performers could handle both
the medium and the message. There was something jarring and
disjointed about a Christian message being delivered, amid smoke
bombs and screeches, by a group like the Chicago-based Resurrection Band, makers of "music to raise the dead." It was like being
handed a bouquet of lilies by a tattooed biker. This was not so
much Christianized culture as encultured Christianity.

THE PRESLEY SYNDROME

In a sense, the grotesque apparition of righteous rockers in glitter gear was the culmination of a long tradition of schizophrenia in pop music that began with Elvis Presley. In his early rockabilly bravado, Presley could jump back and forth from sacred to secular like a hopscotching preacher, following the pelvic unrest of "Hound Dog" with the serenely glistening "Peace in the Valley." Later, as Presley's reflexes slowed, and the puffed-up playboy's piety could hardly keep pace with his pill-popping, both the sacred and the pagan in his music seemed glazed with a thick, sugary sanctimony.

Presley's off-and-on righteousness was symptomatic of a strain of schizophrenia peculiar to certain kinds of Christians—to good country people who could shout "amen" in church and yell "nigger" on the street, to patriotic performers who could shed tears onstage for Mom, Christ, or country and then saunter backstage to dally with underage girls. As Albert Goldman put it, Elvis Presley was "that classic American figure: the totally bifurcated personality. Always professing his undying love and loyalty to Ma, Country, and Corn Pone, always an unregenerate southern redneck who stopped just short of the Klan and the John Birch Society. . . . Accustomed to living in two worlds simultaneously, the day world of the squares and the night world of the cats, he embraces disjunction as the natural and inevitable condition of human existence." For this sort of bifurcated mind, the left hand can remain on the Bible while the right hand reaches toward temptation. As with Elmer Gantry, it's not that one loves Jesus less but that one loves the moment more.

In Presley's defense, however, it must be said that few musicians have been able to resolve the confusion about salvation that lies at the heart of contemporary pop music in America. It did seem as though God had given Satan a license to snare souls in the record business, just as He had allowed the serpent to poison paradise. Nevertheless, if God let Satan have all the good music, the Lord still sat in occasionally for a number or two. Country music was born of valley hymns as well as mountain ballads, and soul music had its roots in the hope of the spiritual as well as the despair of the blues. To entangle things further, rock music was spawned by the pentecostal shaking of rockabilly, itself a product of jazzed-up country music, the jumping jubilation of gospel, and the devilish drive of rhythm and blues. Rock music sought transcendence all right, but it was usually by way of gratifying the senses rather than the spirit. Even rock musicians in search of an angel tended to give the devil his due.

FROM THE STREET TO THE CHURCH

Ironically, it was often the converts from secular success who conquered ambivalence and created the most original religious music. During the mid-to-late seventies, a number of stars from rock and roll, soul, and country music decided to consecrate their sound. For some, like Bob Dylan, this meant breaking new ground; for others, like Johnny Cash, it meant retracing their steps back to their beginnings, returning to roots. While multitudes in the past had fallen from grace—from gospel to pop—the return journey from club to church was rare. It was a risky trip, at least from a marketing standpoint. The gospel circuit, like the chitlin' circuit, was a long, tiring, low-budget bus ride. Gospel albums seldom go gold, and there was no built-in market for repentant rockers, particularly those who expected to retain the secular audience they had built up over the years.

Nevertheless, the barriers between sacred and secular music continued to fall. Some musicians who had no intention of mending their ways made gospel albums. And since so many pop musicians had gotten their start in church choirs, a turning toward Jesus was for many a return to the fold. Donna Summer, who had ruled as the sexy queen of disco, was now ending her concerts with a simple gospel song she dedicated to Christ. Others followed Little Richard's policy of complete abstinence from the profane. In 1981 soul singer Al Green signed a six-album contract with Myrrh, a division of Word, Inc., and vowed to sing nothing but the Lord's music.

Green had become a preacher at his own suburban Memphis church shortly after a jealous woman scalded him with a hot pan of grits and then committed suicide, but he had continued to work the secular soul circuit as well. Now he had come full circle: from early training with his brothers' gospel group, to a pact with producer Willie Mitchell that made him heir apparent to the King of Soul, to the baptism by fire and the stigmata of the grits, to the pulpit of confession, and back to the altar.

Myrrh had already signed the popular black gospel group, the Mighty Clouds of Joy, and Word was willing to take a risk on Green as a gospel singer, even though his popularity in the secular market had waned. Word technicians resisted tampering with Green's self-produced album, *The Lord Will Make a Way,* though they must have been tempted to smooth it out to the tastes of an audience accustomed to the lusher arrangements of Andrae Crouch. Neither did they flinch publicly when Green's wife charged him with physical cruelty as *The Lord Will Make a Way* found its way to the top of the gospel charts.

Fortunately, the Lord appeared to be lenient with the lost sheep of his flock, always keeping the gate open for repentant strays. Country singers, too, did a lot of repenting. Some lost souls, like Jerry Lee Lewis, could feel the breath of hellhounds hot on their trail. They despaired, already smelling the smoke of doom. As hardbitten Johnny Paycheck proclaimed, "I'm the Only Hell My Mother Ever Raised." But some renegades figured it was never too late to put out the flames. It seemed that the Lord was soft on repentant outlaws, particularly the pious outlaws of country music, the prodigal sons who returned to their roots once in a while.

Country stars in the seventies had become more and more explicit about the temptations of the flesh, about what actually happened behind closed doors after the lights went out in the honky tonks. Their morning-after guilt had remained, however. The sense of doom and alienation lingered on like the stain of spilt whiskey on a new linoleum floor, even as suburban malls sprang up around the break-even farms and one-stop towns of the South. Singers who had headed out on the open road found they were still bound by emotional ties to home, family, and church. They suffered the sweetest of all pains—nostalgia—for the past they had lost.

Country music was not so much a music of roots as of uprootedness—the migrant Appalachian jamming coins into a jukebox in Detroit, the lonely truckdriver trying to find a semblance of home at the counter of an all-night diner, the horseless cowboy trying to walk tall in a field of oil derricks. In Tom T. Hall's "Homecoming," a road-weary musician duded up in stage finery and flashy jewelry stops to talk to his aging father, realizing that he is caught in limbo between a vanished rural past and the empty dream of success he has been chasing down the highway.

White gospel music was part of that simpler, painfully remembered tradition. It belonged to the noncommercial strain of country music—the twanging autoharp that had been drowned out by the lush string orchestrations of the Nashville countrypolitans. For many up-and-coming stars, old-time piety was part of the puritanical inhibitions and unpicturesque poverty of a hillbilly past. Yet most country singers continued to make corny Christmas or inspirational albums and to include a token gospel song amid cheatin', yearnin', drinkin', and truckin' songs. In 1966, Elvis Presley, whose career had begun to stagnate, had made a big comeback with his most unctuous album ever, *How Great Thou Art,* which won a Grammy for the best gospel album of the year. Presley's "holy crooning," as Albert Goldman called it, helped to create the new country gospel style that turned the old-time, foot-stompin' gospel quartets into full-chorused, easy-listening productions.

> *If they saw Him riding in*
> *Long hair flying in the wind*
> *Would they love Him down in Shreveport today?*
> *If they heard He was a Jew*
> *And a Palestinian too*
> *Would they love Him down in Nashville today?*

> Bobby Braddock

Ironically, some of the best country gospel albums were those made by singers playing against their rebel images. Jessi Colter, the husky-voiced beauty who married outlaw singer Waylon Jennings, began her shows by kneeling reverently on the stage in a long white gown. Jeanne C. Riley, whose trademark was a miniskirt, managed to make a gospel album that combined old-time religion with her own talent for novelty. Titled, like her autobiography, *From Harper Valley to the Mountain Top,* the album was dedicated to her grandfather, an itinerant "highways and byways" preacher whose message she, "like the prodigal, eventually returned home to." In the title song, she described her odyssey from disillusionment with success to a renewal of faith.

Johnny Cash, too, wanted to sing hymns as well as create his own brand of worship. His two-record set, *A Believer Sings the Truth* (1979), dedicated by Cash to his mother, by whose side he had sung in church, combined traditional black gospel with singing-cowboy music. In "The Greatest Cowboy of Them All," Jesus is described as a benevolent rancher: "He loves any stray that scatters/Like he's the only one that matters."

Despite their early reputations as rebels, Riley and Cash made credible penitents. But Christian disc jockeys hardly knew what to make of gospel albums by Merle Haggard and Willie Nelson. Haggard's "Okie from Muskogee," proclaiming the patriotic values of the silent majority during the heyday of the counterculture, became an instant classic of country conservatism. But Haggard was hardly preacher material, what with his record of prison, pills, and alcohol. Unlike Johnny Cash, who had tempered his brooding man-in-black image by years of testifying and conspicuous clean living, Haggard's intentions weren't so clear. And Willie Nelson, heaven help him, looked like a hippie, what with those long braids, bandanna, and jeans.

Nevertheless, Haggard's *Songs for the Mama That Tried* (1981) and Nelson's *Family Bible* (1980) were among the most moving religious albums of recent years. Both albums were dedicated to loving, long-suffering mothers, and both consisted mostly of familiar hymns and simple, devotional songs sung to humble guitar or piano accompaniment. When Haggard sang Ira Stamphill's "Supper Time," in which the call to heaven comes like a mother's call to supper, it was possible even for a skeptic to understand, for a moment, the psyche of the sentimental redneck and to feel, for a moment, the powerful appeal of both country music and old-time religion. You could feel the pull of tradition and hear the ping of the Sacred Harp. And you could conjure up that sweet hillbilly vision of the close-knit family seated at the hearth, reading from the worn, cherished Bible passed down for generations.

That well-worn vision has lingered like a heartache in the most hardened of rogues. Even the most cynical of cheatin' and hell-

raisin' country songs have been written against a moral backdrop of
conflicting religious impulses: the Calvinistic sense of preordained
destiny and the Arminian notion of free will. That Stoic sense of
doom acts as an undertow of pessimism on even the most optimistic
faith in the value of striving. Hence the country tropes of sentimen-
tality: stolen pleasures, suffering innocents, free-flowing tears,
deathbed and barroom confessions. In country music, you have to
pay the piper, and there's usually hell to pay.

REBORN ROCKERS

Rock and rollers, however, tend to live in the eternal present, so
when the guilt hits, it tends to hit like the change of life. For veteran rock stars, who saw the light in mid-to-late career, a call to
Christianity meant a radical change of scenery.

The fall of 1979 was a triumph for born-again rock, as Bob
Dylan, Van Morrison, and Arlo Guthrie issued albums that represented a musical and spiritual rebirth. "May be a rock 'n roll addict
prancing on the stage," chanted Dylan balefully on *Slow Train Coming,* "But you're gonna have to serve somebody." Arlo Guthrie
announced on *Outlasting the Blues* that he was "satisfied/To sing for
God's own son." Van Morrison vowed on *Into the Music,* "no matter
where I roam/I will find my way back home./I will always return
to the Lord."

For all three musicians, this burst of spiritual fervor also brought
a second wind to careers that had begun to stall. Like born-again
football players who compete with even greater force after their
conversion, they refused to consider themselves hors de combat.
They would put Jesus in their own vernacular, as country and black
singers had done. Morrison's *Into the Music* was actually a kind of
comeback album, as Morrison celebrated a spirit of awakening optimism after a bad year. Morrison rejoiced in a renewal of creativity
that coincided with the overflow of faith. Characteristically, "The
Healing Has Begun" acknowledged romance and rock and roll as
part of a sense of rejuvenation: "When you hear the music ringin'
in your soul/And you feel it in your heart and it grows and grows/
And it comes from the backstreet rock and roll . . . the healing

has begun." In a playful reference to resurrection, he told his love to wear an Easter bonnet. The mood of the album—and of Morrison's faith—was festive.

Because he didn't renounce or relinquish his earthiness, and because he kept things vaguely mystical, Morrison's announcement of spiritual awakening was not as startling as it might have been. At its best, his music had always celebrated an abandon both mystical and primal. *Moondance,* perhaps Morrison's most popular album, was a jumble of crazed eroticism and mystical sprees. Borrowing from Irish folk music and poetry, as well as from basic rhythm and blues, he created songs that danced, like Yeats's Crazy Jane, on the dialectic between body and spirit. His experimental musical odysseys also seemed at times to be spiritual quests. "Listen to the Lion," on *St. Dominic's Preview,* was an extended musing into the mystic, in which a natural musical polyglot searched for a transcendent tongue, then stuttered into silence. The lion of Zion in the song was not only a biblical emblem but an interior voice. Perhaps Bruce Cockburn was listening for the same royal beast in his song "Wondering Where the Lions Are," when he was "thinking about eternity" and "Some kind of ecstasy got a hold on me."

Arlo Guthrie's *Outlasting the Blues* offered a more somber vision of faith. Much of the album was less whimsical and ironic than most of Guthrie's previous work, and it dealt in a simple, succinct way with the terrors of mutability and dark nights of the soul as well as with the bright consolations of faith. He had retraced his folk heritage back from the protest songs of the sixties to the stark fatalism of mountain ballads.

Guthrie felt that this new spiritual direction was a logical extension of rather than a radical departure from the tradition of social protest he inherited from his father Woody and which he had carried on during the Vietnam War. In an interview he commented, "I don't see why this should come as a surprise to anyone. I always thought the battle in the sixties was spiritual anyhow—or at least moral. *Alice's Restaurant* was a morality play, and I've been writing songs all along about who you have to be to have the kind of world you want. The times now are just demanding more of that. It's not that politics are unimportant—it's just that the political side of where we were coming from in the '60s is supported by a spiritual commitment. The gospel deals with things like poverty and exploitation as well as salvation. And with a religious base, it's not just a person singing alone—it's a way of introducing to people a conviction expressed in the gospel."

Nevertheless, said Guthrie, *Outlasting the Blues* had been a kind of experiment. He had been "testing the water to see if anyone else felt the same way. I needed affirmation. It's difficult to establish a new identity, which is the main point of spiritual exercises—you create a new identity, or at least you shift. You don't know how committed you are until you start burning bridges. When I listened to Dylan's album *[Slow Train Coming]* for the first time, what I got from it was a feeling of what I ended up doing on my album—we both burned a lot of bridges."

Though Guthrie wanted to establish a connection between his earlier songs of political protest and his new religious songs, it's hard to claim continuity when you're also burning bridges. His new faith may have been Catholic, but his sense of urgency in spreading the news was evangelical. A song called "Prologue" set forth the need to renounce—or at least redefine—the revolutionary aims of the sixties: "Alone on a hill back in '65/Things looked a lot like changing . . . Fantastic flights once good for your health/Now make you deaf to your calling." Guthrie made the song a legacy, "In the event of my demise"—a condition not altogether rhetorical, since he was haunted by the possibility that he might have inherited Huntington's disease, the crippling genetic disorder that killed his father. Similarly, "Which Side," which echoed an older workers' solidarity song, was a calling for commitment, either for or against the Lord: "I ask you what I ask myself/Which side are you on."

If Guthrie was testing the water with these songs, Bob Dylan was trying to bring it to a boil with *Slow Train Coming*. Like Guthrie, Dylan called for a choice—"Ya either got faith or ya got unbelief and there ain't no neutral ground"—but he was ready to consign the laggards to the inferno. *Slow Train Coming* resonated with the indignation of old-time religion, and his litanies of tyrants and fools thundered like sermons from a pentecostal pulpit.

Because Dylan had boarded the slow train of evangelicalism at a time when it was crowded with flag-raising fundamentalists, his conversion was more incomprehensible to fans and critics than Morrison's indulgence in Christian mysticism and Guthrie's assuaging of his dread of mortality. It was as though the visionary poet of the radical elite had gone slumming in lower-middle America. It had been glorious for Dylan as surrealist-symbolist-seer to toss out oblique references to trainloads of fools, wheels of fire, and gates of Eden from the eclectic bag of images he had picked up in his journey across American folk culture. He had been a kind of scrawny Walt Whitman improvising an American destiny, a rakish Rimbaud blurring the landscape into a drunken symbolist's revery.

Dylan had switched hats and prophetic robes like a quick-change artist. When he had explored his Jewish roots during a Zionist phase, his religiosity had lent a serenity to his sound and simplicity to his lyrics. The album *New Morning* had chronicled a quiet rebirth into values of home, hearth, and reverence. But now he was hurling epithets of fire and brimstone at his former comrades like an Old Testament curmudgeon, like Jonah burped up from the belly of the whale, cursing the fleshpots of Nineveh.

Unlike Morrison and Guthrie, whose work still bore vestiges of their old romanticism, Dylan appeared to be fueling his fervor with a bitter disillusionment with his former life. The man who had himself been a messianic figure to many was attempting to escape the nightmare of history in the Millennium. Discovering the limits of his imagination, the seer who had lost his way called for guidance, and the revolutionary who had despaired of social change called for retribution from on high. Perhaps Dylan felt, as Milton did, that no one could speak for liberty without passing through revolution to apocalypse.

Although Dylan seemed to anticipate that in publicly proclaiming his faith he would be deserted by friends and fans, he still seemed concerned about keeping the multitudes. Always a defender of esoteric causes and a champion of martyrs, perhaps he expected his fans to accept his new passion on faith as they had taken on faith the innocence of jailed boxer Hurricane Carter during the Rolling Thunder crusade. Dylan seemed angry and bewildered that his plain-spoken sermons remained as strange to many of his former fans as his song-song surrealism ever had been to the sixties establishment. As even Jesus discovered, it's hard to be a prophet in your own hometown. The problem was that we knew Dylan too well; we knew him before.

Dylan had refused at first to look back at his past, as though he would be turned into a pillar of salt. But his next two albums were not so resolutely unyielding. In *Saved* (1980), the bitterness had become exhilaration; the corrosive edge of self-righteousness had melted into the wonder and humility of the newly redeemed. In *Shot of Love* (1981), he assessed the price he had paid for his faith and salved his wounds, looking back in regret rather than wrath, picking through the rubble of memories for what could be salvaged.

If secular fans did not respond ecstatically, evangelical followers did. *Shot of Love* made a strong showing on contemporary gospel charts. Booted outside the gates of the garden of rock, Dylan found himself in some unlikely company—amid the sons and daughters of Moral Majority who were swaying to soft-strumming Jesus music. How does it feel to be on your own, like a complete unknown? Unlike the Rolling Stones?

Dylan began singing some of his early songs in concert with a new kind of ruefulness, a new kind of alienation. He still felt that he was more sinned against than sinning. Yet there was a song on *Shot of Love* that took the hands of secular doubting Thomases and placed them in the wounds. In "Every Grain of Sand," the wrath and the rapture were recollected in tranquility, as Dylan became the pilgrim poised at the still point in the turning world: "In the fury of the moment I can see the Master's Hand/In every leaf that trembles, in every grain of sand." The images glowed with the simple poetry of psalms; there were echoes of Blake's "Auguries of Innocence," as well as Matthew 10:29 and 30. As the organ, guitar, and sax accompaniment ebbed and flowed in the background like the tide of an unseen ocean, Dylan's harmonica fluttered like a kestrel in the wind.

This was indeed "healing music," as Dylan had told an interviewer. Perhaps Van Morrison was right, and the time for healing had begun. Although rumors began to circulate in 1982 and 1983 that Dylan was getting ready to change vestments again and return to his Jewish faith, he, like Morrison and Guthrie, had demonstrated for Christians a way in which those who sought the best of both worlds could build rather than burn bridges between the sacred and the secular.

PART II:

CHRIST AND POLITICS

CHAPTER 9

Armies of the Light:
The Washington
for Jesus Rally

Whan that Aprille with his showres soote
The droughte of March hath perced to the roote,
And bathed every veine in swich licour
Of which vertu engendred is the flowr;

Thanne longen folk to goon on pilgrimages.

Geoffrey Chaucer

Tuesday, April 29, 1980. After a cold, dreary morning, the skies over Washington, D.C., have cleared under the bright noon sun, and two joggers head for the comfortable footing of the grassy Mall that stretches between the Capitol and the Lincoln Memorial. As they round the corner of the Smithsonian castle at a brisk clip, they confront a multitude of people in Sunday-best pastels, praying and singing, hands outstretched and upturned like antennae.

Larry, young and bearded, feels conspicuous and suddenly indecent in his cut-offs and "U.S. Justice Gym" T-shirt. He slows awkwardly, as his friend Norm's glowing Adidas flash ahead. Norm charges through the crowd, bare-chested and puffing, his face set in runner's oblivion, but Larry tries to circle the clusters of worshipers. He threads his way through a stream of marchers brandishing banners, led by a muscular long-haired man in jeans bearing a large wooden cross over his shoulder.

For a moment Larry is lost in a mass of smiling Alaskans carrying placards: Juneau for Jesus, the Kenai Peninsula Praises the Lord, God's Frozen Chosen. He breaks free and lands on the sidewalk in front of the National Archives, where a dark-suited, middle-aged civil servant is watching the procession bemusedly and munching a tuna sandwich.

A small crowd of spectators gathers as contingents from each state in the nation walk resolutely down Constitution Avenue in alphabetical order, waving cheerfully toward the sidewalks like dignitaries-for-a-day. The Californians for Christ start singing "Onward Christian Soldiers" a cappella as strains of the hallelujah chorus of Handel's *Messiah* waft across from the huge loudspeakers on the Mall. Helicopters buzz angrily overhead.

The man in the dark suit confides to Larry, who has stopped to watch the procession, "A couple of those people who looked about my age came into the cafeteria where I was eating breakfast this morning. They were wearing those Jesus buttons and smiling like they'd been smoking marijuana for three hours."

"Right," says Larry noncommittally. He muses a moment. "Opiate of the masses and all that."

A couple of skinny teenagers in jeans who have been sitting agawk on the steps of the Archives walk up to Larry. One says, "Does this happen in Washington all the time? We're here from Wisconsin on a class trip, but we weren't expecting this weird scene —those people in wheelchairs and stuff."

A photographer wearing a Washington for Jesus Staff sticker on his lapel overhears as he snaps away at the spectators. "We've come to pray for our hostages in Iran and our nation's leaders," he tells the kid. The boys look at each other uneasily and head up the steps toward a group of girls licking ice-cream cones and chatting, oblivious to all the commotion.

> *Let me count this day, Lord, as the beginning of a new and more vigorous life, as the beginning of a crusade for complete morality and the domination of the Christian church through all the land. Dear Lord, thy work is but begun! We shall yet make these United States a moral nation!*

Sinclair Lewis,
Elmer Gantry

> *Can you tell me where we're headin',
> Lincoln County Road or Armageddon?*

Bob Dylan

In the spring of 1978 the Reverend John Gimenez of Rock Church in Virginia Beach, Virginia, had a vision. During a Bible conference in California, God spoke to the former-drug-addict-turned-evangelist about bringing His legions to Washington D.C. The ghetto-born preacher, sixteen years on drugs and four times in the slammer before his conversion, had been redeemed by a transfusion of the blood of the Lamb to become an ordained minister of the pentecostal Assemblies of God. His 4,000-member Rock Church had expanded within a decade into a chain of twenty-seven spirit-filled sister churches, and now, even as the young David aimed his sling at the giant Goliath's head and slew him, Gimenez would aim God's people at the Capitol—the head of government, where unrighteousness went unregulated.

Gimenez's wife Anne, who had been called by the Holy Spirit from an office job to begin revival preaching several years before her marriage, joined the crusade, and the couple began working toward a goal of 100,000 Christians who would bus to Washington and pray for the deliverance of the nation. Demos Shakarian of the Full Gospel Businessmen's Association, a national lay group who promoted the gospel in men's-club fashion, came aboard, and a nonprofit corporation called One Nation Under God was established for fund-raising.

When Gimenez secured the support of his colleague and neighbor, Pat Robertson, head of the Virginia-Beach-based CBN, the projected numbers swelled. Traditional broadcasting rivalries were overcome, and Jim Bakker's PTL network was enlisted, as was the Trinity Broadcasting Network of Los Angeles. After all, the electronic evangelists of America were said to have the capability to reach half the population of America, and surely a mere million of that number would be willing to show up and be counted in a preliminary for the Roll Call Up Yonder.

In another gesture of unity, Bill Bright, plain-speaking Presbyterian and founder of the Campus Crusade for Christ and the Here's Life campaign, brought in his expertise in rounding up multitudes, and the date of April 29, 1980 was set. The word was spread through the far-flung but increasingly united evangelical communications networks—the electronic preachers, evangelical caucuses, charismatic and pentecostal assemblies, church bulletins, ecumenical steering committees. Regional planning conventions were held in Oakland, California, Montgomery, Alabama, and Burlington, Vermont.

Washington for Jesus would be a momentous event, commemorating the day that the first English settlers landed on the beach of Virginia and knelt on the sand, just a few miles from the current sites of Gimenez's own Rock Church and the CBN's new cross-shaped neocolonial-style headquarters.

The precedents for this national revival meeting would be both scriptural and historical. In 2 Chronicles 7:14, God made a conditional promise to King Solomon to save his kingdom: "If my people, which are called by my name, shall humble themselves, and pray, and seek my face, and turn from their wicked ways; then will I hear from heaven, and will forgive their sin, and will heal their land." And in the dark days of the Civil War, when the nation was awash in blood, Abraham Lincoln declared April 30, 1863, to be a national day of "humiliation, fasting, and prayer." In a formal proclamation, Lincoln deplored the nation's growing aloofness from God: "Intoxicated with unbroken success, we have become too self-sufficient to feel the necessity of redeeming and preserving grace, too proud to pray to the God that made us! It behooves us, then, to humble ourselves before the offended Power, to confess our national sins, and to pray for clemency and forgiveness."

A Preamble for the rally was issued on January 10, 1980, setting forth an imperative for the nation "to return to the dream of our founding fathers." This Christian declaration was a sermon to do a revival preacher proud, vilifying the "adultery, rape, fornication, homosexuality, and filthiness of mind throughout the land," decrying the unbridled sexuality, humanism, and satanism" that "are taught at public expense," and blasting a government that had "become bloated at the expense of the citizens." The declaration concluded with an exhortation to the nation's leaders to "frame laws and statutes and ordinances that are in harmony with God's word" and to "repeal those rulings, laws, statutes, and ordinances which have offended Him."

Gimenez saw many miracles take place as God moved to overcome obstacles and bring together the conservative factions of evangelical Christianity in America: outback fundamentalists, all manner of pentecostals, Catholic and Episcopal charismatics, and even a smattering of mainstream Protestants who hungered for a little old-time brimstone. There was one miracle of a practical nature, too, in the form of a logistical plan. In advance of the Pope's visit to Washington, the mayor's office had put together a tremendous system to cover every contingency in dealing with a million visitors. Although the plan had not been rigorously tested by the moderate turnout for the Pope, the officials gladly passed along the plan to Washington for Jesus. They even agreed to lease the entire Metro system to WFJ (the trains were temporarily dubbed Holy Rollers) in order to transport teenagers from the all-night Christian Woodstock warm-up rally at RFK Stadium to the Mall for the main event.

He was a new Senator, but no stranger to high public office, and he had a remarkable business record in the private sector as well. Ushering his visitors into his private office, he closed the solid door behind them. . . . "America right now is like a plane going down in flames." He paused to let the words sink in. "I'm not a religious man, but you Christians just may be our parachute. If it opens, we'll be saved; if it doesn't . . ." He looked out the window. "But I'll tell you one thing," he said, turning back. "Don't blame the President. Don't blame the politicians, It's your fault," he said, pointing to each of them, one at a time. "You Christians, you've had the answer. You've had the majority. Why did you let it happen? If the Church had been to this country what it should have been, we would never be in the shape we are in today."

David Manuel,
The Gathering

Monday, April 28, 1980. As Daniel Ellsberg and Dr. Benjamin Spock are being arrested and young antinuke demonstrators smear blood on the walls of the Pentagon in the first major peace rally in Washington since the conclusion of the Vietnam War, cadres of conservative Christian men present their congressional representatives with lists of prayerful constituents, and school buses loaded with Christian women head toward Constitution Hall for a Women's Leadership Conference.

Over 4,000 women, who have arrived a day early for the WFJ rally in order for their husbands to besiege the congressional offices, disembark from the buses, exchanging life stories and recipes for faith under pressure. They talk of an immanent God who is with them always, at the supermarket, at the beauty parlor, as well as in church. There are acknowledgments of the power of Providence in all things, inexplicable serendipity, fateful encounters in parking lots, testimonials in laundromats, of success guided by God's invisible but reassuring hand. The women share their experiences in the euphoria of unity with the like-minded. God has settled into their very syntax, such conditionals as "if the Lord is willing" preceding every hope and dream, the emphatic "the Lord willed it" concluding lists of accomplishments even so slight as the repairing of appliances. Even so, there is a giddy sense of freedom, of complicity, of ladies' night out.

The women flow into the hall, ordinarily used as the DAR's national club room, past a man holding a large placard with the legend "Repent or Perish" glossed with bright red-orange Magic Marker flames, past tables piled with copies of *Upon This Rock: The Remarkable Story of Anne and John Gimenez.* Many stop at a table to

buy tiny sackcloth-and-ashes pins for a dollar. A young woman who
is passing out Trilateral Commission conspiracy pamphlets is gently
pushed outside the hall by a rally marshal.

Seated quietly on the stage are the guests of honor. Mrs. Bobbi
James, the first lady of Alabama, leads the meeting in prayer. She
prays that Americans will declare, "Get thee hence, Satan," and
compares the next day's rally to the legions of Joshua marching
around the walls of Jericho. Vonnette Bright, who often joins her
husband, Bill Bright, in work for the Campus Crusade, adds a
lighter touch to the proceedings with a joke about the creation.
Mrs. Bright asserts that God created Eve last of all so she wouldn't
tell him how to create everything else.

Shirley (Mrs. Pat) Boone, always a favorite at evangelical gatherings, follows with a lesson from the book of Esther about maintain-
ing a "meek and quiet spirit." Soft voice trembling, she prays to be
crushed like myrrh in order to release her soul's bittersweet essence. If the husband is the head of the family, she asserts, the
woman is the heart, pumping sustenance to the rest of the body.
She closes to thunderous applause, and the entire hall stands as
Dale Evans Rogers comes to the podium, her face tiny and beaming
under a solid upswept bouffant. "How the holy spirit is falling on
congregation after congregation," she says. "I would give anything
to be with you tomorrow, but I have to be in Minneapolis." Her
voice lowers in solemnity. "There was a time when I was just as
resentful and outspoken as liberationists today. But it was because
my first husband left me. Gals, I learned thirty-two years ago that
there's only one liberation worth talking about, and that's the liberation of Jesus Christ."

Dee Jepsen follows with a testimonial about the tribulations of
being married to a politician. "Being the wife of a senator is like
being sent to Siberia," she says. She herself "came to the fullness of
the Lord ten years ago," but she then had to pray seven years
before her husband Roger, then the lieutenant governor of Iowa,
became born again. And then, lo and behold, in 1978, only a year
after his conversion, Jepsen defeated a moderate Republican in the
senatorial primary and went on to topple liberal Democrat Dick
Clark. Jepsen's campaign was supported by such single-issue groups
as right-to-lifers, antitaxers, and progunners. The new senator im-
mediately engaged himself in such pro-family activities as becoming

cosponsor of the omnibus Family Protection Act, designed to protect the paterfamilias from the government.

Emcee Anne Gimenez interrupts the proceeding with an announcement that the Massachusetts house of representatives has once again passed a law requiring a daily one-minute interval for prayer or meditation in the schools. There is great rejoicing in the hall. Mrs. Gimenez asks that the women pray for the national bill on prayer in the schools proposed by Senator Jesse Helms.

Nancy Thurmond, formerly Miss South Carolina and now wife of the ageless Strom Thurmond, takes the stage and declares, "I feel like the Gerber's ad; babies are my business, my only business." She is followed by Dede (Mrs. Pat) Robertson, who wishes to correct Shirley Boone's anatomy metaphor. The woman is the backbone, not the heart, of the family, she insists, tensing her own vertebrae in demonstration.

As the meeting concludes, many women hold hands, burdens lifted in this shared righteousness. These women, with their auxiliaries, their clubs, their committees, their charities, have found a reason to get through the day.

> *We're gonna stay out all night long*
> *We're gonna dance to the rock and roll*
> *When the healing has begun.*
>
> Van Morrison

Even before the women leave Constitution Hall, a drizzle has darkened the afternoon. It continues until dusk, canceling the plans of the Jumpers for Jesus to parachute into RFK Stadium to kick off the youth session.

As the sun goes down, young, mostly white Christians walk through the rain in a steady stream to the stadium from the nearby Metro stop, clapping and singing, hurrying as they hear the roar from the crowd of early arrivals. Many buy plastic capes from black sidewalk entrepreneurs who also offer commemorative balloons. As they enter the stadium, they are issued programs reminding them that, despite the presence of famous Christian athletes and musicians, this is not to be an evening of "forgetful amusement."

Some of the worshipers are old enough to remember the legendary Explo '72, when 85,000 young people gathered at the Cotton Bowl stadium in Dallas during the height of the Jesus Movement, when Jesus Christ had become a sort of counterculture hero. And some are old enough to speculate excitedly about the rumors that Bob Dylan will show up. A contingent of Jews for Jesus, who prefer to be called Messianic Jews, are particularly hopeful that he will make an appearance.

Out on the field the red, white, and blue colors of the bunting draped around the speakers' platform have run together into an impressionistic blur of pink and purple. The sound equipment is covered with large plastic sheets, and members of the sound crew kneel under umbrellas and ponchos, occasionally taking shelter in a dugout, next to three men who were converted earlier in the day as they worked to erect the platform stage. The downpour persists, but the musicians take their places onstage, braving the threat of electrocution.

The first celebrity of the evening is Pat Boone, who has admitted to a Washington *Post* reporter earlier in the day that he sometimes makes people sick with his wholesomeness. He sets the tone of buoyancy for the rest of the evening. With one arm around his wife Shirley and the other holding an umbrella, Boone tells the audience, "What's happening here is the most important ball game of all." Undaunted by the minimal polite applause, he continues, "It's nice to be on the winning side."

The Jesus-rock groups and athletes who follow draw a more characteristic adolescent response. Christian culture, with its own celebrities and heroes, is not so different from secular culture, and like mainstream rock and roll, Christian pop music depends on the whimsy of teenagers. Tonight there are screams and whistles for the Second Chapter of Acts, a popular folk-rock trio, who lead off with an antiabortion ballad. "I know a lot of you out there have had abortions," says the lead singer. "And I know the enemy has a grip on your guilt. But come to God, and ask His forgiveness, and the enemy will have no power over you."

As the deluge continues, the evening's smorgasbord of youth-specialist evangelists is announced, with the names flashing on the scoreboard. There is Crawford Loritts from the Campus Crusade for Christ, who has stopped briefly on his way to an African ministry; Ron Pritchard, former pro linebacker, now of Professional Athletes Outreach; Danny Buggs of the Washington Redskins (unaware that he is about to be traded to the Tampa Bay Buccaneers); Nicky Cruz, the ex-gang leader from Spanish Harlem whose mother had told him he was the son of the devil; David Allbritton, a leg-flinging pentecostal showman; Bob Birdsong, former Mr. Universe; Arthur Blessitt, the Sunset Strip preacher who has carried a ninety-pound cross over 16,000 miles around the world, including this last stretch to RFK from Virginia Beach; Kyle Rote, Jr., the only "native" American to lead the American Soccer League in scoring.

Most of the evangelists use the testimonial format, emphasizing the before-and-after contrast of their conversion experiences. Nicky Cruz, who still talks with a thick street accent twenty years after his conversion, is the most effective. Kyle Rote, Jr., of the Dallas Tornadoes, who looks like Dudley Do-right, has a harder time convincing anyone of his preconversion depravity. "I am a very special person," says Rote with surprising arrogance, then qualifying his boast, "but it's not because of soccer. I'm important because Jesus loves me."

Other speakers use fear. Keynote speaker Larry Tomsczak tells the kids that we are in the last days, and that everything displeasing to the Lord, including rock records, should be burned in a bonfire. He says with satisfaction, "A number of years ago in this very stadium, Mick Jagger sang 'Sympathy for the Devil.' " He points up at the scoreboard, where the name Jesus is flashing. The kids stomp their feet, creating a sound of thunder, and the scoreboard flashes "Halleluia." Then, as the offering buckets are passed, a giant outstretched hand appears on the board, accompanied by the familiar offertory verse from the sixth chapter of Luke: "Give and it shall be given unto you." Following this reminder of the principle of reciprocity, the board spells out the night's triumph: "Tonight's Score: Jesus: 30,157. The Devil: 0."

Supposing there had been a fourth temptation when our Lord encountered the Devil in the wilderness—this time an offer of network television appearances, in prime time, to proclaim and expound his Gospel. Would this offer, too, have been rejected like the others?

Malcolm Muggeridge

By sunrise the next morning, over two hundred press badges have been issued for the rally on the Mall by Kerr Associates, a nonprofit Christian public-relations firm based in Nashville that has been hired by WFJ to handle publicity. At the behest of the Secret Service, each reporter must show proper identification. Ron Kerr takes this as a sign that Jimmy Carter intends to show up, although the President has made no such commitment, and he has just returned from the bedside of the burned commandos recovering in Texas from the aborted attempt to rescue the American hostages in Tehran.

The secular networks have assigned crews for highlight coverage, including extensive pans across the multitudes, while Christian networks are giving complete live coverage, beginning at 6:00 A.M. As evidence of the miraculous ecumenism being spawned by the rally, all the religious networks have agreed to use the same cameras and equipment.

Except for a few secular reporters who seem to be either baffled or disturbed by the scene, particularly by the propensity of pentecostals to kneel on the soggy ground in prayer or to launch into tongues in midsentence, most of the members of the press in the compound behind the speakers' platform appear to be participant-observers from religious publications who practice a kind of parochial New Journalism. Notes are taken in the first person plural: ". . . and then we knelt and prayed for the redemption of our nation. . . ."

A red-haired woman from *Church and State,* a journal advocating the separation of those entities, clutches the arm of a writer from a secular monthly, confessing, "I can't tell anybody who I write for because they'll try to convert me. We advocate freedom of choice on most issues, and that makes these people mad. They seem to be a pretty fascist bunch under all the Praise the Lord business. Abortion is the real lightning rod issue. And a preacher was telling me he hoped there'd be a war, so the nation would be purged. This is scary."

At the official press conference, the secular press is on firmer ground. They hammer away at Pat Robertson over the political implications of the event. The conference concludes with a question about Robertson's support of the Family Protection Act. Robertson responds, "My wife and I have been married for a quarter of a century. We have four children and a loving family. To call that political is the height of folly."

Meanwhile an adversary ad hoc committee called the April Alliance, made up primarily of liberal clergy, call their own press conference. Dr. James Thinney, a pentecostal preacher, thunders his disapproval of the aims of WFJ with his own peculiar logic: "I reject the idea that America needs to go back to God, because the America I know was never with God, unless God approved of George Washington owning slaves, Thomas Jefferson throwing one of his mulatto children into the Potomac, Puritans burning heretics at the stake, and Jim Crow ruling the South. . . . I reject the idea that a day has been set aside for repentance, only to discover that it is not they who intend to repent, but everyone else who is told to."

The organizers of WFJ, who are themselves mostly from independent fundamentalist or evangelical churches or the Assemblies of God, can take comfort in the fact that their church memberships have, for the most part, been growing steadily in the past five years, while those of their liberal foes have been in decline. And although the failed attempt to rescue the hostages in Iran has stolen the national headlines from them during the last days before the rally, they regard the charred bodies and smoking machines strewn across the desert sands as a further sign of God's wrath toward his unrepentant nation. They fear that the Communists are mustering their forces, just as the Philistines readied themselves to attack a weakened Israel that had forfeited God's protection by its disobedience.

An old, fussily dressed white woman: "Do you think it'll be long before he comes?"

Young black woman in slacks and sweater: "No, it won't be long before he first cracks the sky."

Old woman: "Well, I meant when Jimmy Carter gets here, but I know what you mean. It won't be long."

There are many conspicuous absences at the rally, the most obvious of which is Carter, the second of which is Billy Graham, whose presence could have swelled the turnout considerably, particularly among evangelicals suspicious of the pentecostal participants. On

July 4, 1970, Graham had cosponsored an "Honor America Day" in Washington that drew some 250,000 to the Mall to express support for Nixon's effort to establish "peace with honor" in Vietnam. Today's turnout is only 200,000 or so, as later reported by the National Park Service, even though some of the leaders have given out much higher crowd estimates and attempted to spread the ralliers out over the entire expanse of the Mall. (The following year, a Simon and Garfunkel reunion concert in Manhattan's Central Park will draw twice as many devotees.) Graham has sent a carefully worded statement to the gathering, expressing his regret that "long-standing commitments in Indianapolis for a city-wide crusade" would make it impossible for him to attend in person. However, he supports "the efforts to hold a great nonpolitical demonstration of repentance and prayer for national healing." The key word is "nonpolitical," since Graham has become wary of political causes after being burned by his public camaraderie with that secretive sinner, Richard Nixon.

The rally leaders, too, have become sensitive to charges of a hidden political agenda. The inflammatory Preamble was withdrawn quickly after it aroused a flurry of criticism for its partisan political and economic pronouncements, but the damage had been done. Imprecations that could be flung casually from a Sunday pulpit appeared as Dark Age bigotry in the light of public scrutiny, and WFJ organizers have had to insist rather disingenuously that their aims transcend mere political lobbying.

Despite such wide-eyed disavowals of political intent, these crusading Christians are no more welcome in some circles of Washington than a hornet's nest in a privy. James L. Farmer, founder of the Congress of Racial Equality, after surveying the scene on the Mall, comments to the press that "if the Jesus I knew were looking down on the Mall today he would probably feel compelled to say, 'Thank God I am not a Christian.' " The National Council of Churches has issued a release accusing the rally's sponsors of trying to "Christianize the government." According to the statement from the liberal thirty-two—denomination group, it is "arrogant to assert that one's position on a political issue is Christian and all others are un-Christian."

Although the United States Catholic Conference has not signed the statement, the Roman Catholic church has declined to partici-

pate formally in the rally. Nevertheless a handful of priests involved in the Charismatic Renewal are present on the speakers'
platform at the Mall, and an anonymous nun had been present
onstage at the women's conference. And there are actually some
sixteen congressional representatives on the podium during the
rally, but they are neither introduced nor acknowledged.

The potential danger of political contamination from the event
has kept participation by officeholders to a minimum, but the WFJ
leaders still find it odd that Carter himself fails to show up, since
just three months earlier the President had addressed the convention of the National Religious Broadcasters, where many of these
same evangelists had been present. Carter's eloquence at that time
had been responsible for changing the minds of many Reagan supporters, at least temporarily. Carter told the broadcasters, with a
broad, wincing smile, "Recently we had a famous religious broadcaster at the White House who suggested that before I deliver the
State of the Union address I come to the NRB convention to pick
up a few pointers." And so he had complied, if only to set the
record straight on his own Christian commitment. Said Carter, addressing the packed NRB plenary session, "Since becoming President I have had, as never before, to rely on God's help. Rosalynn
and I read the Bible together every night. We find new insight and
inspiration in the present job in passages we have known and loved
since childhood."

The President had emphasized the power inherent in the broadcast medium, comparing it to that of the Oval Office, calling both
"powerful pulpits" and stressing that serving Christ and America is
"not incompatible." Pamphlets outlining Ronald Reagan's spiritual
positions had fluttered to the floor from participants' laps as they
stood to give Carter a resounding ovation, and the next day many
professed that they had decided to give Carter a second chance, if
not seventy times seven, as Jesus had commanded his disciples in
the matter of forgiveness. But now, already, the pendulum of evangelical approval has begun to swing back toward Reagan, and
Carter's silence behind the doors of the White House, its grounds
easily within shouting distance of the Mall, is taken as a sign of
backsliding.

Sometimes a search for religious faith can lead to terrible acts.

Jimmy Carter

During the early morning hours of the rally, the overcast sky and chill winds dramatize the ominous forecasts of the nation's future by a succession of preachers who mount the pulpit set up on the speakers' platform in the center of the Mall. They intone a litany of the nation's sins—"We're sacrificing our babies on the altar of convenience"—and call for the deliverance of the hostages in Iran. But when the Reverend E. V. Hill, a black pastor from Watts named by *Time* magazine as one of the nation's ten best preachers, takes the microphone to lead the crowd in prayer, the mood shifts from execration to exaltation.

In the tradition of great black orators, Hill reaches into the gutbucket for his timbre and into the Bible for his cadence: "We believe that you're going to save us from the wrath that is sure to come unless we repent. We acknowledge our weaknesses and our wickedness. We acknowledge that we have strayed far from thee, but we know that thou art a loving God, thou art a merciful God, and so we say, in the name of the Lord Jesus, save us, Lord. Restore us, Lord." And as Hill beseeches in a thundering voice, "Bless us, Lord," the sound echoing from the granite monuments around the Mall, the first pale shafts of sunlight appear through the clouds, and the gloom begins to lift.

There are many tears shed at this sign of divine acknowledgement, and the rally begins to splinter into individual prayer groups. People pray in their own way, some silently, some speaking softly in tongues, some shrieking in ecstasy. They feel the presence of God, even amid the imminent threat of evil. Bill Bright shouts, "Unless God does something supernatural, I believe we will lose our freedom to a foreign power." Adrian Rogers, president of the Southern Baptist Convention, intones bitterly, "America, once the mightiest of nations, has become the laughingstock of the nations. The scream of the American eagle has become the twitter of a frightened sparrow." Bishop J. O. Patterson of the Church of God in Christ, selected by *Ebony* magazine as one of the hundred most influential black men in America, warns that "Churches substituting chicken dinners, tea parties, and ice-cream socials for religion will find their faith as weak as tea, as cold as ice cream, and as dead as a chicken."

Circulating among the crowd is the official WFJ newspaper, filled with quotes from famous figures in American history about America's God-driven destiny, including a passage from Christopher Columbus's journal in which he attributes his discovery of America to Divine Providence: "It was the Lord Who put into my mind (I could feel His Hand upon me) to sail from here to the Indies." Many participants fill out orders for the official WFJ poster, which portrays Jesus kneeling in prayer, his head pressed against a cracked Liberty Bell, a copy of the Constitution at his feet, and a dove about to land on his shoulder.

During the waning moments of the rally, from the bird's-eye perspective of the TV cameras perched atop the Washington Monument, the scene becomes an apotheosis of a frightened lower-middle America, deprived of their monopoly on the country's moral consensus, using their faith to find a foothold and build a platform on a culture whose pluralism and changing values are as shifting sands. They find in fundamentalism the connectedness to community they no longer feel in their towns and cities, the immediacy they cannot feel for books, for art, or for an intellectualized, liberalized religion. Like the dreaming legions of Martin Luther King, Jr., the tractor convoys of angry farmers, the desperate armies of the poor, and the bitter crowds of antiwar protestors who have marched on Washington before them during the last two decades, they have come to the seat of the government to make a show of their numbers, to participate in an epiphany of moral power.

Yet the sun is bright, the flowers abundant, the murmuring of the crowd pleasantly lulling. Despite the morning's foreboding clouds, it has become one of those God's-in-his-heaven days, when man and nature seem in perfect balance. The mood has shifted from Sunday morning to Sunday afternoon. As children of the participants clamber onto Lincoln's monumental lap and families open picnic baskets, spreading quilts over the lawn, it becomes difficult to superimpose over this idyll of a day an image of Nineveh, the dark city of fleshpots and corruption, where these Christians have come like Jonah to sound a warning, lest the end come in fire and ice.

Yet these good Christian people who have amassed for the cause of national morality think of America in terms of a kind of medieval topography, dotted with humanist devils, televised angels, and licentious cities. They imagine their ideological enemies burning in grotesque torment, writhing like Jonathan Edwards's spider in the grasp of an angry God. The danger for self-righteous Christians, whose zeal, as John Cotton warned, can become a "wild-fire without knowledge," is their tendency to mistake their own intolerance for the wrath of God, to make of the Bible a bludgeon, to substitute law for love, to smite the nonconformist, to arm to the teeth and make of Armageddon a self-fulfilling prophecy. It is the paradox of conservative Christian gatherings that even when the participants themselves have taken the offensive, they feel themselves to be under siege.

CHAPTER 10

From Subculture
to Counterculture:
The Fundamentalist
Liberation Front

Wake up, America! If you're a God-fearing fundamentalist father living in a house of tracts on a landfill amid the backwaters of prejudice, it's time to load your spiritual guns to fend off the advances of secular humanists, who would: 1) take away your children to teach them the Playboy *way of knowledge in sex education courses; 2) seduce your wife into the white slave trade of a career outside the home; and 3) sell your country down the river of SALT II.*

The prayerful throngs of the 1980 Washington for Jesus rally heralded a turning point for conservative evangelicals in their quest for national recognition. If the Jonestown massacre in 1978 had demonstrated the dangers of fanatic isolationism for charismatic preachers, WFJ dramatized the benefits of public involvement for ambitious ministers. Although the rally had drawn only a quarter of the million marchers its leaders had expected to heed the call, the gathering was one of the largest in the capital's history.

Even more significant than the size of the gathering was its display of hand-clasping, back-pounding brotherhood. With WFJ, fundamentalist leaders had transformed the world of conservative evangelicalism from a dispersed, isolated subculture into a highly visible counterculture. They drew their strength from the two great religious movements that had shaped the American way: Puritanism and revivalism. Their passion for reform compounded a neo-Puritan demand for discipline and law and order with a revivalist call for immediate, emotion-wracked repentance. The repentance, however, was not for themselves but for the religious and political establishment.

Despite the narrow parochialism displayed by many fundamentalists in their dealings with public life, they managed to join some rather unlikely allies in the formation of a powerful new conservative coalition. So formidable did this new alliance appear that the fundamentalist constituency was greatly inflated by the news media. However, fundamentalist leaders not only made some influential new friends; they made some new foes and rekindled some old feuds. Antagonizing leaders of mainstream Protestant churches, they managed to polarize the already divided world of Protestantism into warring camps. The fundamentalist crusade created a backlash among secular and religious liberals alike.

THE COMMON ENEMY

In order to transform fundamentalism in America from a cranky subculture into an effective counterculture, fundamentalist leaders had to translate sectarian issues into ideological issues and ideological issues into political issues. They had to create unity among themselves by identifying a common enemy before they could find common cause with the conservative political leaders who courted them.

Church leaders who could never have agreed on the finer theological issues, such as demonology and the Rapture, found themselves united, for the first time, against a common enemy—secular humanism. And they found themselves united in a common cause —the family. For the fundamentalist crusader, secular humanism had become the source of all the sins of America, the multiformed beast of modern liberalism: the cold idol of godless science; the brazen serpent of pornography and homosexuality; the unpainted temptress of women's liberation; the meddling giant of big government.

By the time Washington for Jesus had gotten under way, secular humanism had taken on the familiar resonance of Godless communism in fundamentalist sermons. But whereas communism had been an unseen menace, whose subversive triumphs in America were evident primarily to the CIA, the threat of secular humanism was right next door, its effects felt in the schools, on TV, and on the newsstands. Preachers fused faith, the flag, and the family, repeating the now-standard tropes of conservative Christianity: *Let there be prayer in the schools, Christians in Congress, and missiles in the silos. Lead us not into temptation, but deliver us from secularism. Lock the homosexuals in the closet, the wives in the kitchen, and the baby-killers behind bars.*

Recharging the old symbols of civil religion with apocalyptic urgency, preachers decried the decay of American might and morality, many citing the foiled rescue mission to Tehran as yet another warning flare before the major conflagration of Armageddon. Most fundamentalists were agreed on the imminence of the Second Coming, and most of them were premillennialists. They believed that the end-time prophecies were coming true, and that Jesus would soon descend from the heavens with a great fanfare of trumpets prior to the earthly shocks of the Tribulation, the showdown at Armageddon, and the golden age of the Millennium when Satan would be safely chained in a bottomless pit.

In the popular millenarian view, every global event, from the fluoridation of water to the Six-Day War, signified another crucial moment in the countdown to Armageddon. If earlier prognosticators had foolishly stuck their necks out with exact dates and were thus left waiting in vain on lonely mesas or their own rooftops, this new crop of seers were only slightly more cautious in their specifics. Preachers peered breathlessly into the Scriptures for new clues, certain that the curtain of the quotidian was about to rise to reveal a supernatural technicolor epic of disaster, judgment, and redemption. That America's own stockpile of nuclear weapons might be the means by which the earthly slate was to be wiped clean was an idea that led, paradoxically, to a position of militancy rather than pacifism.

As each lurid prophecy was unveiled, the smell of brimstone wafted around the edifices of government, and the fundamentalist sense of common cause quickened like the instant camaraderie of soldiers under siege, of survivors in a catastrophe. But there was something new in the chosen-tribe mentality of this gigantic revival meeting that was sweeping the country. The criterion for membership in this private club of the elect was not so much how one stood with God but how one stood on key moral, political, and economic issues. It was not enough to be a Christian, a Protestant, or even a fully dunked Baptist; it was necessary to proclaim oneself a born-again, no-fault, no-doubt, family-loving Bible-believer. In a new form of inquisition, a kindly member of Moral Majority had questioned me about the certainty of my own faith: "But do you know that you know that you know?" A conundrum of election that might have baffled even John Calvin.

TONGUE-SPEAKERS, ISRAELITES, PAPISTS, AND LATTER-DAY SAINTS

In their battle to save the American family, fundamentalists left a number of faithful out in the cold, but welcomed as kin some rather distant relatives in the religious kingdom. During WFJ, all those hands uplifted in prayer, in the traditional pentecostal *orans* posture, signified a breakthrough in conservative evangelicalism: the acceptance of pentecostalism. WFJ marked the first time tongue-speaking, palms-up pentecostals and more tight-lipped, palms-together evangelicals, represented by Bill Bright and his flock, had cooperated in such numbers without sectarian one-upmanship. In fact, some leading conservative evangelicals, including the rock of fundamentalism, Bob Jones III, chancellor of Bob Jones University, had objected to WFJ because of the creeping ecumenism the event portended. And some pentecostals theorized that Jerry Falwell's lack of interest in the gathering reflected his Baptist bias against tongue-speakers.

Historically, since the first stirrings of modern pentecostalism during the early years of the century, fundamentalists and mainstream Protestants alike had tended to regard pentecostals as holy-rolling, snake-handling hicks, despite the fact that the movement had originated in Los Angeles and spread rapidly in urban areas. Scholars had categorized pentecostals as marginal groups seeking emotional consolation for the social or cultural deprivations that had constricted their lives. Theoretically, the babbling tongues and quaking bodies liberated in pentecostal worship would compensate for the lack of culture and comfort in the daily lives of the worshipers. Ironically, pentecostals were the strictest of denominations when it came to one's behavior outside of church. Dancing, drinking, movies, the wearing of makeup, and even sports were all heavily frowned upon.

Generally, tongue-speakers were relegated to the lunatic fringes of Protestantism, with the more exotic forms of worship found in the hills and hollers of Appalachia. In my church, for example, if anyone had tried speaking in tongues or holding out their arms like TV antennae, they probably would have been doused with a bucket of cold water—no baptism intended. And a favorite pastime among bored teenagers in the Bible Belt was cutting the ropes on a pentecostal revival tent while a service was in progress or sitting on a back pew trying to control snorts of laughter at all the strange carryings-on. When healer Oral Roberts abandoned the Pentecostal Holiness church and his portable revival tent for the permanent respectability of Tulsa, Oklahoma, and the United Methodist church, it was regarded as an opportunistic move in spiritual upward mobility.

Those kinds of prejudices are difficult to shed. In the early seventies, when I was researching a story on pentecostalism, I attended a Sunday evening service at a large pentecostal church in New Orleans. At one point I became so disturbed by the unearthly shrieks of one testifier that I fled from the sanctuary, trailed by a solicitous deacon. When I reached my car, I discovered that it was blocked by two sedans and a station wagon. Concerned by my obvious distress, the deacon sent a note up to the preacher, who interrupted the service to request that the drivers of the offending automobiles remove them. When no one appeared to move one of the sedans, the deacon solicited the help of a crew of burly worshipers to lift the vehicle bodily out of my way. I sped from the scene, terrified and guilt-stricken.

Fundamentalist adherents of dispensationalism—the dividing of history into stairstep eras leading to the Second Coming—believed that the pentecostal gifts (charisms) of tongues, healing, and prophecy described in the New Testament in the book of Acts had ceased after the deaths of those first disciples who were touched by the fire of the Holy Spirit. But since 1960, the pentecostal revival known as the Charismatic Renewal had been stirring worshipers of the plain-speaking Protestant denominations into glossolalia and the laying-on of healing hands, and since 1967 members of the Catholic church also began to test the fire. Tongue-speakers who could not comprehend the lingo of the new technology or the highbrow babble of academia found that they could communicate in their own universal language that required no instruction, no special dispensation. They had found, in place of Latin, their own sacred, living language.

Unlike the rural and lower-income members of older pentecostal denominations, who prided themselves on their isolation from secular culture and mainstream religion, the new pentecostals tended to be middle class, Republican, suburban, and well connected in business, social, and political circles. "Imagine their surprise, these tax-paying people . . . these veterans of patio barbecues, when they learned they were carriers of ecstasy."

Pentecostalism had come to mean for the conservative Christian middle class what the Human Potential movement had meant to the secular middle class: a source of immediate community and emotional rebirth. Popular pentecostal speaker General Ralph Haines, Jr., a retired cavalry officer who had become the comedian of the charismatic circuit, liked to describe his staid, complacent role as traditional Episcopalian, before he was "zapped" by pentecostalism: "I was sacramentalized but not evangelized. I was one of God's frozen chosen." Whereas evangelical worship services tended to be predictable and nonparticipatory, except for occasional antiphonal readings and approving amens uttered to punctuate a good sermon, pentecostal prayer meetings were spontaneous and personal, encouraging voluntary testimonials, prayers, and prophecies from the congregation.

Although the new pentecostals seemed to be getting high on Jesus, and they often operated independently of church hierarchies, the movement remained essentially conservative in its ideology. Even communal groups who pooled their incomes and resources emphasized traditional patriarchal social structures. Charismatic leaders continually emphasized spiritual renewal rather than reform as a remedy for social problems such as poverty and injustice. And because it was transdenominational as well as politically conservative, the pentecostal movement laid some of the ecumenical groundwork for the growth of the religiopolitical New Right.

Once they had accepted pentecostals as allies, fundamentalists found themselves embracing even more unlikely bedfellows. Although many fundamentalists still thought of Jews as the murderers of Christ, many fundamentalist leaders were militant supporters of Israel. For one thing, fundamentalists were avid readers of the Old Testament; their ethos had been molded by the eye-for-an-eye God of the Hebrews, and they felt that America's destiny as a chosen nation paralleled the fateful covenant between Jahweh and the Israelites. For another, the state of Israel played a crucial role in the premillennialist scenario of events leading up to the Second Coming of Christ; according to end-time prophecies, the Jews would gather together in Israel and rebuild the temple shortly before Armageddon. And on a more practical level, of course, Israel played a key role in America's current military presence in the Middle East.

When I attended the 1982 National Religious Broadcasters convention, I was surprised to find, among the vendors of broadcast equipment, *Living Bibles,* and prophetic cassettes, a booth operated by representatives of Americans for a Safe Israel, a strongly Zionist group based in New York. The ASI representatives may have felt a bit uncomfortable among all the gospel paraphernalia, but they secured a ready ally at the convention in the Roundtable, the ultraconservative religious lobbying group. On the last day of the convention, the Roundtable sponsored a prayer breakfast for Israel during which the theme from *Exodus* was played, bagels were served, and "God Bless America" sung by a blind Korean War orphan. Bobbi James, the first lady of Alabama, recounted the story of a birthday party she had sponsored for Israel at the governor's mansion that coincided more or less with the discovery of oil in Mobile Bay, the state treasury thereby being blessed to the tune of over $400 million. God blesses those who bless Israel, reminded Mrs. James.

A surprise guest at the breakfast was Bailey Smith, president of the Southern Baptist Convention. The man "who had fired a shot that went all the way to Israel" (in the words of Roundtable founder Ed McAteer) apparently had come to rectify his ill-considered statement the previous year that "God does not hear the prayer of a Jew." Smith told of his recent trip with a group of rabbis to the Holy Land, where he stayed in a kibbutz and "wept as we toured the Holocaust Center." There were in fact many tears shed at that meeting as evangelicals and Jews recalled their common heritage.

A Baptist wanders into a cathedral during a mass and sits down. Getting carried away with the service, he shouts "Amen!" and everyone turns around and stares disapprovingly. As the liturgy proceeds, he again forgets himself and yells "Halleluia!" Two deacons then appear at his side and lead him out of the sanctuary. "I couldn't help it," the man expostulates. "I got religion." The Catholics glare at him and say, "Well, you didn't get it here."

an old Baptist joke

Fundamentalists seemed to be hopping into the bunker with almost any ideologues they found to be lodging in the same conservative camp. Even though many fundamentalists still regarded Catholics as the legions of Babylon and the Mormons as members of a demonic cult, pro-family fundamentalist tacticians joined forces with leaders of the long-standing Roman Catholic crusade against abortion and the discreetly organized Mormon campaign against the ERA. In fact, many of the principal strategists of the new conservative right turned out to be Catholic. Clearly, for fundamentalist leaders, it had come down to choosing the lesser of evils—the

Pope and Joseph Smith being currently less dangerous than the sybarites of secular humanism.

This ex officio ecumenism indicated that the fundamentalist identity had become more ideological than theological. If one ignored such troublesome issues as the status of the Virgin Mary and the authority of the Pope, fundamentalists seemed to have more in common with conservative Catholics than they did with liberal Protestants. The key to such ideological unity amid serious religious differences was placing the big, symbolic issues—abortion, prayer in the schools, etc.—on a Manichaean battleground of good and evil, and talking about unity of purpose without sounding overly ecumenical. Thus politics would become a morality play, and the embattled family a rallying point for conservative Protestants, Catholics, and Jews alike.

The crusade by conservative Christians to "save" America had in fact become a last-ditch attempt to preserve their traditional values and carry out their obligations as God's people in an increasingly pluralistic society. The coincidental resurgence of the political and religious right—two discrete if overlapping movements—pointed to common causes of discontent. Conservative middle-class Americans, once complacent in their status within the moral and social—if silent—majority, had come to feel like voices in the wilderness. Upward-bound evangelicals who had moved into suburban respectability from farms or factories felt like second-class citizens whose concerns were being either ignored or assaulted by the government at every level.

These were not the grievances of a marginal group, as the Far Right had been perceived in the fifties and sixties, when Billy James Hargis was raving about Communist conspiracies and Richard Hofstadter was writing about the paranoid style in American politics. Such factors as "status anxiety" put forth by Daniel Bell and Seymour Martin Lipset no longer seemed entirely adequate to account for the growing restiveness and power of conservative Christians. By the late seventies, evangelicals had come a long way from revival tents, streetcorner pamphleteering, backwoods camp meetings, and Bible-verse billboards. Their churches had grown, and they had prospered, as had the fundamentalist faction within the loosely allied National Association of Evangelicals.

Even as conservative Christians consolidated their numbers and their power, the quality of life around them continued to deterio-rate, and the stench of corruption was everywhere. As they saw it, their hard-earned prosperity was being eaten away by taxes that were redistributed as handouts to the idle or as contributions to the legal-services funds for the flagrantly sinful. Unless good Christian people shelled out non-tax-exempt tuition for private Christian schools, their sons and daughters would be taught values in the classroom that assailed the book of Genesis and mocked the strict morality of their parents. Even sheltered parochial-school students were being lured into a corrupt secular world with the switch of a TV channel or the flip of a magazine page. There was crime in the streets, lenience in the courts, mutiny in the home, apathy on the job, abortion on demand. One did not have to be paranoid to perceive that the close-knit family, the tightly woven fabric of com-munity, had frayed into loose ends.

The time was ripe for another Great Awakening, or at least an-other eruption of the scapegoating populism that had been popping up on the American scene since the Know-Nothings set out to curb the Catholics in the midnineteenth century. The fact that America had entered the age of high technology was no assurance that prim-itive religious instincts would die out like the dodo bird. Popular religious movements, in fact, often flourish within a context of ra-tionalism. The first Great Awakening in America coincided with the first rays of the Enlightenment.

THE NEW CONSERVATIVE ALLIANCE

The conservative awakening of the late seventies contained ele-ments of both revivalist piety and reactionary populism. The new coalition of preachers and politicos was linked by religious fervor and an extrapolitical network. It was an alliance that wedded old-style populism, with its ruling trinity of patriotism, Protestantism, and paranoia, with the new-style, single-issue politics of action com-mittees and computerized mailing lists. As Peter Ross Range ob-served in the New York *Times,* the coalition "overcame historic regional differences, linking Washington-haters in the Southern Bi-

ble Belt with the Middle Western Farm Belt and the Sagebrush
Rebellion of the West."

But even more important than this resolution of regional differences was the reordering of moral priorities that allowed conservative evangelicals to find loopholes in the wall between church and
state. Fundamentalists had to do some rationalizing to overcome
their wariness of worldly matters—specifically, political activism.
During the civil rights movement, most white evangelicals had de-
nounced the political involvement of black ministers and white
Northern liberal pastors. In a sermon called "Ministers and
Marches," Jerry Falwell himself had attacked all religious reform
movements: "Nowhere are we commissioned to reform the ex-
ternals. We are not told to wage war against bootleggers, liquor
stores, gamblers, murderers, prostitutes, racketeers, prejudiced persons, or institutions, or any other existing evil as such."

Falwell's position reflected the traditional fundamentalist denial
of the Social Gospel, the reform movement that took root in post-
Civil War Protestantism in response to the excesses of the industrial
system, but it also repudiated the more conservative reform movements initiated during the Awakening of 1800–35 and the revivals
of 1875–1914, which had inspired crusades against the sins and
corruptions of city life. Churches and preachers generally had not
participated directly in politics, but if issues were formulated in
moral terms and set forth as right or wrong within a Christian
framework, churchgoers felt bound to speak out or use their influence as concerned citizens. The reform-minded frequently joined
together in temperance unions or charitable societies, smashing sa-
loons or building soup kitchens in the slums.

By the late 1970s, fundamentalists had returned to those early
roots of reform. Falwell had resolved the church-state separation
issue with a little historical revisionism: "Our Founding Fathers separated church and state in function, but never intended to establish
a government void of God. As is evidenced by our Constitution,
good people in America must exert an influence and provide a
conscience and climate of morality in which it is difficult to go
wrong, not difficult for people to go right in America." Ironically,
conservative Christians had learned a lesson in strategy from Martin
Luther King, Jr., and other black ministers. They had learned that
moral conviction could be translated into legislation and social

change; they had learned that those who seemed powerless in the face of an unheeding society could, like Joshua, cause walls to crumble, barriers to fall. And they learned from the antiwar movement that even military policy was vulnerable to public protest.

However, the new social gospel for conservative evangelicals had little to do with concern for the poor and disadvantaged or for the cause of peace. The social concerns of most conservative evangelicals constituted a collection of single issues that, taken together, made up a complete, self-enclosed worldview, ostensibly drawn from the Scriptures. The Bible had become not only a moral guide and spiritual history but also an economics textbook, a political handbook, and a science abstract. The ideological shift toward political activism by many fundamentalist leaders was directed not by hoary prophets brandishing tablets of stone but by a Washington-based tactical group composed of former businessmen, educators, and professional political strategists. The agenda for this group combined the neofundamentalist family issues of abortion, the ERA, and prayer in the schools with the economic and military priorities of the Old Right.

Not only were these leaders quick to find loopholes in their own church-vs.-state tradition; they were also, from my point of view, quick to find loopholes in the New Testament. During the 1982 National Religious Broadcasters convention, I was discussing the political gains of conservative Christians with Ed McAteer, the man who claims to have created the new Religious Right. Said McAteer, a former field director for the CFF who began as a traveling salesman for Colgate-Palmolive, "I'm the guy that introduced the big-name preachers to the activists." A jovial, pink-cheeked man with a men's-club smile and a just-folks Tennessee accent, McAteer told me that the Roundtable (formerly the Religious Roundtable), of which he was a cofounder, "uses the Bible as our operations manual."

Then, as we discussed the advocacy by the Roundtable of a military buildup and a cutback in services to the poor, we exchanged Bible verses, as those with an evangelical training are wont to do. I brought up the Beatitudes (from the fifth chapter of Matthew), with their ringing blessing of the poor and the peacemakers as well as the pure in heart. McAteer's response, after asserting that there is a difference between quoting the Bible and understanding it, was to refer me to the Old Testament and the "many instances where God destroyed cities. Loving-kindness and righteousness" are called for in a Christian, he said, but "so is judgment. God judges evil. I'd like to love, but I'm a realist."

While conservative evangelicals were managing to conquer their prejudices against political involvement, secular conservatives were endeavoring to overcome their reluctance to associate themselves with politically primitive evangelicals. Sometimes such allies could do a cause as much harm as good, particularly when that cause already had experienced its share of notoriety. Fundamentalists shared with political conservatives a pessimistic view of human nature; both groups believed that the essentially brutish nature of man required the strong imposition of moral order. But frequently they disagreed on the measures that had to be taken to impose that order.

Fundamentalist preachers, unfortunately, were prone to get worked up and call for the death penalty for homosexuality or advocate such bizarre forms of discipline for children as electric dunce chairs. In January 1980, a member of the American Conservative Union who was manning a booth at the National Religious Broadcasters convention told me that a prominent member of Moral Majority had proved an "embarrassment" in a speech to the ACU. The man had gotten carried away with an encomium on discipline and had described in acoustic detail the difference between spanking a girl and walloping a boy. Also an "embarrassment" were the frank opinions of the Reverend Dan Fore, Moral Majority's spokesman in New York. Fore told the New York *Times* that "Jews have a God-given ability to make money" and *New York* magazine that the Spanish Inquisition had not represented Christian persecution of the Jews because "those weren't Christians. Those were Roman Catholics." Despite such indiscretions, though, conservative organizations were willing to tolerate a little backwoods zealotry in order to court the evangelical vote.

Aside from McAteer, the key figures in bringing together the Bible zealots and lovers of laissez-faire were: Robert J. Billings, the former roving Christian-school organizer who acted as director of Moral Majority before becoming Ronald Reagan's campaign liaison to the religious community; Paul Weyrich, an Eastern Rite Catholic

who had worked as a Senate aide in Washington and who had been
the prime mover in such conservative groups as the Heritage Foundation and the Committee for the Survival of a Free Congress; and,
most important, Richard Viguerie, the direct-mail fund-raising whiz
who had learned about coalition politics while raising money for
George Wallace in the early seventies. It was Viguerie and his master list of single-issue supporters that enabled the New Right to
build multi-issue coalitions independent of traditional party politics.
And it was Viguerie who foresaw the importance of conservative
evangelicals in the creation of the new conservative coalition. In a
1976 interview with *Sojourners* magazine, Viguerie made a self-fulfilling prophecy: "The next real major area of growth for the conservative ideology and philosophy is among evangelical people. I
would be surprised if in the next year you did not see a massive
effort to involve them, utilizing direct mail and other techniques."

Raised a Catholic, Viguerie manifested the evangelical zeal of a
born fundamentalist. He was known to keep a Bible on his desk. In
his self-congratulatory manifesto, *The New Right: We're Ready to
Lead,* he showered Moral Majority with praise for its role in showing the "enormous power religious people can have for good in
America—if only they rouse themselves and don't leave the field to
the Reverend Jesse Jackson, the Reverend William Sloane Coffin,
Father Robert Drinan, and the National Council of Churches."
However, according to conservative journalist Alan Crawford,
Viguerie, whose fund-raising operation, RAVCO, was grossing $15
million annually by 1981, had not always been a successful dunner
for the cause of morality. In 1971 and 1972, he raised $2.3 million
for the Citizens for Decent Literature, but his own costs devoured
81 percent of the money. In 1976, he reportedly raised $802,028
for the Bibles of the World Society and then charged them
$889,225 for his services.

Nevertheless, RAVCO's computerized list of 4.5 million conservative boosters, which Viguerie had been compiling since 1964,
when he started his business with the YAF (Young Americans for
Freedom) as his only customer, brought money and power to
groups and individuals that might otherwise have languished on the
fringes of political discourse. Viguerie's scare-and-entreat form letters made NCPAC (the National Conservative Political Action
Committee) one of the most powerful PACs in the capital and

drummed up support for such satellite groups as the Conservative Caucus. Said Viguerie of the New Right's fund-raising prowess: "We've surpassed our early goals by so much that I've learned to quit expecting to run up against a final limit."

By the end of 1978, the growing network of New Right lobbies, political action committees, and think tanks, spearheaded by Paul Weyrich's Committee for the Survival of a Free Congress, had begun to produce results, and a small squad of inexperienced but gung-ho conservatives took their seats in Congress, their hands poised above the voting buttons, ready to blast liberal programs out of the water.

Ed McAteer and Robert Billings had brought Jerry Falwell and other members of the electronic brigade together with Richard Viguerie and Conservative Caucus leader Howard Phillips—a more perfect match-up could not have been designed by a computer dating service—and the mutual evangelization that followed eventually produced Moral Majority. If Falwell had been coy at first, he soon became the aggressor in the relationship. His decision to bring the pulpit into politics had been gradual but inevitable. Beginning in 1975, he had been involved in patriotic rallies to coincide with the nation's bicentennial, and he had warned then that America, a nation under God, was flouting "His principles and His heritage." Although he had turned down an overture by Billings in 1977 to establish an affiliation similar to what would become Moral Majority, by 1979 he was ready to join forces with the big-gun conservatives Billings had lined up in support. The papers for Moral Majority were drawn up in June 1979, and in September of that year Falwell inaugurated his organization on the steps of the state capitol in Richmond, Virginia. From there he set off across America with a clean-cut choir from his own Liberty Baptist College to lead a series of "I Love America" rallies. During the following January, he began publishing the Moral Majority *Report,* and by August 1980, when Ronald Reagan joined Falwell, Senator Jesse Helms, and other conservative all-stars in Dallas to brief conservative clergymen on the subject of church and state, the mailing list had been beefed up to 400,000.

By the time of the National Affairs Briefing, sponsored by Ed McAteer's Roundtable, Reagan had become the messiah of the New Right, pledged to deliver them from the evils of government regulation and lead them not into the temptation of taxation. In a miracle of clerical legerdemain, Reagan, a divorced ex-movie star and practitioner of casual California ecumenism, displaced Jimmy Carter as the born-again candidate, attacking FCC regulations on behalf of religious broadcasters, assailing the IRS persecution of Christian schools, casting doubt on Darwin, and enshrining the Bible. He told an enthralled clergy at the briefing that "it is an incontrovertible fact that all the complex and horrendous questions confronting us at home and worldwide have their answers in that single book." Although he had done some backsliding in appointing George Bush as his running mate, he had at least conferred with Falwell in his hotel suite during the GOP convention. Falwell had kept the faith by printing articles favorable to Reagan in the Moral Majority *Report* and restricting mention of Carter to articles associating the President with gay rights and opposition to school prayer. Moral Majority continued to maintain that it could not endorse candidates directly, but the July 30, 1980, cover of the *Report* featured a picture of Falwell and Reagan.

It must have seemed to Carter that conservative Christian groups were springing up like summer crabgrass around the White House lawn. Even more open in its embrace of Reagan than Moral Majority was Christian Voice, a group headquartered in Pacific Grove, California, that came together during the 1978 statewide battle for Proposition 6, a statute designed to restrict the rights of homosexuals. Organized in the now typical Washington triad of lobby, political action committee, and educational foundation, the Voice was primarily a direct-mail concern—all hay and no grass roots. As part of its Christians-for-Reagan campaign, Christian Voice distributed *The Faith of Reagan* pamphlets claiming that "Ronald Reagan is the only candidate that has firmly stood behind his Christian principles at the risk of political loss." And to clarify issues in congressional races, CV issued the Congressional Report Card, which tattled on members of the House and Senate who voted the wrong way on such issues as busing, SALT II, affirmative action, and foreign aid. Oddly enough, Congressman Richard Kelly of Florida, who was convicted of accepting a bribe from an ABSCAM operative, scored 100, while Father Robert Drinan of Massachusetts rated a zero and Presbyterian minister Robert Edgar of Pennsylvania chalked up an 8 on this moral achievement test.

INFLATING THE FAITH

If the religious right had lent Christian credibility to Ronald Reagan, he had in turn brought political credibility to conservative Christians, and to Jerry Falwell in particular. While Carter's reassurances on the subject of church and state had been designed to reinforce the boundaries and downplay his devotion, thus allaying fears that he would render unto Christ what was Caesar's, Reagan's pronouncements on the subject were calculated to adjust those boundaries and inflate his faith. As Reagan publicly telegraphed messages to his enthused new constituency, with charged references to the Scriptures and fundamentalist issues, the press finally began to intercept. When Reagan concluded his acceptance speech at the GOP convention with a moment of silent prayer, prefaced by dramatic trepidation, reporters knew that something had changed in American politics.

If the national media had been slow initially to respond to the emergence of this new political faction, they compensated subsequently by frequently exaggerating the strength and numbers of the fundamentalist front. The Washington for Jesus rally itself had received rather cursory coverage, particularly compared to the outpouring of print that followed the Pope's tour of America. Much of the coverage of WFJ focused on denunciations of the event by the liberal clergy. However, by the time of the National Affairs Briefing, the press was prepared. Moral Majority was becoming a household epithet, and liberal drivers were sporting bumper stickers proclaiming "Moral Majority, My Ass!" Over 250 reporters turned up, representing most of the major networks, newspapers, and newsmagazines in the country, and another 100 accompanied Reagan to the closing ceremonies.

On August 17, on the eve of the Briefing, the New York *Times* began a four-part series "on the rise of ultraconservative Christians as a political force in the nation." In the first installment, John Herbers wrote that "The television preachers, a new breed of independent evangelists, have largely created the climate for the movement by building huge new audiences in urban America." In short order, demonstrating the domino theory of media coverage, Falwell made guest appearances on "Meet the Press," "Today," and "Donahue" and addressed the National Press Club. The media were quick to focus on a leader who seemed to personify this growing faction of political activists, and Falwell certainly gave more pungent quotes than the distinctly uncharismatic behind-the-scenes organizers. Falwell, the man of the hour, became the figurehead of the conservative coalition.

On September 15, Falwell's picture adorned the cover of *Newsweek*. The accompanying story announced, "Over the past 18 months a new and potent political force has been taking shape—a 'New Christian Right,' in the words of theologian Martin E. Marty. Led by religious-TV stars such as Falwell, whose 'Old-Time Gospel Hour' reaches an estimated 18 million viewers each week, this movement is attempting to enlist the nation's 30 million to 65 million evangelical Christians in an unabashedly political crusade based on fundamentalist morality." The article recounted Falwell's prediction—which would later prove to be 80 percent accurate—of the fall of George McGovern of South Dakota, Frank Church of Idaho, John Culver of Iowa, Alan Cranston of California, Birch Bayh of Indiana, and Gaylord Nelson of Wisconsin. Only Cranston survived the carnage in November, and Falwell appeared to be a proven Jeremiah.

Moreover, Falwell had accomplished a feat of multiplication similar to the miracle of the loaves and fishes—he had swelled the numbers of his actual viewing audience to many times its actual size. Frequently he claimed an audience of 25 million, and during the GOP convention one of his spokesmen upped the count to 50 million. The secular media, caught up in the hysteria and hype, swallowed this fish story, with 18 million being the average published estimate. *Playboy* implied that as many as 30 million Americans watched Falwell's "Old-Time Gospel Hour."

Falwell and his allies were becoming so successful in manipulating public opinion that they resembled the warlord in Kurosawa's film *Kagemusha* who simply had to make a ritual show of his army in order to defeat his enemies. This was particularly true in the case of the Reverend Donald E. Wildmon and his campaign against the TV networks. In February 1981, Wildmon, a mild-mannered Methodist minister from Tupelo, Mississippi, who had for many years been coordinating audience protests against violence and indecency on TV, formed the Coalition for Better Television, counting among his supporters Jerry Falwell, Phyllis Schlafly, and other conservative leaders. During the summer of that year, after CBTV volunteers had monitored prime-time network shows for "obscenity" (which included the categories of "skin scenes," "sexual innuendo," and "implied sexual intercourse"), "profanity," and "violence," Wildmon announced that the group intended to single out for a boycott the sponsor whose commercials were paying for the most offensive shows. Wildmon also argued, as had the Gablers with respect to the secular classroom, that Christian values, Christian characters, and Christian culture had been censored out of network TV. Even worse than television's gratuitous sex and violence, he said, was the anti-Christian "bigotry" he found on the secular airwaves.

Two weeks before Wildmon was to announce the unlucky target of CBTV's boycott at a national press conference, TV's biggest sponsor, Procter & Gamble, announced that the coalition was "expressing some very important and broadly held views about gratuitous sex, violence, and profanity." Already nervous about a series of rumors connecting their logo to demonic powers, P&G decided to play it safe. If Wildmon had been bluffing, the bluff had worked. The "galvanizing specter" of the religious right, as NBC's Grant Tinker branded Falwell and his followers, had begun to cause tremors of fear and anger across the land.

DEFLATING THE FAITH

Nevertheless, not everyone in the media took Falwell, Wildmon, et al. at their word when it came to the size and power of their following. By 1981, it had become apparent to many experts that Falwell's strength was more in zeal than in numbers. Jeffrey Hadden, a sociologist at the University of Virginia, and Charles E. Swann, a Presbyterian minister and radio-station manager, revealed in their book, *Prime Time Preachers: The Rising Power of Televangelism* that the figures from the Arbitron Company, an independent audience auditor, showed the *total* audience for evangelists in 1980 to be 20,538,000—a drop from 22,538,000 in 1978. They concluded that a probable source of the inflated audience estimates was the practice of counting the same viewer more than once. The single viewer who tuned in to both Oral Roberts and Jerry Falwell was thus counted twice. Similarly, sociologist William Martin reported in the *Atlantic* that after a decade of research on polls and audience surveys he had found the audience estimates purveyed by Falwell and his critics alike to be "absurd." Even the National Religious Broadcasters counted the total number of devout watchers at 14 million.

The figures for individual preachers and shows were considerably more modest. Hadden and Swann reported that in an average week, as measured in February 1980 by Arbitron, Falwell reached an audience of 1,455,720. Ironically, "The Old-Time Gospel Hour" was beaten out by five other religious broadcasts: Oral Roberts (2,719,250), Rex Humbard (2,409,960), "Hour of Power" (2,069,210), Jimmy Swaggart (1,986,000), and "Day of Discovery" (1,519,400). To put these numbers in their proper perspective, one had only to compare Falwell's following with the viewing audience devoted to less uplifting shows during the same ratings period. The seething Southern-gothic soap, "Flamingo Road," for example, a target of the Reverend Donald E. Wildmon's CBTV, averaged 14.8 million viewers a week during that February. And according to a report in the Boston *Globe,* "Fallen Angel," a TV movie about a child pornographer, reached 34 million viewers when it was broadcast on February 24.

Beware, America! If you're a progressive liberal male living in a high-tech loft amid the secular spires of modernism, it's time to disarm the charging army of fundamentalists who would: 1) burn your Kurt Vonnegut, Jr. books, your Rolling Stones albums, and your stash of sensamilla; 2) force you to spank your children, sing "Onward Christian Soldiers" before every sporting event, and swear on the Bible that Noah's ark accommodated more beasts than the Bronx Zoo; and 3) turn your carefree spouse-equivalent into a slavish Total Woman.

As liberals began to recover from shock and disbelief at their losses, attacks on the new religiopolitical right began to mount. A number of liberal groups and individuals began to develop their own propaganda techniques, using direct-mail appeals, TV specials, and ad campaigns. The American Civil Liberties Union, for example, took out several full-page newspaper ads, including one which contained a sketch of a cross-wielding preacher riding on Uncle Sam's back. The headline read: "If the Moral Majority has its way, you'd better start praying."

In June 1981, I received a form letter from a group called People for the American Way that began with a Falwellesque flourish: "If I live to be a thousand—and I would like that—I may never write a letter more important to me than this one. The future of our pluralistic society is at stake. . . ." The letter was signed by Norman Lear, the TV producer, who had founded American Way as a "broadly based, non-partisan national committee" dedicated to wresting the "American way" from the religious right. Wrote Lear, ". . . unless we who value the diversity of our religious faiths, the variety of our cultural and ethnic backgrounds and our freedom to differ politically unite, we stand a very real chance of seeing this glorious free nation turned over to those who would dictate exactly how we should think . . . or even *if* we should think!"

Elsewhere, Lear described the New Right as a "new breed of robber barons who have organized to corner the market on morals." In October 1982 the Rev. Msgr. George Higgins, a longtime social justice advocate, ended his connection with American Way, saying that the group used the same "emotional scare tactics" that had been associated with the religious right.

In order to beat the fundamentalists at their own game of schmaltzy patriotism, Lear organized a TV special in honor of George Washington called "I Love Liberty." The special featured a cameo performance by comedian Robin Williams as the tattered but vocal American flag, a recital of the First Amendment by Jane Fonda, and a rendition by Barbra Streisand of "America the Beautiful." Emcee Martin Sheen spun a few stories about his Irish grandmother, then asked how many blacks were in the audience, how many Italians, how many Chinese. After each group had applauded, Sheen called for another round: "Come on, let's hear it for us!" As critic James Wolcott described it, the show was itself "something of an evangelical spectacular, a cross between a political convention (bunting, cascading balloons) and a Christian fundamentalist crusade." Commenting on the show's parade-of-stars approach, Wolcott observed that, rather than touting liberty and tolerance, the show seemed to celebrate "the rewards and adulation that stardom brings."

Writers, too, took aim at the religious right, often matching the apocalyptic warnings and righteous pronouncements by the fundamentalists with their own form of rhetorical overkill and banner-waving sanctimony. Journalism professor Andrew Merton noted in his book *Enemies of Choice* that antiabortion groups resembled Nazis: "In its emotional appeals and its disregard of logic, the right-to-life movement resembles many other oppressive crusades in human history, from the earliest witch hunts to the Spanish Inquisition to the Nazis' persecution of Jews and other *Untermenschen* (subhumans)."

Writers Flo Conway and Jim Siegelman, the authors of *Snapping,* an investigation of the brainwashing techniques of religious cults, followed up that first attack on blind faith with *Holy Terror: Religion Run Amok in Politics and Our Private Lives.* They seemed to regard the fervent religious faith of fundamentalists as a mental condition similar to that of the Moonies they had previously observed. After traveling 10,000 miles over a period of five months during 1981, Conway and Siegelman concluded that America "had already taken dramatic steps toward becoming a fundamentalist nation." Fundamentalist leaders, asserted Conway and Siegelman, were guilty of "mass manipulation on a scale that we believe is unprecedented in both religion and politics."

The authors made an impassioned case for the impending take-over of statehouses, schools, bedrooms, and minds by the likes of Falwell and Pat Robertson of the 700 Club. Comparing the propaganda efforts of fundamentalist preachers to the brainwashing methods used in Hitler's Germany, Stalin's Russia, and Mao's China, Conway and Siegelman contended that America was undergoing a siege of "total propaganda" rivaling the will-crushing tactics of those regimes. Behind this campaign of terror, however, sat "no single maniacal leader, no lone rebel, visionary or even a formal ruling clique, but the syndrome of fundamentalism."

Remarkably, Conway and Siegelman succeeded in matching the

hyperventilated tone of the TV preachers themselves. In a fund-raising letter, Jerry Falwell had warned, "Our Grand Old Flag is going down the drain. . . . One day the Russians may pick up the telephone and call Washington, D.C., and dictate the terms of our surrender to them." Similarly, Conway and Siegelman warned, "As Americans, we must face squarely . . . the prospect that very soon we may be living in an America reborn of total propaganda and surrender to the supernatural."

Perry Deane Young, the author of *God's Bullies: Power Politics and Religious Tyranny,* took a different line of attack. Young, an excellent reporter, set out to document the personal failings and hypocrisy of New Right leaders, particularly the conservative Catholics like Richard Viguerie who were trying to build a conservative empire based on fear and resentment of minority groups. The most startling of Young's allegations was that some prominent members of the New Right were gay. Young wrote in defense of this and other similar disclosures, "It is not their homosexuality I am disclosing, but their repression of feelings I regard as natural. It is . . . not their homosexuality that is worth noting, but their hypocrisy."

It seemed that the hostility and intolerance shown by members of the New Right were contagious. In his own study of the new religious right called *The New Subversives: Anti-Americanism of the Religious Right,* Daniel Maguire, professor of ethics at Marquette University, warned that the first temptation to be guarded against was paranoia, lest opponents of the New Right themselves get caught up in the heat of epithet-flinging and endow the "threat with demonic powers." Maguire quoted Richard Hofstadter on the danger of attributing to one's political opponents "some especially effective source of power; he controls the press; he directs the public mind through 'managed news'; he has unlimited funds; he has a new secret for influencing the mind; he has a special technique for seduction; he is gaining a stranglehold on the educational system."

The fundamentalists had been no more effective than other groups in achieving those sources of power. And, as Maguire conceded, they were raising many basic issues that deserved serious attention: "The rightists are addressing real problems when they speak of things like the legitimate place of religion in political and social life, the decline of family stability, the hidden value-assumptions of supposedly neutral public education, the chaotic sexual mores of the day, and issues like pornography, drug abuse, and abortion."

For Maguire, as for many liberal religious leaders, the proper response to preachers who invaded politics was not to send them scuttling back to their pulpits but to reclaim the social issues they had appropriated. Yet liberal clerics fell short of the fundamentalists when it came to confidence about seizing moral and political prerogatives. As representatives of fifteen Protestant denominations declared in an official statement critical of the radical right, "On theological and ethical grounds, we reject the assumption that human beings can know with absolute certainty the will of God on particular public policy issues. Many in the religious right seem to have forgotten the clear Biblical witness and central Christian acknowledgment that all of us are finite, fallible, and sinful."

CHAPTER 11

Of God, Marx, and Mammon: The Way of Radical Evangelicalism

If the Christian is not being revolutionary, then in some way or another he has been unfaithful to his calling.

Jacques Ellul

If today's church does not recapture the sacrificial spirit of the early church, it will lose its authenticity, forfeit the loyalty of millions, and be dismissed as an irrelevant social club with no meaning.

Martin Luther King, Jr.

Despite the rattle of tambourines and the growing of beards that announced the greening of Christianity on the West Coast during the late sixties, most of the locusts-and-honey freaks and sidewalk seers of the Jesus movement remained simple Armageddonists at heart. The gleeful folk-rock gospel of the Jesus festivals was co-opted by Christian entrepreneurs as inevitably as the secular counterculture had been absorbed by Madison Avenue. The prophetic raptures of the Jesus People, which had appeared at first to be the latest flowering of ecstatic-communard gnosticism, faded into the sober conventions of fundamentalism.

Typical of this transformation was Gospel Outreach, a pentecostal church headquartered in a lighthouse in Eureka, California, which got its start in 1970 as a refuge for runaways, ex-drug addicts, and other street people. As the church grew and stabilized into a permanent congregation, members mounted a missionary outreach in a number of countries around the world. In 1983, the church numbered between 3,000 and 4,000 members worldwide, its most prominent spokesman being the deposed president of Guatemala, Brigadier General Efraín Ríos Montt.

Yet the spiritual turbulence of the sixties and seventies created a new radical movement as well as a strengthened fundamentalist contingent within the ranks of evangelicals. Young radicals, like older fundamentalists, smelled corruption in the political, religious, and economic institutions of America. Like fundamentalists, radical Christians had an idea what Jesus would do if he were to materialize suddenly in America—if he were to walk through the fleshpots of Manhattan's Times Square, the labyrinthine halls of the Pentagon, or the boardroom of a Madison Avenue ad agency. They found themselves at odds with a culture that promoted self-gratification over self-sacrifice, that stressed neighborhood gentrification over communal harmony, that sold brand-name trendiness over spiritual verities. They, too, wanted to build a New Jerusalem in the ashes of the American dream.

Radical evangelicals, however, rejected the prosperity and power that conservative evangelicals felt to be their just reward for living good Christian lives. Unlike fundamentalists, who wanted to fight fire with fire by banning and burning, Christianizing the culture, and hoarding arms for Armageddon, radical evangelicals called for a scaling down of Christian enterprise, a rejection of the arms race, and a buildup of social concerns. And unlike secular radicals, who shared many of their aims, most radical evangelicals placed more faith in such atavistic measures as voluntary poverty than in visions of political reform. Nevertheless, they were not isolationists in the older Christ-against-culture mode; they attempted to act as catalysts within the larger communities into which they settled, and on key issues they entered the political fray.

This new radical movement drew members from both conservative and liberal churches. Not satisfied with such concessions from conservative churches as "contemporary Christian music" in the choir lofts, nor with the tepid social activism of more liberal churches, a number of young evangelicals involved in the Jesus movement developed a permanent sense of estrangement from established churches. The Christian World Liberation Front, for example, founded at the University of California at Berkeley as a kind of counterculture facade for the Campus Crusade for Christ, became genuinely radicalized. Evolving into the Berkeley Christian Coalition, the group, through their journal *Radix,* proclaimed true Christians to be "a people radically set apart from the world system" because of their "rootedness in Jesus Christ."

Similarly, evangelicals who had been involved in the civil rights and antiwar movements, and who had become disillusioned with religious as well as political institutions, began to try to reconcile their social and political activism with their lingering faith in Christ. Just as fundamentalists learned from civil rights leaders whose roots were in the church that Christian activism could actually bring about changes in the social order, young white evangelicals learned from black ministers how Christian faith might become the basis for resistance to social injustice.

After their immersion in the free communal bath of the secular counterculture, these evangelicals had retained a number of radical notions that seemed to coincide with the Scriptures—chiefly, the importance of peace and community and the dangers of complacency. They found in Jesus not only an apostle of peace but a radical savior who had met his fate for casting his lot with the oppressed and opposing the powers of business, church, and state. Wary of wealthy churches as of secular establishments, they began to band together in experimental communities and collectives and to publish magazines setting forth their views on Christ and culture.

In a manifesto called *Agenda for Biblical People,* Jim Wallis, a cofounder of the Sojourners community in Washington, D.C., and editor of *Sojourners* magazine, indicted "establishment Christianity" for its cultural enslavement, asserting that institutionalized Christianity and biblical faith were mutually exclusive: "Establishment Christianity has made its peace with the established order. It no longer feels itself to be in conflict with the pretensions of the state, with the designs of economic and political power, or with the values and style of life enshrined in the national culture. Establishment Christianity is a religion of accommodation and conformity, which values realism and success more than faithfulness and obedience. It is heavily invested in the political order, the social consensus, and the ideology of the economic system. Its leaders are more comfortable as chaplains than as prophets. . . ."

For a small minority of radical Christians, the alternative to complicity in a captive religion was participation in radical politics. The Radical Religion Collective of Berkeley, publisher of the journal *Radical Religion,* announced its intention "to play an active role in political movements for liberation" and "to work for a socialist alternative." The editors of the journal solicited articles from radical academics in the fields of history and sociology as well as theology. A favorite subject was Antonio Gramsci, the martyred Italian Communist who disagreed with Marx's dismissal of religion as an opiate, contending that popular religion, which expressed the worldview by which most people actually lived, had to be taken seriously by intellectuals seeking political change.

This new wave of Christian socialists traced their roots back to the Society of Christian Socialists, founded in Boston in 1889 by Episcopal priest William D. P. Bliss, and to Congregational pastor George D. Herron's Christian Socialist weekly, *The Kingdom,* first published in Grinnell, Iowa, in 1894. They tended not to mention such precedents as Reinhold Niebuhr's Fellowship of Socialist Christians, formed in the thirties, largely in response to the Depression. Niebuhr eventually found that history dictated a choice between lesser evils, and as the greater evils of Stalinism became apparent, Christian Socialism became Christian Realism. The Fellowship of Socialist Christians changed its name in 1948 to the Frontier Fellowship: Christians for Social Reconstruction, and Niebuhr's journal, *Radical Religion,* became *Christianity and Society* and eventually *Christianity and Crisis.*

Niebuhr's disillusionment with socialism, fed by his deepening Augustinian conviction of the corruptibility of men and systems, led, at its extreme, to a kind of cold-war-Christian posture: "Everybody understands the obvious meaning of the world struggle in which we are engaged. We are defending freedom against tyranny and are trying to preserve justice against a system which has, demonically, distilled injustice and cruelty out of its original promise of a higher justice." Niebuhr, though he continued to advocate reform and to assail the defenders of the status quo, tempered his support of liberal democratic politics with a conservative social philosophy. His concern for the unintended side effects and unfortunate consequences of social policy led to a critical view of the utopian visions of both left and right.

By contrast, such groups as the Christians for Socialism, whose American chapter was founded in 1974, found socialist ideology "useful for understanding our own historical movement" and for "uncovering the Christian symbols and thought forms and laying bare their revolutionary implications." These Left Christians, as they sometimes called themselves, attempted to merge Christ and Marx in their critique of capitalism, allying themselves with the liberation theology emanating from radical priests in Latin America. Theology was to be found in praxis rather than contemplation, in political action rather than personal piety.

Most radical evangelical groups in the seventies, however, were less interested in creating a dialogue between Christ and Marx than in reexamining the original dialogue between Christ and his disciples. In an early issue of *The Other Side,* a journal published by members of the Jubilee Fellowship in Philadelphia, Mark Olson wrote that "revolution in today's world is the opiate of intellectuals." After living and working among the poor, he had become concerned about the gap between rhetoric and reality in socialist ideology: "Among the poor 'n' oppressed there's little if any interest, for example, in finding the 'root causes' of oppression, in building 'intentional community,' or in developing new patterns of 'economic sharing.' "

The new social gospel for these evangelical groups was grounded in the New Testament rather than in *Das Kapital.* They found in the teachings of Jesus, particularly in the Sermon on the Mount, an imperative to act as peacemakers as well as to plead the cause of the poor:

Blessed are the poor in spirit: for theirs is the kingdom of heaven.

Blessed are they that mourn: for they shall be comforted.

Blessed are the meek: for they shall inherit the earth.

Blessed are they which do hunger and thirst after righteousness: for they shall be filled.

Blessed are the merciful: for they shall obtain mercy.

Blessed are the pure in heart: for they shall see God.

Blessed are the peacemakers: for they shall be called the children of God.

Jim Wallis, who had entered the seminary after years of involvement in protest movements, described his disillusionment with secular political solutions: "At first it was a heady feeling to get thousands of people in the streets, thinking we could bring down the system. But the system ultimately brought down the movement. People got co-opted. My friends from that time are doing things like teaching courses on the New Left in graduate schools. But I went back to the New Testament, to give it one more chance. It wasn't that I got burned out by the movement. I realized that here was a God among the weak, the expendable, the marginal. There was nothing in secular literature to compare with that."

Mennonite theologian John Howard Yoder had also turned to the New Testament with questions about contemporary social and political problems. Provoked by the claims of young radicals that Jesus was, like themselves, a social critic, a dropout from the social climb, and the spokesman of a counterculture, Yoder attempted in *The Politics of Jesus* to bridge the gap between biblical exegesis and Christian ethics. Beginning with Mary's Magnificat in the book of Luke, which echoes Hannah's song in the Old Testament book of Samuel, Yoder found that the message embodied in the life and words of Christ was indeed radical:

He hath put down the mighty from their seats, and exalted them of low degree.

He hath filled the hungry with good things; and the rich he hath sent empty away.

Yoder pointed out that the messianic prophecy from Isaiah that Jesus claimed to fulfill was directed explicitly toward the poor, oppressed, and lowly:

The Spirit of the Lord is upon me, because he hath anointed me to preach the gospel to the poor; he hath sent me to heal the broken-hearted, to preach deliverance to the captives, and recovering of sight to the blind, to set at liberty them that are bruised.

Countering traditional interpretations of these and other seemingly revolutionary passages as largely symbolic in import, Yoder asserted that Jesus was setting forth a social ethic that specifically addressed the uses of wealth, weapons, and power.

The new radical communities of young evangelicals that were being organized in cities and rural areas around the country were closer to the Mennonite than to the Marxist model. The emphasis was on "costly discipleship"—a form of Protestant Christianity that antedated liberalism, humanism, and fundamentalism alike, harking back to the simpler, imperiled days of the early church. Drawing on the German crisis theology of Dietrich Bonhoeffer, the neo-orthodoxy of Karl Barth, and the benign pragmatism of William Booth, the young evangelical left attempted to avoid the seductive glamor of utopianism.

Bonhoeffer, who had been martyred in Nazi Germany, had characterized the Sunday morning rituals of modern Christianity as cheap discipleship, while Barth had emphasized the "disheartening fact" of sin in modern life. Booth, cofounder of the Salvation Army, with his wife, Catherine Mumford Booth, had assailed both the otherworldly piety and subversive spirit spawned by the Gilded Age: "This religious cant which rids itself of all the importunity of suffering humanity by drawing unnegotiable bills payable on the other side of the grave is not more impracticable than the socialist clap-trap which postpones all redress of human suffering until after the general overturn."

Concerned with the growing influence of conservative evangelical preachers, young evangelicals began discovering their own radical heritage—the tradition of social reform that was associated with evangelicalism before the Great Reversal of the late nineteenth and early twentieth centuries that left conservative Christians on the side of regressive pietism and liberal Protestants on the side of progressive humanism. Religious historian Timothy L. Smith had argued in his book *Revivalism and Social Reform in Mid-Nineteenth-Century America* that "far from disdaining earthly affairs, the evangelicals played a key role in the widespread attack upon slavery, poverty, and greed. They thus helped prepare the way both in theory and in practice for what later became known as the social gospel." Concluded Smith, "The quest for perfection joined with compassion for poor and needy sinners and a rebirth of millennial expectation to make popular Protestantism a mighty social force."

It was a force that seemed to be held in abeyance in the twentieth century until the black ministers of the civil rights movement reminded evangelicals of their promise "to preach liberty to the captives." As historian Donald G. Mathews argued, "White Evangelicals were too conscious of their own respectability and too crippled by their ethnocentrism or racism to sense the agony and alienation of the cross and therefore to understand the Gospel as a truly liberating force. . . ."

The outbreaks of revivalism in evangelical churches in the eighteenth and nineteenth centuries had affirmed the powerful bonds of love and care between all men and women in the Christian community. Revivals were a leveling force, as distinctions of social standing and learning were cast aside in the intensity of religious experience. Despite the emphasis by evangelists on the sin and depravity of humanity, the worth of the individual was constantly upheld; the proof of God's presence could be seen in the transformation of the lives of the worshipers. The revival spirit led to reform movements that were both uplifting and repressive—to abolitionism as well as the temperance movement.

Donald Dayton, an assistant professor of theology at North Park Theological Seminary in Chicago, wrote a series of articles for the *Post-American*, eventually published in book form, establishing the tradition of reform in revivalist Protestantism and analyzing the loss of that radical spirit in modern evangelicalism. Dayton suggested that the intensity of such early reform movements as abolitionism had been difficult to maintain, even over a single generation. Moreover, the Civil War had destroyed earlier utopian visions, and in the post-Civil War era the issues that replaced slavery tended to be based on questions of personal piety, detached from the larger social framework. Waves of immigration and massive urbanization brought problems too complex for the revivalist/reform vision. And with the growing popularity of premillennialism, notions of long-range social improvement were abandoned in favor of preaching the gospel to as many lost souls as possible before the trumpets sounded, heralding the Second Coming.

With the emergence of Darwinism and higher biblical criticism, conservatives of the old school, the practitioners of what became known as Princeton theology, became hostile to the spirit of modernity and to those clerics who sought scientific sources of religious affirmation, believing religion to be the soul of culture. As George Gordon observed bitterly in 1915, "During the last three light-hearted decades, we have been smoking the opium pipe of evolution, telling the world how far it has risen."

And all that believed were together, and had all things common; And sold their possessions and goods, and parted them to all men, as every man had need.

Acts 2:4,5

Generally, the new radical communities that came together during the seventies were set up as combinations of rescue missions and models of economic sharing. As if to counterbalance the conspicuous wealth of established churches, these evangelicals lived in conspicuous poverty. They embraced the poor, in the spirit of Dorothy Day and the *Catholic Worker* movement. As Jim Wallis described it, echoing Isaiah 61:1 and Luke 4:18, Christianity was a calling that meant "feeding the hungry, meeting the needs of the homeless and the refugees, supporting the imprisoned, befriending the lonely, standing with the poor and the outcasts, loving the unloved . . . confronting with our lives the institutional and root causes of the wretched condition of the oppressed."

The Sojourners community, which grew out of a group of dissidents at Trinity Evangelical Seminary in Illinois who had published the radical journal *Post-American,* made its home in Columbia Heights, the "riot corridor" of Washington, D.C. One of ten such radical groups loosely allied in an affiliation called the Community of Communities, the Sojourners community grew in the first year from fifteen adults to a total of fifty people, including children. They renovated several run-down dwellings into extended-family households, where both incomes and chores were shared. In 1979, when I first visited the Sojourners, each person in the community received only $15 a month in spending money from the central fund into which they pooled their incomes. The rest of the money, after minimal allocations for food and housing, went into various community projects. Members of the community opened day-care, tenant-organizing, and food co-op facilities in the single worst housing project in the city. The office of *Sojourners* magazine was set up near Washington's porno corridor of "adult" bookstores, where limos slid up briefly to the curb and prostitutes displayed their wares.

Similarly, the Jubilee Fellowship of Philadelphia, publishers of *The Other Side,* settled in the dilapidated Germantown section of the city. Explaining his voluntary abandonment of the American dream of upward mobility, editor John Alexander wrote, "God hates our lofty self-confidence, our commitment to success. What he's telling us is that he wants us to be toilet cleaners. The world doesn't need more big shots, but more servants like our Lord, more footwashers, more broken people who will clean up the human ruin the big shots leave behind."

The Sojourners were, in fact, no more optimistic about the redeeming powers of culture than the old Princetonites. And they, too, regarded themselves as biblical conservatives. They found that the power of culture to enslave had become even greater with the growth of a technological environment. They felt that the individual American's sense of covenant—of sacred alliance—with neighbors, with the earth, and with God had been lost. And they felt that the evangelical mandate for stewardship, taken from the book of Genesis, when God bade humans to have dominion over the earth, had been abused by fundamentalists. For radical as well as many moderate evangelicals, that mandate meant cultivation and conservation of the natural world rather than manipulation or exploitation of the world's resources. For these evangelicals, the stewardship mandate implied a kind of spiritual ecology.

Embracing the theology of Jacques Ellul, for whom technological society was the modern Babylon, the Sojourners sought to smash the idols and illusions of contemporary culture—the new Mammon of consumerism, the new Baal of military might, the new golden calf of greed. Sometimes that mission simply meant tracking down absentee slumlords, sometimes pursuing the purveyors of nuclear weapons. And sometimes it meant confronting Christians whom they felt had become infused with the spirit of the age: liberal Protestants as well as conservative evangelicals.

Sojourners was the only major evangelical publication that did not endorse Jimmy Carter in the 1976 election. But the magazine reported regularly on the excesses of the religious right. In the April 1976 issue, an article entitled "The Plan to Save America: A Disclosure of an Alarming Initiative by the Evangelical Far Right" revealed the grand scale of conservative Christian ambitions, including the political underpinnings of Bill Bright's Christian embassy. The article was extremely embarrassing to Bright. Eventually the embassy was shut down, the building sold to the government of Oman.

Even so, the Sojourners, with their emphasis on biblical imperatives and the decadence of modern culture, sometimes seemed closer to old-time fundamentalists than to mainstream Protestants. Jim Wallis would start feeling "prophetic," he told me, when, as guest speaker at a liberal church, he would walk past a cloakroom full of fur coats on his way to the pulpit. By the time he reached the pulpit, he was ready to talk about Cadillacs getting through the eye of the needle. He was the untonsured avatar of a fourteenth-century Fraticello, a heretical friar preaching poverty to the Benedictine abbots who had accumulated the wealth and power of princes.

Because of their positions on such issues as wealth and sexual morality, the Sojourners remained outside the liberal consensus. Social activists like the Reverend Bob Davidson of West Park Presbyterian Church in Manhattan found the group's views on morality repressive. Said Davidson, otherwise an admirer and ally, "In personal morality they are more traditional, more captive to the culture than the faith. They rely too heavily on scripture—if the bible didn't say it, it can't be right."

Most controversial to liberals was the Sojourners' disapproval of sex outside of marriage. Along with the group's adoption of voluntary poverty, it implied a self-denial that many Christians would find hard to practice. When I asked Barbara Tamales, who is Jim Wallis's sister, what would happen if someone in the community disagreed with the general consensus on sexual morality, she replied that those kinds of problems came up often in group discussions. "In our household," she said, "a woman has been romantically involved with a man outside the community, so we've talked about it a lot. It's not that we have an absolute moral code; all our decisions are shared, and we feel we can negotiate on individual cases." In that particular case, the woman eventually left the community, her loyalties torn. She married the man in question, and they joined the community as a couple.

Because Sojourners tended to take such uncompromising, prophetic stances on most issues, the magazine seldom reflected the difficulties involved in belonging to an intense, sacrificial Christian community—the bickering, the burn out, the disillusionment. Typically, *Sojourners* would focus on issues like torture in El Salvador while *The Other Side* would devote a special issue to the pros and cons of Christian communities. In the April 1982 issue of *The Other Side*, a former member of a Christian community described the stifling of personal needs and ambitions that ultimately caused her to choose a more individual form of worship: "Little time was available for personal reflection in the accelerated pace of our community. When you live with anywhere from twelve to twenty-five people, work full-time in an outside job, dash from meeting to meeting, and lead worship and other music programs, the years escape quickly."

The Sojourners community itself had undergone a number of transformations, as members dropped out and others joined. Wallis described those phases as prophetic, pastoral, and contemplative. In the prophetic phase, he said, "we were young, single, and intense. It was not really a community," although "there was a lot of bickering about the ideal form of community." In the pastoral phase, "we really became a church, and there was a nurturing of relationships within the community." And in the current contemporary phase, "there is more emphasis on prayer and thought." And more emphasis on privacy. The community has been broken down into smaller living units, and some families live alone. Wallis stressed, however, that all three phases are necessary in the life of a Christian community: "If it's all action, you burn out. If you spend all your time loving one another, you go around in circles. If you spend all your time praying, you don't know what to pray for."

The problems of women in such communities were particularly troublesome. Because the Sojourners community had been started by male seminarians, the role of women in the group at first tended to be secondary, despite the recognition of the problem by the men as well as the women. And on an issue like abortion, the Sojourners eventually took a pro-life position that angered a number of evangelical as well as secular feminists. For several years they remained neutral as part of their profeminist stance, but in 1980 the editors devoted an entire issue of the magazine to a pro-life prolegomena. Setting out to wrest the issue from the ideological agenda of the New Right, they placed it in a larger context of life-and-death issues involving the peace movement and opposition to capital punishment. Cathy Stentzel, a member of the community, wrote of her own conversion from a pro-abortion to pro-life stance as part of her own commitment to nonviolence: "I am wholeheartedly in support of the Equal Rights Amendment. Feminists who use a pro-choice position on abortion as a litmus test for membership in the women's movement must re-examine that position. There have been almost seven million abortions in this country since 1973. As a woman and as a Christian I do not want to be identified with that measure of liberation."

Daniel Berrigan, the Catholic peace activist, examined the issue from the point of view of his antiwar activities and his work with cancer patients at St. Rose's hospital in New York City: "So I go from the Pentagon and being arrested there, to the cancer hospital, and then I think of abortion clinics, and I see an 'interlocking directorate' of death that binds the whole culture; that is, an unspoken agreement that we will solve our problems by killing people in various ways, a declaration that certain people are expendable, outside the pale. . . ."

The Sojourners, for all their radical austerity, were not voices in the wilderness. Surprisingly, Jim Wallis had been chosen by *Time* magazine in 1979 as one of its list of "50 Faces for America's Future." Although the loosely affiliated network of radical Christian communities known as the Community of Communities was hardly gaining members at the rate of the booming conservative churches, the influence exerted by these radical groups on the world of evangelicalism was disproportionate to their numbers. The unrelenting earnestness of *Sojourners* magazine was parodied by *The Wittenberg Door,* a kind of evangelical *National Lampoon,* in a mock-up issue called *Sobouring* that featured such articles as "Here's Justice America" and "The Politics of Santa." However, evangelical writer Richard Quebedeaux asserted that *Sojourners* had replaced *Christianity and Crisis* as the most influential magazine on the Christian left. For many evangelicals, the Sojourners community had become the exemplary city on the hill that Christ had spoken of in the Beatitudes.

If the Great Reversal early in the century had set fundamentalists at odds with social reformers, the second Great Reversal in the sixties had turned many moderate evangelicals as well as liberal Protestants toward the causes of peace and social justice.

In 1947, a number of young evangelical leaders who were contemporaries and, in some cases, colleagues of Billy Graham had attempted to counter the isolationist and anti-intellectual tendencies of fundamentalism by steering evangelicals back toward the mainstream of American cultural and religious life. Evangelical theologian Carl F. H. Henry expressed a concern that evangelicals, in their fervor to differentiate themselves from their more liberal brethren, had opted out of social and political issues. In his book *The Uneasy Conscience of Fundamentalism,* he suggested that evangelicals had been induced by the fundamentalists in their midst to stress evangelistic over humanitarian missions. Said Henry, paving the way for social involvement by Moral Majority theocrats as well as moderate evangelicals, "Though the modern crisis is not basically political, economic or social—fundamentally it is religious—yet evangelicalism must be armed to declare the implications of its proposed religious solution for the politico-economic and sociological context of modern life."

In 1973, Henry joined a number of other elder evangelical statesmen for a summit conference on social issues. The resulting Chicago Declaration of Evangelical Social Concern was a confession of evangelical complicity in problems of racism, sexism, militarism, and economic injustice. The Declaration articulated a grave if vague concern over the growing gap between poor and prosperous nations: "Before God and a billion hungry neighbors, we must rethink our values regarding our present standard of living and promote more just acquisition and distribution of the world's resources."

This evangelical movement toward social concern paralleled a similar pattern within ecumenical Protestant groups that had not yet been swept up into the social concerns of the World Council of Churches. In the spring of 1973, a group of religious-retreat directors, gathered for an annual fellowship at the site of a restored Shaker village near Lexington, Kentucky, turned their religious discussions toward a "global perspective," concluding that further consideration of such issues was needed. During a follow-up meeting at the Yokefellow Institute in Richmond, Indiana, participants agreed on a common pledge that came to be known as the Shakertown Pledge, advocating practices of "creative simplicity," in keeping with the Simple Living movement that was growing within mainstream Protestant denominations.

The Shakertown Pledge, calling for a "more just global society in which all people have full access to the needed resources for their physical, emotional, intellectual, and spiritual growth," was largely a middle-class manifesto, since its stance of divestiture and scaling down implied a prior heedless prosperity. Shakertown participant Adam Daniel Finnerty's *No More Plastic Jesus: Global Justice and Christian Lifestyle,* published in 1977, was not actually an attack on the idolatry of dashboard relics but on complacent Christians and churches who consumed the glutton's share of world resources. Like the secular small-planet movement, the Christian Simple Living movement focused on the conscience of the prosperous, whose rejection of kitchen conveniences and substitution of soybeans for steak presumably would mean a significant step toward alleviating Third World poverty.

No More Plastic Jesus captured the growing sense of unease with prosperity felt by a number of Christians. But for many evangelicals, the pledge was neither Christian enough nor specific enough. The concern of conscience-stricken evangelicals was often expressed in more urgent and more biblical terms. In 1977, Ronald J. Sider, a professor of theology at Eastern Baptist Theological Seminary who headed a group called Evangelicals for Social Action, which grew in part from conferences and workshops on social issues that followed up the Chicago Declaration of 1973, published the influential *Rich Christians in an Age of Hunger: A Biblical Study.* Applying the apocalyptic urgency of such Armageddonists as Hal Lindsey to the problem of world hunger, Sider reminded his readers that "Famine is alive and well on planet earth," and that countries whose populations faced starvation might be tempted to try nuclear blackmail against well-fed nations. Sider attempted to demonstrate to his presumably middle-class readers the kind of grinding poverty faced by the multitudes of the Third World, contrasting the consumption of resources in America to that of underdeveloped nations. Citing God's apparent bias toward the poor, as revealed in the Scriptures, Sider concluded that "Present economic relationships in the worldwide body of Christ are unbiblical, sinful, a hindrance to evangelism and a desecration of the body and blood of Jesus Christ." Far from being a measure of God's blessing, accumulated wealth was an abomination; it brought indifference to God and to the poor:

Come now, ye rich men, weep and howl for your miseries that shall come upon you.

Your riches are corrupted, and your garments are moth-eaten.

Your gold and silver is cankered; and the rust of them shall be a witness against you, and shall eat your flesh as it were fire.

If Christian entrepreneurs claimed to be practicing a kind of biblical capitalism, based on the parable of the talents, Sider was advocating another kind of biblical economics, based on the kind of radical banking described by Jesus: *Give to him that asketh thee, and from him that would borrow of thee turn not thou away.* Like Finnerty, Sider proposed a kind of small-is-beautiful Christianity, with prosperous Christians adopting a simpler, scaled-down lifestyle. Sider, however, outlined a specific plan for immediate and fairly radical divestiture, based on a "graduated" tithe. Rather than the traditional straight 10 percent tithe of one's earnings, Christians would donate an increasing percentage of all their earnings over the absolute minimum required to survive. Thus a family with an income of $8,000 would give $800, while a family earning $26,000 would give $11,150. By 1980, such views were almost commonplace, in theory if not in practice. That year, members of the World Evangelical Fellowship published a rather general manifesto on the subject called *An Evangelical Commitment to Simple Lifestyle.*

As an example of the changing patterns of Christian fellowship, Sider described the transformation of the Gospel Temple in Philadelphia, a thriving pentecostal church that jettisoned all its activities except the Sunday morning worship service, dividing its huge congregation into small home-meeting groups. Tithes were channeled into mission activities rather than building funds. Ironically, this emphasis on small, intimate groups led to rapid growth in church membership, and home-meeting groups had to be subdivided as soon as they reached twenty-five persons.

Gospel Temple was one of many churches whose members began to emphasize fellowship and social service over bigger sanctuaries and better facilities. Members of my own church back home, who were already outgrowing their new sanctuary, decided to postpone constructing a larger building. Instead, they decided to concentrate more on charity and missionary work and on social programs for the community.

Clearly, moderate and radical evangelicals agreed that wealth was an issue. Where they differed was on the measure of divestiture required. For moderates, souped-up personal and institutional charity was sufficient. For radicals, the institutions themselves were the problem. But if radical and moderate evangelicals frequently disagreed on priorities, they at least agreed in theory on the need for commitment to social justice. Consequently, the Sojourners and other radical groups sometimes found themselves with some rather unlikely evangelical allies. One of the strangest and strongest of such alliances was between the Sojourners and Republican Senator Mark Hatfield. In the late seventies, Hatfield, a devout evangelical and former boy-wonder governor of Oregon, was fast becoming one of the most powerful Republicans in the Senate. He was the heir apparent to Milton Young, the ranking Republican on the Senate Appropriations Committee, and already the ranking member of the Energy and Natural Resources Committee. On bread-and-butter issues, he voted as a typical Republican. But on the matter of armaments, he was willing to become a pariah for peace, sometimes casting a lone vote against military appropriations.

When I first met Jim Wallis and the Sojourners, on a bright, cold December day in 1979, they were demonstrating on the steps of the Capitol as members of Congress hurried by. With a kind of quixotic innocence born of faith and the sixties, they were trying to muster support for Hatfield's moratorium amendment to the SALT II treaty that called for a freeze on the building and proliferation of nuclear weapons. They had been joined by the Fisherfolk, a radical Episcopalian community from Colorado who specialize in drama and storytelling.

As the Sojourners brandished banners that included a topsy-turvy flag emblazoned Disarm and Live, the Fisherfolk performed a playful skit satirizing senators Gary Hart, Howard Baker, Frank Church, and Henry Jackson for their various equivocations on the arms race. Hatfield appeared on the steps, glinting with the steel-gray patina of authority amid the brightly-costumed Fisherfolk and sensibly attired Sojourners. Hatfield, who called himself a "radical peacenik," told his small crowd of supporters and a smattering of curious tourists, "The apostolic church infiltrated the institutions of Rome. I'm very hopeful you'll have that kind of impact today."

Hatfield had been affiliated with the Sojourners since 1971, when the first issue of the magazine (then called the *Post-American*) appeared. What Hatfield and the Sojourners had in common were their evangelical roots and an opposition to the Vietnam War. In his book, *Between a Rock and a Hard Place,* Hatfield wrote of the Sojourners, "Here was a group of committed evangelicals articulating the imperatives of the Gospel for our time in a compelling biblical fashion." Their message, as Hatfield interpreted it, was a critique of established churches as well as political institutions: "Our church was encultured, and our message was frequently far more an echoing of society's dominant values rather than a clear proclamation of the whole Gospel." Because so many evangelicals had supported Richard Nixon and the Vietnam War, Hatfield felt, as did the Sojourners, that the church was being used as a "tool of national self-righteousness."

Civil religion, of the God-bless-America kind, he said, "enshrines our political order. . . . We are given a sense of righteous mission to the world." In an interview, he told me that he felt that civil religion, "which pounds the drums and blows the bugles, leads to the dangerous political attitude that God is ratifying everything the United States does. I reject the idea of a Christian political platform." Conservative evangelicals, he felt, "have not understood the notion of corporate sin, that we are accountable as individuals for what the state does." Yet Hatfield himself had merged moral and political issues with his freeze amendment. And it seemed that he sometimes diluted his effectiveness in both realms—the moral and political. His conscience remained torn between Christ and Caesar, as he continued to vote right on most economic matters and left on most military issues.

I was laughing at myself, at twenty years of a ministry which had become, without my realizing it, a ministry of liberal sophistication. An attempted negation of Jesus, of human engineering, of riding the coattails of Caesar, of playing on his ballpark, by his rules, and with his ball, of looking to government to make and verify and authenticate our morality, of worshiping at the shrine of enlightenment and academia, of making an idol of the Supreme Court, a theology of law and order, and of denying not only the Faith I professed to hold but my history and my people. . . .

Will Campbell

Another unlikely ally of the young radical evangelicals who wanted to change Christianity from an institution to a force was a former Southern Baptist preacher from Mississippi named Will Campbell, a "solitary country-evangelist Quixote" and country singer who operated a kind of guerrilla ministry from his small, rock-ridden farm near Nashville, Tennessee. Campbell, who grew up on a farm in the Mississippi Delta, returned home from Yale Divinity School in the fifties to become a leader in the civil rights movement, joining with Martin Luther King, Jr., in the formation of the Southern Christian Leadership Conference. Campbell, however, was becoming disillusioned with the institutions of church and government as means of change, and with liberal white Northerners as redeemers of Southern transgressions. He had come to see redneck racists as victims as well as perpetrators of an inequitable economic system, and he began to minister to Ku Klux Klanners as well as civil rights activists. As he explained it in his book *Brother to a Dragonfly,* "The romance of 'black and white together, we shall overcome' was wearing thin and more and more blacks were telling us that if we wanted to do something in race relations maybe we should go and work with our own people." Campbell's Calvinistic pessimism was tempered by a doctrine of unconditional grace: "Black, white, Kluxer, preacher, banker, Teamster, murderer, chairman of General Motors, head of the Ford Foundation—we are all bastards, but God loves us anyway."

Like Jacques Ellul, Campbell found the real tyranny in "technique": "We are the prisoners of the technological concentration camp of our own doing. . . ." With a small company of his fellow

Christian irregulars, the Committee of Southern Churchmen, an affiliation revived from the ashes of the Reinhold-Niebuhr-inspired Fellowship of Southern Churchmen, Campbell began to advocate a kind of primitive, ad hoc Christianity: "pulpitless, roofless, unpropertied, uncodified, but catholic in what could be considered the fullest sense." Like the members of the original Fellowship that had flourished in the thirties, Campbell and his committee spoke of a "hidden" church—a church that existed wherever the faithful gathered. Institutions, including the church, actually impeded the practice of faith: "What institutions actually institute, in the end, is inhumanity, by advancing the illusion that form is substance, the means are the doing, doing is being, procedure is redemption—and so they can only further dehumanize the relationships between those they were instituted to reconcile."

Campbell, who had come to resemble an Amish elder, with his broad-brimmed black hat clamped down over a wispily fringed bald pate, operated a spontaneous, have-guitar-will-travel ministry that interrupted his farming chores, performing marriages for country singers, comforting Kluxers in trouble, speaking to divinity students from Vanderbilt, witnessing to intransigent bureaucrats and Episcopal priests on retreat.

In *Katallagete* ("Be reconciled"), the journal of the Committee of Southern Churchmen, Campbell began to take on the "Astrodome Isaiahs" of evangelism. In 1971, Campbell published an open letter to Billy Graham, accusing Graham of becoming a captive "court prophet" to Richard Nixon and his regime: "We believe that the only way you, or any of us, can *minister* to the White House or the Pentagon is in the tradition of Micaiah, son of Imlah." As for the massive crusades led by Graham, Campbell charged that "Politics and culture are the 'Christ' for all crusades. . . . There can be no 'decisions' for Christ in crusades. There can only be *enlistments* by individuals, institutions, structures, and movements into ideological causes, into the political maneuverings which are a fundamental part of the suffering, slavery, and death in our, and every, civilization."

Campbell, a full-fledged "character," had become such a wise, lovable, carrying-on Southern curmudgeon that he inspired the cartoonist Doug Marlette to add the eccentric preacher Will B. Dunne to the cast of rednecks in his strip "Kudzu." In one installment, the preacher stands at a pulpit, nearly paralyzed by doubt and humility, wondering, "Who am I to preach to these people?" His interior monologue continues, "If I just had a sign to ease my doubt/ . . . A sign to buoy my faith! . . ." and so on, until a bolt of lightning strikes, leaving the hapless preacher holding a "No Parking" sign.

Despite such whimsies, Campbell was as much a Bible-thumping fundamentalist as Graham had ever been, full of the woe wrought by an awareness of the ornery, fallen nature of men and women and their institutions. But Campbell had been almost as stunned as St. Paul had been on the road to Damascus by the forgiving grace of God, by a grace that was offered to the unworthiest of sinners, to the lowliest of sufferers, to all the racists and persecutors and whores and tax collectors and victims of the earth. For Campbell, as for most radical evangelicals, it was a recognition of this unconditional grace that would bring about revolution—revolution in the human heart, if not in the body politic.

Conclusion

Brother Earl Bigg grew so powerful that he was sure that by 1984, instead of Big Brother watching everyone, everyone would be watching Brother Bigg. That was the difference between godless totalitarianism and Christian capitalism. Brother Bigg was dissatisfied, however, with the laggardly pace of moral reform in America; it was barely outstripping the creeping secular humanism that was corrupting the minds of children and politicians. Brother Bigg decided to back a baseball-player-turned-staunch-conservative for U.S. senator. Brother Bigg coached the aging Republican athlete in his new role, and the former outfielder shagged questions from reporters as skillfully as he had once caught flies on the run. Brother Bigg looked forward to hobnobbing with the Big Boys in the Big Time, and wielding great influence in the government. But once the baseball player took office, he no longer needed Brother Bigg. Brother Bigg returned to his station by the sea and began to preach about corruption in high places.

During the stormy winter of 1980–81, as Ronald Reagan's legions sacked Washington, D.C., and Democrats prepared for an extended siege by cold warriors, cowboy industrialists, and Christian soldiers intent on carrying out a scorched-earth policy, it seemed that Reagan had been elected ruler of a Christianized republic whose central rituals were the business lunch and the pregame prayer, whose economic policies were directed by political action committees, and whose sins were washed away by the sweat and tears of power-hungry preachers. It was open season on liberals, as lame ducks and doves flew South. Conservative Christians looked forward to a born-again nation of prayerful schools, plentiful armaments, and chastened humanists.

But two years later, after the Ninety-seventh Congress had adjourned for its long winter nap, the cause of Christian culture had not made many practical gains. Republicans had lost twenty-six seats in the House of Representatives as a result of the November 1982 elections, and the toll was particularly high among New Right ideologues. Among the conservatives who fell from grace were Moral Majority's Albert Lee Smith in Alabama and the entire Congressional Club slate supported by Jesse Helms in North Carolina. The ERA had been defeated, but the new Arkansas statute granting creationism equal billing with evolution in science classrooms had been overturned, and efforts to undermine Supreme Court decisions protecting civil rights and civil liberties—particularly those on abortion and school prayer—had been stymied in Congress. In Mount Diablo, California, *Ms* magazine had been removed from the school library shelves and stashed behind the counter, but in Austin, Texas, Mel and Norma Gabler, the nation's most prominent book-banners, were given just six minutes of testimony on proposed school textbooks; the previous year they had carried on for three and a half hours. The omnibus Family Protection Act had made little headway, although Reagan had managed to pare federal funding to the primary target of the bill—the Legal Services Corporation.

It had begun to appear as though the coalition between the religious right and the secular right was more a marriage of convenience than a match of long-term compatibility. Reagan had left the frumpy moral agenda of the religious right to stew in the kitchen while he squired his more glamorous economic programs around town. He had flouted Jerry Falwell in appointing Sandra Day

O'Connor to the Supreme Court, and he had flinched in the controversy over tax-exempt status for segregated Christian schools. Institutions like Bob Jones University were having to pay taxes just like corporations and private citizens.

Moreover, there was evidence not only that the overall viewing audience for the Super Savers of the Electronic Kingdom had been exaggerated but that it was actually beginning to wane. The emotional tide of the nation had begun to turn away from the "far righteous," as one writer called them, and the promise of economic recovery did not offer much opportunity for significant advances. Even Jesse Helms, the great white political hope of conservative Christians, could hardly hold the fort alone, much less charge the citadel.

Early in 1984, however, as Ronald Reagan prepared to announce his run for re-election, his speechwriters dusted off their Bibles in preparation for a religious crusade. Addressing the convened members of the National Association of Evangelicals in Columbus, Ohio, on the morning after the official declaration of his candidacy, Reagan asserted that during his presidency the nation had experienced a spiritual as well as economic renewal. America, he said, was recovering from the sinful excesses of governmental and sexual promiscuity that had been encouraged by liberals during the seventies: "The American people decided to put a stop to that long decline, and today our country is seeing a rebirth of freedom and faith —a great national renewal." News photographers snapped away as Reagan bowed his head and tensed his face in prayer.

Subsequently, setting aside his pretensions to humility, the President quoted a line of dialogue from the film *Chariots of Fire,* implying a parallel between Olympic runner Eric Lydell's race for divine glory and his own run for office: "God made me for a purpose, and I will run for His pleasure."

Reagan soon established abortion and school prayer as the cornerstones of his early re-election campaign. It seemed that he was now stumping for God rather than Reaganomics. In case anyone had missed the point, he co-authored a book called *Abortion and the Conscience of a Nation,* scheduled to be published in May 1984 by Thomas Nelson, the nation's leading publisher of Bibles.

In his 1984 State of the Union address, Reagan demanded of Congress, "If you can begin your day with a member of the clergy standing right here to lead you in prayer, then why can't freedom to acknowledge God be enjoyed again by children in every school-room across this land?" And in March 1984, when Senator Howard Baker, Jr., of Tennessee was encountering difficulty in mustering enough votes to pass his constitutional amendment permitting offi-cially sanctioned prayer in public schools, Reagan telephoned unde-cided legislators, using recollections of his own childhood school experiences as evidence that the young need not feel stigmatized by classroom prayers.

House Speaker Tip O'Neill responded with a certain incredulity to this outpouring of religious sentiment: "Here's a man who doesn't go to church and he talks about prayer." The last time Reagan had attended services in the capital was on June 26, 1983. Since his inauguration, he had attended church services a total of nine times, including on Inauguration Day. O'Neill might also have mentioned Reagan's negligible contributions to churches and charities, as reported to the IRS on his income tax returns.

Reagan's highly publicized protestations of faith, which put Jimmy Carter and Jesse Jackson to shame, reminded me of the New Testament teachings of Christ on the subject of public prayer and hypocrisy. In the book of Matthew, chapter three, Jesus cautions his disciples, "And when thou prayest, thou shalt not be as the hypo-crites are: for they love to pray standing in the synagogues and in the corners of the streets, that they may be seen of men . . . But thou, when thou prayest, enter into thy closet, and when thou has shut thy door, pray to thy Father which is in secret. . . ."

THE PEACE REVIVAL

Meanwhile, as conservative evangelicals continued to push the pop-ular issues of abortion and school prayer, moderate and radical evangelicals were pushing another Christian concern: peace. A little more than two years after the revivalist ruckus of Washington for Jesus and nearly two and a half years after the Sojourners' quiet remonstrations on the steps of the Capitol, there was another public showing forth of faith and dissent that seemed to eclipse both events. On June 12, 1982, some 800,000 demonstrators assembled on the streets of Manhattan in support of the second United Nations Special Session on Disarmament. Far more ecumenical than WFJ and far more visible than the Sojourners' demonstration, the New York peace march, composed of both secular and religious groups—orating preachers, concerned scientists, pacifist priests, socially responsible physicians, activist architects, antinuke artists, visionary puppeteers, a hundred-year-old Hopi shaman—signaled a fear of nuclear war in America that counterbalanced the premillennialist longing for Armageddon.

The Sojourners and such groups as the Fellowship of Reconciliation, an ecumenical peace group from Nyack, New York, that had been one of the principal organizers of the June 12 march, had become participants in a scattered, diverse, nationwide peace movement that affected evangelical as well as liberal mainstream churches. Nuclear weapons had become an issue with as much emotional impact for evangelicals as the endangered nuclear family. And peace, if not economic and social justice, was an issue on which liberal Protestants and moderate evangelicals could confront fundamentalists with biblical authority.

Even as Reagan was calling for a step-up in defense spending, churches across the country began to organize conferences and study groups on the subject of arms control and disarmament. A lively middle-aged Methodist woman from Iowa whom I met at a festival organized to commemorate Charles Grandison Finney, the great nineteenth-century revival preacher, told me that the peace study group that she had helped to organize in her church was part of a network of such groups across the Midwest. A packet of material entitled *The Nuclear Challenge to Christian Conscience: A Study Guide for Churches,* put together by the Sojourners for the use of such groups, sold 60,000 copies in less than a year, and Jim Wallis was approached by a major publisher interested in distributing the Sojourners' study. A similar publication from the ecumenical Institute for Peace and Justice in St. Louis had sold 30,000 copies by May 1983. And between September 1982 and May 1983, more than 50,000 copies of the Episcopal church's antiwar document *To Make Peace* were distributed around the country.

Even traditionally conservative evangelical groups were calling for new initiatives on controlling the arms race. The theme of the 1982 annual convention of the National Association of Evangelicals echoed the familiar conservative battle cry "Save the Family," and a number of speakers during the convention praised the Reagan administration for its social and economic policies. But delegates also voted unanimously to urge "our national leaders to rededicate their efforts to obtain a meaningful arms control agreement that will scale down the nuclear arms race." In the summer of 1973, a Gallup survey conducted for the NAE revealed that 60 percent of the evangelicals who were queried supported the idea of a nuclear arms freeze.

According to the Reverend John Perkins, chairman of the NAE's social action commission, the 1982 delegates had been influenced by two different factors in their decision to confront the administration over the arms control issue. First was simply the concern they shared with many Americans about the development of alarming new weapons systems and about the failure of past initiatives at arms control. Second and perhaps more important was the support for arms control expressed by the most famous evangelical of all, the former sanctifier of Richard Nixon, the Super Saver who, as a gangling young revivalist, had thrilled William Randolph Hearst by declaring that the world was divided into two armed camps: "On the one side, we see communism. On the other, we see Western culture, with its foundation in the Bible, the word of God. . . . Communism, on the other hand, has declared war against God, against Christ, against the Bible."

THE PILGRIMAGE OF BILLY GRAHAM

Billy Graham had always been drawn like a taxman to men of commerce and power. As his biographer Marshall Frady described it, Graham's "beguilement over the years with sirens singing in the national empyrean of power, his own gradual Assumption up into those high altitudes through Hearst and Luce and Eisenhower and Johnson, reached its apogee with the presidency of Richard Nixon." And as Nixon fell, so fell Graham. Tainted by the unholy revelations of the White House tapes, his innocence and certitude finally breached, he had retreated to the more limited limelight of his stadium crusades.

Initially, Graham refused to face the implications of Nixon's crimes against decency. He told Marshall Frady that Nixon "took all those sleeping pills that would give him a low in the morning and a high in the evening. . . . My conclusion is that it was just all those sleeping pills, they just let a demon-power come in and play over him. . . ." The fault, then, as Frady expressed it, was "not in Nixon, but in the dark stars and dark winds of the otherworld." Chemical and demonic intervention, not power, was the problem. Yet Graham's discovery of unexpected corruptibility in high places led to his withdrawal from the political arena and eventually to a controversial pilgrimage in quest of peace. During his post-Watergate travels around the world, from Auschwitz to Bangladesh and Eastern Europe, Graham came to a different understanding of his own mission as well as that of America.

The first glimmerings of that shift in priorities came in a 1979 interview printed in *Sojourners* magazine. Titled "A Change of Heart," the interview revealed Graham's growing if still vague concern with such global issues as hunger and the threat of war. Graham began to formulate his own coda to the SALT agreements which he called SALT X, calling for the destruction of all nuclear weapons. It seemed that slowly he was coming to a broader vision of human fallibility, of the social evils—poverty, warmongering—that were the collective sins of mankind. (It was a vision that did not coincide with that of Jerry Falwell, as he was always careful to point out. Graham told *Newsweek*, when asked what he thought of Falwell, "I've met Mr. Falwell once, for a minute at a prayer breakfast, and I've talked to him once, I think, by phone. I don't know what Falwell's following is, but I don't think that the Moral Majority would represent more than 10 percent of the evangelicals in America.") Even more slowly, Graham was coming to a broader vision of the responsibility for those collective sins. Not even a boatload of sleeping pills and demons could account for the suffering and shortcomings he saw around him.

Billy Graham had come to epitomize contemporary evangelicalism at its strongest and weakest, precariously balanced between Christ and culture, between peace and the principalities and powers. In the spring of 1982, he delivered two remarkable orations that epitomized the transformation that was occurring among many evangelicals. The first, at Harvard University, was more a confession than a sermon, and the second, in Moscow, was more a beatitude than a jeremiad.

On April 20, at the beginning of a big stadium-by-stadium New England crusade, his first since 1964, Graham took the podium for an hour at Harvard's Kennedy School of Government, awed, he said, by the aura of learning that surrounded him, all those Ph.D.'s and whatnot. Even dressed in a dark, conservative suit that seemed a bit somber for early spring (he had long since muted his taste for landing-strip ties and bright-colored socks), he felt outclassed, like the man who had entered a mule in the Kentucky Derby. Harvard, after all, was the pinnacle of liberal enlightenment, the hothouse of the Northeastern intellectual establishment, located all the way across the wilderness of middle America from the Know-Nothing, antiegghead, creation-believing, Bible-armed fortresses of fundamentalism that had nurtured him. Graham himself, who probably owned more honorary diplomas than Walter Cronkite or the late Eubie Blake, habitually listed only two alma maters on his résumé —the Florida Bible Institute and Wheaton College in Illinois.

In his ingenuousness, Graham seemed to forget that under Harvard's mythic ivy vines was a solid sacred foundation, that Harvard had once had been ruled by Puritan divines, including both Cotton and Increase Mather, those dour and learned theocrats. The Kennedy School, its dean reminded Graham, was just down the road from the spot where Jonathan Edwards had delivered that most chilling of all fire-and-brimstone texts, "Sinners in the Hands of an Angry God."

Graham's courtly, gee-whiz presence seemed a reminder that it was in the cold, rocky soil of New England that the notion of America as God's country first took root, that it was primarily from the Puritan devotion to individual, direct congress with God that both the radical and conservative strains of evangelicalism had grown. Moreover, the crowds that had been lined up by Graham's advance team to fill the stadiums for his crusade were evidence of surprising evangelical strength in the Northeast.

Despite New England's dismal church-attendance statistics (70 percent of the 13 million souls in the region were considered either "unchurched" or "inactive Christians"), evangelical churches were thriving there amid the declining glories of Congregationalism. Of the 250 or so new churches established in New England in the past decade, some 91 percent were designated fundamentalist or evangelical. All this in the region that was also a stronghold of Roman Catholicism and the center of Unitarian Universalism. As Richard Lovelace, a church historian at the evangelical Gordon-Conwell Seminary, told a *Newsweek* reporter, mainstream Protestants had been deeply affected by "the popularity of the evangelicals. It's like now, when everybody is buying Japanese cars, Detroit has to ask, 'What are they doing that we're not?'" Harvey Cox, Harvard's best known liberal theologian, always at the forefront of new religious developments, had offered a course on evangelicalism and social action the previous semester, and there were plans to establish an evangelical chair at Harvard Divinity School, perhaps to be named after Graham. (In his new book *Religion in the Secular City,* Cox compared fundamentalism and liberation theology, concluding that both movements, which had evolved on the periphery of mainstream cultural and religious life, were emerging as powerful forces. Fundamentalism, however, Cox found to be too rigid and intolerant to offer a new vision to a pluralistic society.)

But Graham had not come to Harvard to debate theology or to reveal his secrets of soul-winning; he had come to talk about his own "pilgrimage" and what he had learned from his mistakes. Said Graham, recalling his early days as a tent-rattling evangelist, "I often spoke on the wonderful little story in the tenth chapter of Luke where Jesus told the story of the good Samaritan, teaching us our social responsibilities. From the very beginning, I felt that if I came upon a person who had been beaten and robbed and left for dead that I'd do my best to help him. I also felt that this applied to my relatives and friends and immediate neighbors. But I never thought of it in terms of corporate responsibility. I had no real idea that millions of people throughout the world lived on the knife-edge of starvation and that the teachings of my reference point demanded that I have a responsibility toward them. Later, as I traveled and studied the Bible more, I changed. . . ."

Graham went on from there to talk about the arms race and call for negotiations that would lead to the extinction of nuclear weapons. It was an eloquent speech that drew much acclaim from liberal preachers and theologians. Graham's penchant for name-dropping had undergone a change; he was now telling anecdotes about Oscar Wilde and Blaise Pascal instead of Richard Nixon and Henry Kissinger. But less than a month later, Graham's trip to Moscow to address an international religious conference on nuclear disarmament earned him the disapproval of liberals and conservatives alike. He angered conservatives by glossing over the Soviet regime's treatment of religious dissidents ("I think there is a lot more freedom here than has been given the impression in the United States . . ."), thus becoming a pawn of Soviet propaganda, and he disappointed liberals by not being more specific in his support for nuclear arms negotiation. Jim Wallis criticized Graham in an article in the New York *Times* for his "lack of clarity" on the issue.

Yet Graham's speech from the pulpit of Moscow's Patriarchal Cathedral on May 11 had the powerful ring of prophecy: "Let us call the nations and leaders of our world to repentance. We need to repent as nations and as people over our past failures—the failure to accept each other, the failure to be concerned about the needs of the poor and the starving of the world, the failure to place top priority on peace instead of war. . . ." Even Will Campbell, who had once been Graham's most pointed critic, was encouraged by Graham's new prophetic role. Campbell told reporter Frye Gaillard, "I once accused him of being the court prophet to Richard Nixon. But I have to say he's God's prophet now."

THE PROPHETIC CENTER

If, as Jerry Falwell had claimed, fundamentalists had managed to hijack the jumbo jet of evangelicalism, it appeared that by 1984 the less fanatic passengers on the plane were beginning to reassert control. Instead of flying off to the right, evangelicalism appeared to be moving toward what Robert E. Webber called the "prophetic center," toward churches whose membership included supporters of the Sojourners as well as of Moral Majority. Webber, a professor of theology at Billy Graham's alma mater, Wheaton College, sought to steer a course between the World Council of Churches on the left and the fundamentalist fringe on the right. Said Webber, "The solution to the world's problems does not lie in an economic or political system, nor does it lie in the predominance of America." He called for social activism without the submergence of faith into a civil religion and invited both Moral Majority and the World Council of Churches to "forsake their economic and political alignments and to return to a Christocentric understanding of the church as the presence of Jesus in the world."

Even Falwell himself sometimes appeared to be edging cautiously toward the center. Once the ERA was dead, he declared that Christians should support equal rights for women, and he acknowledged that abortion was permissible in cases where a mother's life was in jeopardy. One day in October 1983, he even found himself hosting Ted Kennedy in Lynchburg. It seems that Kennedy, whose personal life had provided Falwell with steady fodder for his sermons, had inadvertently been sent a Moral Majority membership card inviting him to join the crusade against "ultraliberals such as Ted Kennedy." Hearing of the blunder, Moral Majority spokesman Cal Thomas sent Kennedy a note telling him that he did not have to give up the card, concluding with a suggestion that Kennedy speak at Falwell's Liberty Baptist College. Kennedy responded positively, and though Falwell, according to Thomas, turned white as a sheet when he was informed about the proceedings, he realized that giving a foe like Kennedy equal time in Lynchburg might improve Moral Majority image.

When Kennedy arrived, he told Falwell's students that a number of people in Washington had been surprised that he accepted the invitation to speak on Falwell's home turf: "They seemed to think that it's easier for a camel to pass through the eye of a needle than for a Kennedy to come to the campus of Liberty Baptist College." Kennedy was received courteously by the students, leading him to acknowledge that his own alma mater, Harvard, had not been so tolerant when Falwell spoke there a few months earlier. Students had shouted out "Nazi!" before Falwell could get out a word.

Falwell was still poised at the crossroads that Frances Fitzgerald had described two years before: "In one direction lay the rugged narrow valleys of the old-time religion, with its absolute truths, its puritanism, and its ferocities, where he could be King of the Outsiders. In the other lay the broad plains where the majority of Americans lived, with all their liberal uncertainties, and where he might have some influence if he joined the general, confusing din."

Falwell, like so many populist heroes before him, had emerged as a leader by playing on the needs and fears of a group of Americans who felt alienated from the mainstream of American life. Recognizing that the concerns of many blue-collar workers, small-property owners, and family-business entrepreneurs were not being met by churches preoccupied with the Third World and politicians sold on *detente,* he had rushed in where liberals feared to tread. Americans needed a focus for their fears, a solution to their unease. Falwell provided both.

As his influence grew, Falwell hoped to inherit the robes of evangelical leadership from Billy Graham, once Graham finally ended his long, winding pilgrimage. *Newsweek's* Kenneth Woodward noted that at one point Falwell flew to Washington, D.C., to meet with evangelical leaders who might have a say in such a succession. Yet until Falwell broadened his appeal, thus endangering his strength with fundamentalists, he could not hope to follow in Billy Graham's footsteps; he didn't have the charisma. Moreover, it was highly unlikely that any single Super Saver could ever rule the world of evangelicalism again; it had grown too diverse, too far-flung.

Evangelicalism was still a house divided against itself. It was a community that was torn between those who were trying to learn how to live the good life, Christian style, surrounded by other Christians in a total Christian culture; those who were trying to return America to some mythical age of God-fearing virtue, bristling with guns and burdened with guilt; and those who were simply trying to live by the light of the gospel, simply and earnestly, one day at a time.

It appeared now that only a moderate center could hold the fragmented world of evangelicalism together. Yet many of the multiministried Super Savers were operating from a position of permanent marginality. They had built their huge Christian complexes on shifting sands, not on solid rock—on a sense of emergency and panic, with letters and TV appeals announcing alternately that Jesus offered success and that Christianity was going out of business. If one believed what Jesus had to say about such matters, those preachers who thrived on storms of fear and swells of pride would inherit the wind, not the earth.

Notes

INTRODUCTION

Epigraph: Quoted by Jim Wallis in *Sojourners* magazine, November 1977.

Prediction of a national religious revival: "Religion in America," *The Gallup Opinion Index,* 1977–78, p. 2.

Description of Carter's conversion and mission work: From James and Marti Hefley, *The Church That Produced a President: The Remarkable Spiritual Roots of Jimmy Carter* (New York: Wyden Books, 1977). Also, from Perry Deane Young, *God's Bullies: Power Politics and Religious Tyranny* (New York: Holt, Rinehart, & Winston, 1982), p. 21.

Carter's speech at Winston-Salem: Quoted by Young in *God's Bullies,* p. 21.

"Most politicians have typically . . .": *Sojourners,* October 1976.

A boon in "being different": Dotson Rader, *Parade,* July 19, 1981.

Benefit for Holovita: Rusty Unger, *Village Voice,* November 27, 1978.

Carter had "surrounded himself": Richard A. Viguerie, *The New Right: We're Ready to Lead,* rev. ed. (Falls Church, Va.: The Viguerie Co., 1981), p. 125.

The Dade County controversy: See *God's Bullies,* pp. 36–54. Fundamentalist hijacking: *The Fundamentalist Phenomenon: The Resurgence of Conservative Christianity,* edited by Jerry Falwell (Garden City, N.Y.: Doubleday/ Galilee, 1981).

Christ and culture: H. Richard Niebuhr, *Christ and Culture* (New York: Harper & Row, 1951).

Age of the superchurch: Falwell, *Fundamentalist Phenomenon,* p. 140.

Mega-sanctuaries: Thomas Trumball Howard, *Christianity Today,* August 17, 1979.

"I'd rather be in Heaven . . .": Rex Humbard, sermon at the NRB convention, January 1981.

Artificial camaraderie: Ralph Keyes, *We the Lonely People* (New York: Harper & Row, 1973).

Christian theme park: Jamie Buckingham, *Jesus World* (Lincoln, Va.: Chosen Books, 1981). Also, *The Wittenburg Door,* June/July 1983.

Attitude of early fundamentalists: George M. Marsden, *Fundamentalism and American Culture: The Shaping of Twentieth-Century Evangelicalism: 1870– 1925* (New York: Oxford University Press, 1980).

Sense of national calling: Robert N. Bellah, "Civil Religion in America," in *American Civil Religion,* edited by Rusell E. Rickey and Donald G. Jones (New York: Harper & Row, 1974), p. 25.

CHAPTER 1. IN DEFENSE OF IGNORANCE

Epigraph: Quoted by Marsden, *Fundamentalism,* p. 130. "the doctrine of persecution . . .": Quoted by Young, *God's Bullies,* p. 183.

Lyman Beecher's warnings: Quoted by Sandra S. Sizer in *Gospel Hymns and Social Religion: The Rhetoric of Nineteenth-Century Revivalism* (Philadelphia: Temple University Press, 1978), p. 63.

Henry Ward Beecher's warning: Quoted by Timothy P. Weber in *Living in the Shadow of the Second Coming: American Premillennialism 1875–1925* (New York: Oxford University Press, 1979).

Barth's analysis of Schleiermacher: Niebuhr, *Christ and Culture,* p. 93.

"The Bible is absolutely infallible . . .": Jerry Falwell, *Listen, America!* (New York: Bantam, 1981), p. 54 (originally published by Doubleday, 1980).

"the city men who had laughed . . ." and "to put Bryan in his place . . .": Quoted by Marsden, *Fundamentalism,* p. 187.

Fundamentalism hardening into political paranoia: See Richard Hofstadter, *Anti-Intellectualism in American Life* (New York: Alfred A. Knopf, 1962), pp. 117–136. Also, *The Paranoid Style in American Politics, and Other Essays* (New York: Alfred A. Knopf, 1963), p. 29.

Ban on school prayers leading to crime: Bill Bright, *Come Help Change Our World* (San Bernardino, Cal.: Campus Crusade for Christ, 1979).

Raids on library shelves: Dena Kleinman, New York *Times,* May 17, 1981.

Solzhenitsyn on humanism: Commencement address, Harvard University, 1978.

Whitehead and Conlan: Quoted by Martin E. Marty, New York *Times*, July 22, 1981.

LaHaye on humanism: Tim LaHaye, *The Battle for the Mind* (Old Tappan, N.J.: Fleming H. Revell, 1980).

The Gablers' crusade: William Martin, *Texas Monthly*, November 1982; Donna Hilts, Washington *Post*, April 19, 1981; Falwell, *Listen*, pp. 180–185.

The Kanawha County book-burning: Curtis Selzer, *The Nation*, November 2, 1974.

Description of the Arkansas "creationism trial": Installments by Reginald Stuart in the New York *Times;* James Gorman, *Discover*, February 1982; Gene Lyons, *Harper's*, April 1982.

Creationism book: Phyllis and Monty Kester, *What's All This Monkey Business?* (Harrison, Ark.: New Leaf Press, 1981).

The ACE program: Kenneth L. Woodward, *Newsweek*, February 28, 1983.

Falwell on education: *Listen*, p. 190.

Falwell at Louisville: Donna Hilts, Washington *Post*, April 19, 1981.

Frances Fitzgerald on Falwell: *New Yorker*, May 18, 1981.

"I want you to know . . .": Quoted by Jere Real, Boston *Phoenix*, August 4, 1981.

CHAPTER 2. THE LORD HAS MANY MANSIONS

Bill Sharp's vision: Robert G. Kaiser and Jon Lowell, New York *Times*, June 21, 1979.

Anita Bryant's crusades: From promotional brochures issued by Anita Bryant Ministries.

Lloyd Tomer's plan: Reported in *Wittenberg Door*, June/July, 1978.

Fisher and Van Koevering: from brochures distributed during the National Religious Broadcasters convention, January 1980.

"Every time a group of Christians . . .": Quoted by Thomas L. Connelly in *Will Campbell and the Soul of the South* (New York: Continuum, 1982), pp. 33–34.

"the age of the Super Church": Falwell, *Fundamentalist Phenomenon*, p. 140.

First Baptist Church of Dallas: William Martin, *Texas Monthly,* September 1979.

"global responsibilities": C. Peter Wagner, *Church Growth and the Whole Gospel: A Biblical Mandate* (San Francisco: Harper & Row, 1981), p. 13.

Social concerns of Protestant leaders: Jeffrey K. Hadden, *The Gathering Storm in the Churches* (Garden City, N.Y.: Doubleday, 1969).

Possibility Thinker's Creed: Quoted by Jan Roorda in *Saturday Evening Post,* April 1978.

"the gloomy cathedrals of Christendom . . .": Quoted by Roorda, ibid.

"We are trying to make a big . . .": Robert Schuller, *Your Church Has Real Possibilities* (Glendale, Cal.: Regal Books, 1974), p. 117.

Hyles's church manual: Quoted by Alfredo S. Lanier, *Chicago* magazine, June 1981.

"The essence of the system . . .": R. H. Tawney, *Religion and the Rise of Capitalism: A Historical Study* (New York: New American Library, 1947). (Originally published by Harcourt, Brace, & World, 1926).

The *Yellow Pages* legal imbroglio: Wayne King, New York *Times,* November 8, 1981.

CHAPTER 3.   THE TOTAL WOMAN VS. THE WHOLE WOMAN

"It is popular for the modern woman . . .": Ella May Miller, *Happiness Is Homemaking* (Harrison, Va.: Choice Books, 1974), p. 11.

Woman as little girl: Helen B. Andelin, *Fascinating Womanhood* (Santa Barbara, Cal.: Pacific Press, 1965).

"all-American Cinderella story": Marabel Morgan, *The Total Woman* (Tappan, N.J.: Fleming H. Revell, 1973), pp. 8, 14, 51–102.

"how to cater to male pornographic fantasies . . .": Andrea Dworkin, *Right-Wing Women* (New York: G. P. Putnam's Sons, 1983), p. 25.

"The Total Woman is in heaven . . .": Morgan, *Total Woman,* p. 105.

"The girls really listened well . . .": Ibid., pp. 250–251.

"happiness merchants": Barbara G. Harrison, *McCall's,* June 1975.

Susan Key and Eve Reborn: Gregory Curtis, *Texas Monthly,* June 1975.

"a new incarnate picture . . .": Judith M. Miles, *The Feminine Principle: A Woman's Discovery of the Key to Total Fulfillment* (St. Louis: Bethany Press, 1975), pp. 51, 151, 44.

"I believe the Bible is truth . . .": Marabel Morgan, *Total Joy* (Old Tappan, N.J.: Fleming H. Revell, 1976), p. 53.

"Only as I practice yielding . . .": Anita Bryant, *Bless This House* (New York: Bantam Books, 1976), pp. 51–52.

"violated my most precious asset . . .": New York *Times,* May 4, 1980.

"gripped with the illusion . . .": Ruth Carter Stapleton, *The Gift of Inner Healing* (Waco, Tex.: Word Books, 1976), p. 7.

"walk into the graveyard . . .": Ibid., pp. 2, 11.

Mary Ann's visualization: Ibid., p. 32.

Stapleton targeted by preachers: Flo Conway and Jim Siegelman, *Holy Terror: The Fundamentalist War on America's Freedoms in Religion, Politics and Our Private Lives* (Garden City, N.Y.: Doubleday, 1982), p. 226.

"Roger and I shared . . .": Jeannie C. Riley, with Jamie Buckingham, *From Harper Valley to the Mountain Top* (New York: Ballantine Books, 1982), pp. 143, 165.

Sense of resignation: Martha Tomhave Blauvelt, "Women and Revivalism," in *Women and Religion in America,* edited by Rosemary Radford Ruether and Rosemary Skinner Keller, vol. 1 (San Francisco: Harper & Row, 1982), p. 4.

"All of our studies . . .": George Gallup, Jr., and David Poling, *The Search for America's Faith* (Nashville: Abingdon Press, 1980), p. 112.

Women comprising two thirds of the congregation: *Women and Religion,* pp. 314–315.

"evangelical religion would remain women's domain . . .": Ibid., p. 9.

"You are the devil's gateway": Quoted by Rosemary Radford Ruether, *Sexism and God-Talk: Toward a Feminist Theology* (Boston: Beacon Press, 1983), p. 167.

EWC's Statement of Faith: From brochure issued by the Evangelical Women's Caucus.

"Much as the ancient housekeeper . . .": Phyllis Trible, *God and the Rhetoric of Sexuality* (Philadelphia: Fortress Press, 1978), p. 200.

Use of word "head": Letha Scanzoni and Nancy Hardesty, *All We're Meant to Be: A Biblical Approach to Women's Liberation* (Waco, Tex.: Word Books, 1974), p. 31.

"I don't blame the women . . .": Patricia Gundry, *The Complete Woman: Living Beyond Total Womanhood at Home, On the Job, and All by Yourself* (Garden City, N.Y.: Doubleday/Galilee, 1981), p. 13.

"The critical principle of feminist theology . . .": Ruether, *Sexism,* pp. 18–19.

"Once the mythology about Jesus . . .": Ibid., p. 135.

"an antidote and medicine . . .": Quoted by George H. Tavard, *Woman in Christian Tradition* (South Bend, Ind.: Notre Dame Press, 1973), p. 173.

Adam "saw himself complete . . .": Ibid., p. 176.

Catherine Beecher's *Treatise* and the cult of true womanhood: Barbara Welter, "The Cult of True Womanhood, 1820–60," *American Quarterly* 18 (1966).

feminization of culture: See Ann Douglas, *The Feminization of American Culture* (New York: Alfred A. Knopf, 1977).

"To American mothers . . .": Margaret Coxe, *The Claims of the Country on American Females* (Columbus, Ohio: Isaac N. Whiting, 1842), p. 6.

"Sex is beautiful . . .": Kevin Leman, *Sex Begins in the Kitchen: Renewing Emotional and Physical Intimacy* (Ventura, Cal.: Regal Books, 1981), pp. 119, 118.

"the titanic emotional . . .": Tim and Beverly LaHaye, *The Act of Marriage: The Beauty of Sexual Love* (Grand Rapids, Mich.: Zondervan, 1976), p. 30.

Redbook's survey: LaHaye, *The Act,* p. 9.

"spirit-filled Christians do not have . . .": Ibid., p. 21.

"When a person's sins are forgiven . . .": Ibid., p. 134.

"Pastor, I never dreamed . . .": Ibid., p. 133.

Dr. Robinson's clinical pronouncements: Ibid., p. 144.

The choleric woman: Ibid., p. 143.

On women carrying the ball: Ibid., p. 192.

Schlafly's presentation at Falwell's church: Falwell, *Listen,* pp. 130–132.

housewife as "patriot and defender of our Judeo-Christian civilization . . .": Phyllis Schlafly, *The Power of the Positive Woman* (New Rochelle, N.Y.: Arlington House, 1977), p. 166.

General Gatsis on the horrors of women on the battlefield: Quoted in Falwell, *Listen,* p. 141.

Distrust of men and fear of feminists: See Barbara Ehrenreich, *The Hearts of Men: American Dreams and the Flight from Commitment* (Garden City, N.Y.: Anchor/Doubleday, 1983).

"husbands support their wives . . .": Schlafly, *Positive Woman,* p. 76.

CHAPTER 4. THE SPIRIT OF WINNING

On the alienation of men from female-dominated church and culture: See Douglas, *Feminization;* Jackson Lears, *No Place of Grace: Antimodernism and the Transformation of American Culture 1880–1920* (New York: Pantheon, 1981); Alan Trachtenberg, *The Incorporation of America: Culture and Society in the Gilded Age* (New York: Hill & Wang, 1982).

"In its very success . . .": Trachtenberg, *Incorporation,* p. 141.

Peter Cartwright and the wealthy man: Quoted in *Women and Religion,* p. 23.

John Tanner and the jealous husband: Donald G. Mathews, *Religion in the Old South* (Chicago: University of Chicago Press, 1977), p. 103.

"For their part, perhaps the sinful males . . .": Shirley Abbott, *Womenfolks: Growing Up Down South* (New York: Ticknor & Fields, 1983), p. 142.

FCA motto: from a brochure issued by the FCA, Kansas City, Missouri.

Dr. Tom Bennett's bargain: Peter Gent, *North Dallas Forty* (New York: William Morrow, 1973), p. 27.

"God loathes mediocrity." Quoted by Bill Glass in *Don't Blame the Game* (Waco, Tex.: Word Books, 1972).

"I ran on . . .": Quoted by William G. McLoughlin, Jr., in *Billy Sunday Was His Real Name* (Chicago: University of Chicago Press, 1955), p. 28.

Sunday as "man's man": William T. Ellis, *Billy Sunday: The Man and His Message* (Chicago: The Moody Press, 1959), pp. 25 and 59.

Puritan ban on sports: Foster Rhea Dulles, *America Learns to Play* (New York: Appleton-Century-Crofts, 1940), p. 6.

Rockne's fight talk: Robert Harron, *Rockne: Idol of American Football* (New York: A. L. Burt, 1931), p. 27.

Roberts's efforts to build a basketball team: See Jerry Sholes, *Give Me That Prime-Time Religion: An Insider's Report on the Oral Roberts Evangelistic Association* (Tulsa, Okla.: Oklahoma Book Publishing, 1979).

ORU in New York: James Michener *Sports in America* (New York: Random House, 1976), p. 187.

Sports as "natural religions": Michael Novak, *The Joy of Sports: End Zones, Bases, Baskets, Balls, and the Consecration of the American Spirit* (New York: Basic Books, 1976), p. xiv.

"Church and stadium alike . . .": Charles Prebish, New York *Times,* January 17, 1982.

Fritz Peterson on sliding: George Vecsey, New York *Times,* May 10, 1981.

Interviews with born-again players: Bob Hill, *The Making of a Super Pro* (Atlanta, Ga.: Cross Roads Books, 1979).

Peale on William James: Norman Vincent Peale, *The Power of Positive Thinking* (New York: Prentice-Hall, 1952), p. 94.

Hannah on consistency: Quoted by Bob Hill in *Christian Review* 7, no. 8.

Born-again bodybuilder. Quoted in *Us,* May 25, 1982.

Golfer Larry Nelson: Quoted in *Christian Life,* August 1982.

"How do I lift weights . . .": Wes Neal, *The Handbook on Athletic Perfection* (Milford, Mich.: Mott Media, 1981), p. ix.

Steve Largent's vow: Quoted in *Christian Life,* July 1982.

"When it comes to religion . . .": Roger Staubach, *First Down, Lifetime to Go* (Waco, Tex.: Word Books, 1974), p. 280.

Warner E. Sallman's head of Christ: Cynthia Pearl Maus, *The Church and the Fine Arts* (New York: Harper & Row, 1960).

"The athlete and his coach . . .": James Michener, *Sports,* p. 265.

Meggyesy's exposé: Dave Meggyesy, *Out of Their League* (Berkeley, Cal.: Ramparts Press, 1970).

"For we wrestle not . . .": Ephesians 6:12.

CHAPTER 5. GOD AND MONEY

"Indeed, so far has the church . . .": Rollo Ogden, *The Nation,* Dec. 16, 1886. See also Lears, *No Place* and Henry May, *Protestant Churches and Industrial America* (New York: Harper Torchbooks, 1967).

"For religion must necessarily . . .": Quoted by H. Richard Niebuhr in *The Social Sources of Denominationalism* (New York: World Publishing, 1929), p. 70.

"So far from there being . . .": R. H. Tawney, Foreword, in Max Weber, *The Protestant Ethic and the Spirit of Capitalism* (London: Scribner's, 1930), p. 2.

"to erase the notion . . .": From an ad in *Publishers Weekly,* May 14, 1982.

"But as riches increase . . .": Niebuhr, *Social Sources,* p. 70.

"not only beneficial . . .": Andrew Carnegie, "Wealth," *North American Review,* June 1889.

"the mainspring of activity . . .": Lyman Abbott, *How to Succeed* (New York, 1882), p. v.

"It is a wonderful fact . . .": Quoted by Richard V. Pierard, *The Unequal Yoke* (Philadelphia: J. B. Lippincott, 1970), p. 31.

"As he stood on the platform . . .": Lyman Abbott, in *Echoes from the Pulpit and Platform,* by Dwight L. Moody (Hartford, Conn., 1900), p. 31.

Peale's eulogy to Andrews: Peale, *Positive Thinking,* p. 17.

"the price ratio of gold . . .": Harry Hurt III, *Texas Rich: The Hunt Dynasty from the Early Oil Days Through the Silver Crash* (New York: W. W. Norton, 1981), p. 406.

"believe in capitalism . . .": George Gilder, *Wealth and Poverty* (New York: Bantam Books, 1982), pp. 119–120. (First published by Basic Books, 1981).

"Capitalism begins with giving . . .": Gilder, *Wealth,* p. 23.

"The attempt of the welfare state . . .": Ibid., p. 296.

"Respect for the transcendence . . .": Michael Novak, *The Spirit of Democratic Capitalism* (New York: Simon and Schuster, 1982), pp. 67–68.

"Under free enterprise . . .": Harold Lindsell, *Free Enterprise: A Judeo-Christian Defense* (Wheaton, Ill.: Tyndale House Publishers, 1982), p. 21.

"The biblical stewardship mandate . . .": Ibid., p. 77.

"capitalist miracle . . .": William E. Simon, *A Time for Truth* (New York: McGraw-Hill, 1978), p. 5.

Falwell on Friedman: *Listen,* pp. 11–12.

"I say to the rich men . . .": Quoted by Jeremy Rifkin and Ted Howard in *The Emerging Order: God in the Age of Scarcity* (New York: G. P. Putnam's, 1979), p. 154.

"Businessmen who found . . .": Ellis, *Sunday,* p. 8.

"When the capitalist . . .": "The Capitalists and the Premillenarians," *Christian Century,* April 4, 1921.

Billy Graham's capitalist crusade: See Marshall Frady, *Billy Graham: A Parable of American Righteousness* (Boston: Little, Brown & Company, 1979), pp. 197–234.

"Back in Jerusalem . . .": Quoted by Arthur Unger, *Christian Science Monitor,* July 13, 1977.

Bright's blitz: Group Research Report to the World Student Christian Federation, June 25, 1980.

Robison's backers: Grant Simmons, *Texas Business,* December 1979.

Robison's battle with WFAA: See William Martin, *Texas Monthly*, April 1981.

CHAPTER 6. STATIONS OF THE CROSS

"We need to get into the arts . . .": *Sojourners*, September 1979.

"I'm a great believer . . .": Jane Meredith Meyer, *Wall Street Journal*, September 11, 1981.

The difference between CBN's soap and others: Terry Ann Knopf, Boston *Globe*, May 31, 1981.

Aaron's takeover of the project: Kenneth A Briggs, New York *Times*, May 31, 1981.

"We're on the verge . . .": Pat Robertson, *Shout It from the Housetops* (Plainfield, N.J.: Logos International, 1972), pp. 188–189.

CHAPTER 7. SELLING THE WORD

The Salesman from Nazareth . . .": Josef Daikeler, *The Salesman from Nazareth* (Philadelphia: Dyco Institute of Tested Selling, 1946), p. 69.

The explosion in Christian publishing: Fact sheet distributed by the CBA, 1981.

"Would Jesus have drunk . . .": Abbott, *Womenfolks*, p. 125.

"A physical weakling!": Bruce Barton, *The Man Nobody Knows* (Indianapolis, 1925), unnumbered preface.

"Since they are excluded . . .": Harold Pickett, *Publishers Weekly*, October 2, 1981.

"God is like the Chairman . . .": Pat Boone, *Pray to Win: God Wants You to Succeed* (New York: Popular Library, 1982), 97–98. (Originally published by G. P. Putnam's, 1980).

"Where the spirit needs . . .": Virginia Stem Owens, *The Total Image: Or Selling Jesus in the Modern Age* (Grand Rapids: Eerdmans Publishing, 1980), p. 11.

"To all that shall be . . .": Leon Jaworski and Dick Schneider, *Crossroads* (Elgin, Ill.: David C. Cook, 1981), p. 216.

The causes of humanist dominance: John W. Whitehead, *The Second American Revolution* (Elgin, Ill.: David C. Cook, 1982).

"the idea that the final reality . . .": Francis A. Schaeffer, *A Christian Manifesto* (Westchester, Ill.: Crossway Books, 1982), p. 18.

Christian publishing as "Negro league": Cal Thomas, *Book Burning* (Westchester, Ill.: Crossway Books, 1983), pp. 100–101.

"If you don't look . . .": Young, *God's Bullies*, p. 237.

Failing "to articulate . . .": Klaus Runia, *Christianity Today*, June 19, 1970.

CHAPTER 8.   MAKING A JOYFUL NOISE

"I ain't knockin' the hymns": Larry Norman, "Why Should the Devil Have All the Good Music?" © 1973 by Glenwood Music Corporation/ Straw Bed Music.

"Jesus is alive . . .": *Time*, June 21, 1971.

"In the true spirit . . ." Paul Baker, *Why Should the Devil Have All the Good Music?* (Waco, Tex.: Word Books, 1979), p. 80. Baker's book contains a detailed account of this era.

"Jesus loves me . . .": Tom Paxton, "Jesus Christ, S.R.O. (Standing Room Only)." © 1972 by United Artists Music Co., inc.

"slow month's budget . . .": Mark Humphrey, Los Angeles *Reader*, December 4, 1981.

Ralph Carmichael's deal with Warner's: Reported in *Contemporary Christian Music*, October 1981.

Jimmy Swaggart's dealings with God, the devil, and Jerry Lee Lewis: Nick Tosches, *Hellfire* (New York: Delacorte/Dell, 1982).

"achieved a new low . . .": Tosches, *Vanity Fair*, April 1983.

"her creative impulses . . .": Bob Larson, *Rock: Practical Help for Those Who Listen to the Words and Don't Like What They Hear* (Wheaton, Ill.: Tyndale House, 1980), p. 41.

"featured pictures of demons . . .": Ibid., p. 43.

Hart on the dangers of rock: Lowell Hart, *Satan's Music Exposed* (Salem Kirban, Inc., 1980).

"the words were Christian . . .": Richard Stanislaw, *Eternity*, November 1978.

"During the dynamic days . . .": Preface, *Baptist Hymnal* (Nashville: Convention Press, 1975), p. v.

"Here Is My Life": Ed Seabough and Gene Bartlett. ©1970, Broadman Press.

"that classic American figure . . .": Albert Goldman, *Elvis* (New York: McGraw-Hill, 1981), p. 349.

"If they saw Him . . .": "Would They Love Him Down in Shreveport" by Bobby Braddock. ©Tree Publishing Co.

"He loves any stray . . .": Johnny Cash, "The Greatest Cowboy of Them All." ©House of Cash, Inc.

"May be a rock and roll band . . .": Bob Dylan, "Gotta Serve Some-body." ©1979, Special Rider Music.

"satisfied to sing . . .": Arlo Guthrie, "Which Side." ©1979, Arloco Music.

"no matter where I roam . . .": Van Morrison, "Full Force Gale." ©1979, Essential Music.

"When you hear the music . . .": Van Morrison, "And the Healing Has Begun." ©1979, Essential Music.

"thinking about eternity . . .": Bruce Cockburn, "Wondering Where the Lions Are." ©1981, Golden Mountain Music.

"Alone on a hill . . .": Arlo Guthrie, "Prologue," 1979, ©Arloco Music.

"I ask you what I ask . . .": "Which Side." ©1979, Arloco Music.

"You either got faith . . .": Bob Dylan, "Precious Angel," ©1979, Special Rider Music.

"In the fury of the moment . . .": Bob Dylan, "Every Grain of Sand." ©1981, Special Rider Music.

CHAPTER 9.   ARMIES OF THE LIGHT

"Let me count this day . . .": Sinclair Lewis, *Elmer Gantry* (New York: New American Library, 1979), p. 416. (Originally published in 1925 by Harcourt, Brace).

"Can you tell me . . .": Bob Dylan, "Señor (Tales of Yankee Power)." ©1978, Ram's Horn Music.

"He was a new Senator . . .": David Manuel, *The Gathering* (Hyannis, Mass.: Rock Harbor Press, 1980), 1980, p. 9.

"We're gonna stay out . . .": Van Morrison, "And the Healing Has Be-gun." ©1979, Essential Music.

"Supposing there had been . . .": Malcolm Muggeridge, *Christ and the Media;* Grand Rapids, Mich.: W. B. Eerdman's, 1977, p. 30.

CHAPTER 10. FROM SUBCULTURE TO COUNTERCULTURE

"Imagine their surprise . . .": Don DeLillo, *The Names* (New York: Alfred A. Knopf, 1982), p. 173.

"Ministers and Marches": Quoted by Frances Fitzgerald, *New Yorker,* May 18, 1981.

Fore's indiscretions: Joe Klein, *New York,* May 18, 1981.

"enormous power religious people . . .": Viguerie, *New Right.*

RAVCO's fund-raising: Alan Crawford, *Thunder on the Right: The "New Right" and the Politics of Resentment* (New York: Pantheon, 1980), pp. 62–63.

Wildmon and Procter & Gamble: For a more complete account, see Todd Gitlin, *Inside Prime Time* (New York: Pantheon, 1983).

The audience for TV evangelists: See Jeffrey K. Hadden and Charles E. Swann, *Prime Time Preachers: The Rising Power of Televangelism* (Reading, Mass.: Addison-Wesley, 1981). Also, William Martin, *Atlantic,* June 1981.

Antiabortion groups and Nazis: Andrew Merton, *Enemies of Choice: The Right-To-Life Movement and Its Threat to Abortion* (Boston: Beacon Press, 1981), p. 10.

America "had already taken dramatic steps . . .": Conway and Siegelman, *Holy Terror,* p. 341.

"unprecedented in both religion . . .": Ibid., p. 8.

"syndrome of fundamentalism . . .": Ibid., p. 276.

"surrender to the supernatural . . .": Ibid., p. 341.

"It is not their homosexuality . . .": Young, *God's Bullies,* p. xi.

Hofstadter and paranoia: Daniel Maguire, *The New Subversives: Anti-Americanism of the Religious Right* (New York: Continuum, 1982), p. 5.

Protestant declaration: Quoted by Maguire, ibid., p. 86.

CHAPTER 11.   OF GOD, MARX, AND MAMMON

"Establishment Christianity has made its peace . . .": Jim Wallis, *Agenda for Biblical People: A New Focus for Developing a Life-Style of Discipleship* (New York: Harper & Row, 1976), p. 1.

Niebuhr's assault on communism: Reinhold Niebuhr, *The Irony of American History* (New York: Scribner's, 1952).

Booth's assault on the Gilded Age: See Donald Dayton, *Discovering an Evangelical Heritage* (New York: Harper & Row, 1976).

"far from disdaining earthly affairs . . .": Timothy L. Smith, *Revivalism and Social Reform in Mid-Nineteenth-Century America* (Nashville, Tenn.: Abingdon, 1957), pp. 8, 149.

"white Evangelicals were too conscious . . .": Mathews, *South,* p. 185.

"during the last three light-hearted . . .": Quoted by William R. Hutchison in *The Modernist Impulse in American Protestantism* (Cambridge, Mass.: Harvard University Press, 1976), p. 260.

"God hates our lofty . . .": John Alexander, *The Other Side,* January 1978.

The Sojourners on abortion: *Sojourners,* November 1980.

"Though the modern crisis is not . . .": Carl F. H. Henry, *The Uneasy Conscience of Modern Fundamentalism* (Grand Rapids: Eerdman's, 1947), p. 84.

"Famine is alive and well . . .": Ronald J. Sider, *Rich Christians in an Age of Hunger* (Downers Grove, Ill.: Inter-Varsity Press, 1977), pp. 13–16.

Mark Hatfield and the Sojourners: Mark Hatfield, *Between a Rock and a Hard Place* (Waco, Tex.: Word Books, 1976).

"I was laughing at myself . . .": Will D. Campbell, *Brother to a Dragonfly* (New York: Continuum, 1977), p. 222.

"the romance of 'black and white' . . .": Ibid., p. 246.

"Black, white, Kluxer . . .": Frady, p. 380.

"We are the prisoners . . .": Quoted by Connelly, *Campbell,* p. 39.

"pulpitless, roofless . . .": Frady, *Graham.* For Campbell's critique of Graham and of institutionalized Christianity, see Frady, pp. 374–395.

CONCLUSION

"beguilement over the years . . .": Frady, *Graham,* p. 437.

Graham's brief conversation with Falwell: *Newsweek,* April 26, 1982.

Campbell on Graham's trip to Moscow: Frye Gaillard, *The Progressive*, August 1982.

"the solution to the world's problems . . .": Robert E. Webber, *The Moral Majority: Right or Wrong?* (Westchester, Ill.: Cornerstone Books, 1981), pp. 155–156.

Account of Kennedy's visit to Lynchburg: New York *Times*, October 4, 1983; New York *Daily News*, October 4, 1983.

Falwell at the crossroads: Fitzgerald, *New Yorker*, May 18, 1981.

INDEX